The Trial of Warren Hastings

The Trial of Warren Hastings

*Classical Oratory and Reception in
Eighteenth-Century England*

Chiara Rolli

BLOOMSBURY ACADEMIC
LONDON • NEW YORK • OXFORD • NEW DELHI • SYDNEY

BLOOMSBURY ACADEMIC
Bloomsbury Publishing Plc
50 Bedford Square, London, WC1B 3DP, UK
1385 Broadway, New York, NY 10018, USA

BLOOMSBURY, BLOOMSBURY ACADEMIC and the Diana logo
are trademarks of Bloomsbury Publishing Plc

First published in Great Britain 2019
Paperback edition first published 2021

Copyright © Chiara Rolli, 2019

Chiara Rolli has asserted her right under the Copyright,
Designs and Patents Act, 1988, to be identified as Author of this work.

For legal purposes the Acknowledgements on p. vii constitute
an extension of this copyright page.

Cover design: Alice Marwick
Cover image: Impeachment ticket. For the trial of W-rr-n H-st-ngs Esqr,
James Gillray, hand coloured etching, circa February 1788 © National Portrait Gallery, London

All rights reserved. No part of this publication may be reproduced or
transmitted in any form or by any means, electronic or mechanical,
including photocopying, recording, or any information storage or retrieval
system, without prior permission in writing from the publishers.

Bloomsbury Publishing Plc does not have any control over, or responsibility for,
any third-party websites referred to or in this book. All internet addresses
given in this book were correct at the time of going to press. The author and publisher
regret any inconvenience caused if addresses have changed or sites have
ceased to exist, but can accept no responsibility for any such changes.

A catalogue record for this book is available from the British Library.

Library of Congress Cataloging-in-Publication Data
Names: Rolli, Chiara, author.
Title: The trial of Warren Hastings: classical oratory and reception in
eighteenth-century England / Chiara Rolli.
Other titles: Tullius Indianus. English
Description: London, UK; New York, NY: Bloomsbury Academic, 2019. |
Series: Library of classical studies | Revision and translation of author's thesis
(doctoral)–Universitáa di Parma, 2012, titled Tullius Indianus: Edmund
Burke, Cicerone ela romanitáa nel processo a Warren Hastings. |
Includes bibliographical references and index. |
Identifiers: LCCN 2018053306 (print) | LCCN 2019003227 (ebook) |
ISBN 9781350112759 (epub) | ISBN 9781350112742 (epdt) | ISBN 9781784539221 |
ISBN 9781784539221 (hb) | ISBN 9781350112742 (ePDF) | ISBN 9781350112759 (eBook)
Subjects: LCSH: Burke, Edmund, 1729–1797. | Political oratory–Great
Britain–History–18th century. | English language–18th century–Rhetoric. |
Rhetoric–England–History–18th century. | Hastings, Warren, 1732–1818–Trials,
litigation, etc. | Hastings, Warren, 1732–1818–Impeachment.
Classification: LCC PR3334.B4 (ebook) | LCC PR3334.B4 Z8713 2019 (print) |
DDC 825/.609–dc 3
LC record available at https://lccn.loc.gov/2018053306

ISBN: HB: 978-1-7845-3922-1
PB: 978-1-3501-9062-7
ePDF: 978-1-3501-1274-2
eBook: 978-1-3501-1275-9

Typeset by RefineCatch Limited, Bungay, Suffolk

To find out more about our authors and books visit
www.bloomsbury.com and sign up for our newsletters.

Contents

List of Figures		vi
Acknowledgements		vii
	Introduction	1
1	Cicero, Verres and the Classics in Eighteenth-Century Britain	11
2	A Clash of Characters	29
3	Classical Oratory and Theatricality in the Trial against Warren Hastings	47
4	Spectacles of Passion: Cicero's *In Verrem* and Burke's 'Speech on the Opening of the Impeachment'	85
5	The Reception of the Hastings Trial in the Newspapers and Satirical Prints	113
	Conclusion	133
Notes		137
Bibliography		185
Index		201

Figures

3.1 Anon., *Print/fan*, 1788. BM 1891,0713.387. © Trustees of the British Museum — 48

3.2 Thomas Prattent, *A view of the court sitting on the trial of Warren Hastings Esq.*, 1788. BM 1880,0911.1217. © Trustees of the British Museum — 48

3.3 Admission-ticket for day 28 of the trial of Warren Hastings, 1787. BM J,9.46. © Trustees of the British Museum — 57

3.4 Admission-ticket, 1787 c. BM J,9.21. © Trustees of the British Museum — 59

3.5 James Sayers, *For the Trial of Warren Has[tings]/Seventh Day*, 1788. BM 1868,0808.5692. © Trustees of the British Museum — 60

3.6 *Refreshments to be had in the Hall*, 1788. BM J,9.17. © Trustees of the British Museum — 62

3.7 Admission-ticket, 1788 c. BM J,9.8. © Trustees of the British Museum — 63

3.8 Admission-ticket, 1787 c. BM J,9.3. © Trustees of the British Museum — 65

5.1 James Sayers, *The Impeachment*, 17 March 1786. BM 1868,0808.5488. © Trustees of the British Museum — 127

5.2 John Boyne, *Cicero against Verres*, 7 February 1787. BM 7138. © Trustees of the British Museum — 128

Acknowledgements

This book began as my doctoral dissertation, completed at the University of Parma in 2012. I have many people to thank from that period and from the years since then. First of all, I would like to thank Diego Saglia, for invaluable direction and constant support throughout. The gratitude I owe to Diego for his numerous suggestions, advice and criticism is far greater than can be expressed here. I am also deeply indebted to Phiroze Vasunia for the many conversations – encouraging and challenging in equal measure – that helped me refine the terms of this study. The Department of Classics at the University of Reading, where I was visiting scholar in 2011 and where this book began life, provided me with a stimulating research environment and a passionate interest in classical reception studies.

I am profoundly grateful to Jo Brown, who read the manuscript in draft and offered numerous comments. She was extremely generous with her time and assistance. Special thanks go to Sheila O'Connell for showing me Sarah Sophia Banks's collection of 'Tickets of the Warren Hastings Trial' and for her generous help at the Department of Prints and Drawings of the British Museum; to Matthew Fox, who kindly shared his research with me; and to Daphne Ayles and Anastasia Bakogianni, for their wonderful hospitality and friendship during my stays in London. I owe much to Anastasia for all her support and encouragement and for never tiring of discussing the issues we are both so interested in.

Tom Stottor started to work with me on the editing of the book and I am deeply obliged for his enthusiasm and interest in the work. I am also indebted to several people at Bloomsbury, particularly to Alice Wright, Rachel Singleton, Lily Mac Mahon, and Terry Woodley, for their professionalism and skill. My thanks then go to the anonymous readers who commented on the manuscript, for their astute observations and suggestions. At the closing stages, the vigilant solicitude of Merv Honeywood of RefineCatch was greatly appreciated.

The staff of the Biblioteca Pier Giorgio Negro of the University of Parma have been exceptionally efficient in the assistance they have extended to me over the years. I have also been helped by staff at the British Library, the British Museum, Senate House Library of the University of London, the Bodleian Library and the Library of the University of Reading.

The section of the book on Sarah Sophia Banks's collection of passes is a revised version of part of my article 'An impeachment turned into a show: Sarah Sophia Banks's collection of "Tickets for Warren Hastings Trial"', *Il lettore di provincia* 150 (2018), pp. 49–66. I am particularly grateful to the publisher for granting permission to reuse this material.

Finally, I would like to thank my family. My brother's deep and passionate love for unstained snowy mountain-tops has been a constant source of inspiration. Marco, Sven and my parents lived through all the highs and lows of this book and I cannot say how grateful I am for their unwavering and loving support throughout the years. This book is dedicated to them, with love.

Introduction

A fashionable spectacle

Yesterday the great World *attended the trial of* WARREN HASTINGS, *Esq. – and whether he be convicted, or whether he be acquitted, his accusers are entitled to the thanks of the ladies mantua-makers and milliners.* [...] *About twelve at night* hair-dressing *commenced. What an hour for* hair-dressing! *And the operators continued* twisting of curls *till nine the next morning. Poor Devils, what a night of labour they must have experienced!*
The Times (14 February 1788)

The trial of Mr. Hastings [...] *swallows up everything – no spectacle was ever so much resorted to. The manners, at least the hours of London, are completely changed.*
Anthony Morris Storer to William Eden (22 February 1788)¹

The adjournment of the trial has indeed been felt by this whole metropolis as a breaking up for the holidays is by schoolboys and schoolgirls, for besides the managers, the Lords, and the person accused, all the fine ladies and many of the fine gentlemen were on duty, which, considering the revolution in their hours and ways of life, must have been as severe a campaign as Coxheath or Warley were to the militia. The ladies were up at six every morning, to dress and breakfast so as to be at Westminster Hall by nine o'clock.
Sir Gilbert Elliot to Lady Elliot (3 March 1788)²

Penned by three very different individuals – a newspaper reporter, a politician, and a future Governor-General of Bengal – these three reports give us an idea of the profound impact that the impeachment of Warren Hastings (1732–1818), first Governor-General of Bengal between 1773 and 1785, had on the 'hours and way of life' of the British and foreign elites in London. During the early months of 1788, the impeachment of Hastings became a national sensation and the public's appetite for this extraordinary spectacle was insatiable.

Hastings had served for two long periods in India and each time had come back to Britain with a considerable fortune. Though he was 'treated as something of a celebrity' after his return to England for the second time,[3] his enemies persecuted him with the utmost ferocity, and in 1786 he was impeached before the House of Commons on twenty-two 'Articles of Charge of High Crimes and Misdemeanors'. Most articles were rejected, but seven were passed by the Commons.

If some of the charges, such as the awarding of corrupt contracts or the illegal receipt of presents, were of a traditional sort, the two principal charges concerned the Governor-General's relations with Indian rulers. In the first charge, Burke held that Hastings had provoked Raja Chait Singh of Benares to revolt in 1781. In the second charge, the Anglo-Irish orator argued that Hastings had confiscated the landed income and treasure of the mother and grandmother of the *nawab* of Awadh (who were also known as the Begums of Oudh).[4]

Six of the seven charges were then redrafted as 'Articles of Impeachment' and on 10 May 1787 the House of Commons voted that Hastings was to be prosecuted before the Lords. One of the most spectacular of the eighteenth century's public events, the trial opened in 1788 and ended in Hastings's acquittal in 1795.

The prosecution of the Governor-General was brought by a cast of star orators, which included three of the most brilliant speakers of the period: the politician and philosopher Edmund Burke (1729/30–97), the Whig leader Charles James Fox (1749–1806) and the celebrated playwright and manager of Drury Lane Theatre, Richard Brinsley Sheridan (1751–1816). For the occasion, the austere edifice where the trial took place, Westminster Hall, was draped in scarlet and turned into a 'huge theatrical auditorium'.[5]

Besides nearly 170 Lords, the large number of auditors present in Westminster Hall comprised many of the most distinguished figures of the time, such as, notably, the historian Edward Gibbon (1737–94), the painter Joshua Reynolds (1723–92), the actress Sarah Siddons (1755–1831), the soprano Elizabeth Ann Linley (1754–92) and the naturalist and long-time president of the Royal Society, Sir Joseph Banks (1743–1820). For at least the first half of 1788, the galleries of the debating chamber were packed with refined ladies and gentlemen who squashed together to catch a glimpse of the Governor-General or to enjoy Burke's and Sheridan's extraordinary performances.

From a twenty-first-century perspective, it may be puzzling to think of a grave parliamentary debate in terms of a fashionable spectacle. Yet it was in a blaze of splendour and publicity that the trial against the Governor-General opened on the morning of 13 February 1788. As Thomas Babington Macaulay (1800–1859), historian, politician and member of the Supreme Council of India, recalled about fifty years later:

> The long galleries were crowded by such an audience as has rarely excited the fears or the emulation of an orator. There were gathered together, from all parts of a great, free, enlightened, and prosperous realm, grace and female loveliness, wit and learning, the representatives of every science and of every art. [...] There the historian of the Roman Empire thought of the days when Cicero pleaded the cause of Sicily against Verres.[6]

In contrast to the general atmosphere of excitement in the courtroom, the defendant looked 'pale, ill, and altered' – or, at least, so he seemed to the novelist Frances Burney (1752–1840), a self-declared supporter of Hastings.[7] While Burney's impression may have been exaggerated as a result of her feeling for him, there is no doubt that the endurance of so interminable a judicial action caused Hastings much excruciating pain, as he indicated in a letter of 17 July 1788: 'if any friend of mine shall be hereafter brought to a similar trial, shall I advise him to plead guilty to the charge, to avoid the torture of the process'.[8] Indeed, Hastings was judged not only by the House of Lords but also symbolically by the whole nation.

From the opening speeches to its final verdict, the trial was covered in contemporary newspapers, inspired popular doggerels and was often represented in satirical prints as a theatrical spectacle. That the managers' speeches were intentionally dramatic rather than legalistic – Burke and his colleagues often omitted canons of evidence, opting instead for sudden indispositions and swoons (sometimes real and sometimes feigned) – is a point worth stressing. One of the most striking examples, in this sense, is Burke's account of the so-called Rangpur episode (18 February 1788). His graphic description of tortures allegedly inflicted by revenue collectors in the district of Rangpur shocked the audience and caused a sensation at the time. The orator himself was taken ill and the session had to be adjourned. Although a company official, John Paterson (d. 1809), and, later, a committee of three were sent to India to investigate, exactly what atrocities had been committed was not clearly determined. F. P. Lock has persuasively argued that, even if all the allegations were true, 'Hastings neither committed nor authorized them, nor could he reasonably be held responsible for them'.[9] Some four months after Burke's melodramatic performance, Sheridan complemented his celebrated four-day speech in defence of the Begums of Oudh with similar dramatic gestures: a (feigned) illness (10 June 1788) and a well-timed fainting spell (13 June 1788).

Scholars have been quick to seize on the vast resonance and theatricality of the impeachment as well as on its intricate combination of spectatorship, histrionics and conspicuous consumption. In recent years, in particular, commentators have variously remarked on the ubiquity of correlations between the impeachment and the theatre. Siraj Ahmed's 2002 article on Burke and 'the theater of the civilized self', for example, contended that the Anglo-Irish orator's exaggerated performance – especially in its descriptions of the horrors perpetrated at Rangpur – 'had all the sensationalism of the contemporary vogue for sentimental drama'.[10] Focusing on the politics of visuality both in the prosecutors' performance at the trial and in the trial's satirical reception, Daniel O'Quinn's 2005 study on the 'raree show of impeachment' has equally demonstrated that the *cause célèbre* shared many tropes with 'the lowest forms of theatrical presentation'.[11]

The spectacle of the event has, in fact, been explored from a variety of perspectives, either historical, philosophical-political, or postcolonial. Notably, Sara Suleri's 1992 reading of the Hastings trial has placed Burke's and his fellow manager's spectacular performances alongside 'the inscribability of colonial guilt'.[12] From different angles, and yet similarly, historians and political scientists have stressed that Burke's carefully crafted staged-production was designed to explore – as Jennifer Pitts has put it – 'the "incorrigibility" of the Company, the tendency to abuse inherent in any attempt to govern a distant colony, and the particular evils of British rule over a people the British were content to regard as lawless and benighted'.[13]

In this book, I hope to bring a new critical energy to the discussion of the pervasive presence of theatricality in the trial, registering the ways in which the managers, in particular Burke and Sheridan, were influenced by classical oratory. In doing so, I excavate a wide range of eighteenth-century sources – journals, correspondence, reports in newspapers and satirical engravings – that show how profoundly Graeco-Roman culture permeated the managers' most spectacular performances.

It is important to stress that this study does not offer a political assessment of the trial, nor does it evaluate the veracity of Burke's accusations against Hastings; those who wish to know more about the articles of charge against the Governor-General and to get a firm grasp of the long and intricate phases of the impeachment should consult P. J. Marshall's 1965 seminal monograph or Richard Bourke's more recent analysis.[14] Rather, each chapter of *The Trial of Warren Hastings* offers an analytical snapshot of the multi-layered classical influences that pervaded and informed the impeachment, its context and eighteenth-century reception, and illuminates their significance both for British parliamentary oratory and, on a more symbolic level, for the British rule in India.

Classical presences

Starting with P. J. Marshall, a number of scholars have noticed that Burke 'knew that he needed not only to convince the British public that a peril existed but also to excite them into supporting his cause'.[15] Were the charges against Hastings rendered into tedious legal discourses (that is, without theatrical histrionics), they would become incomprehensible and would fail to capture most Britons' interest: 'If we proceed under the publick [sic] eye' – the Irish-born orator wrote on 1 November 1787 – 'I have no more doubt than I entertain of my existence, that all the ability, influence and power that can accompany a decided partiality in that tribunal can [not] save our criminal from a condemnation'.[16] From that perspective, attracting the continuous attention of the audience at large was crucial to the success of the impeachment.

Burke's and his colleagues' exaggerated performances may be ascribed to contemporary modes of delivery or – in the words of Tillman W. Nechtman – to 'a tradition of English theatrics that dated back to Shakespeare'.[17] In his perceptive comment on Sheridan's tragic body at the trial, David Francis Taylor has significantly noted that many came to Westminster Hall expecting 'Shakespearian pathos'.[18] For example, it was 'only within the vicarious economy of tragedy' that 'spectators-consumers – uninterested in legal argumentation and unfamiliar with the process of impeachment –' could read Sheridan's June 1788 flamboyant delivery.[19] Nonetheless, the managers' theatrical shows can also be ascribed to classical, especially Roman, rhetorical prescriptions, which recommended that the orator should transform into an *actor*, namely a performer. Classical authors had repeatedly argued for the importance of an affecting body language. It was by means of a tragic body that the orator could, indeed, become the emotional puppet-master of his spectators.

By calling attention to key passages from Cicero's and Quintilian's rhetorical treatises, this book shows how pervasively classical and, especially, Roman models informed the trial's dramatic atmosphere. In particular, Cicero's recommendation that a highly emotional performance is fundamental to stir the feelings of the audience seems to have had a far-reaching impact on the managers' theatrical gestures. Among all classical orators, I have chosen to focus on Cicero and Quintilian for two main reasons. As I show in Chapter 1, it was especially Roman models that counted in the education of the eighteenth-century British elite. And secondly, of all Roman orators, it was Cicero and Quintilian who took the lion's share. In this sense, the exhortation of the 4th Earl of Chesterfield (1694–1773) to his seventeen-year-old son in 1749 is quite emblematic: 'You have read Quintilian; the best book in the world to form an orator; pray read Cicero, *de Oratore*; the best book in the world to finish one'.[20]

This leads us a step further. In spite of the copious number of studies already existing on the trial, heretofore the impeachment of Hastings has never been thoroughly considered through the framework of classical reception studies. It is true that scholars have frequently drawn attention to the close correspondence between Cicero's orations against Verres and Burke's speeches against the Governor-General. But their observations are rather limited to rapid allusions or brief remarks. Specific similarities and differences between the impeachments of Verres and Hastings have been noted and analysed by H. V. Canter and Geoffrey Carnall in 1914 and 1998, respectively.[21] And yet, where both articles have the merit of emphasizing the importance of Burke's rhetorical borrowings from Cicero, neither offers an in-depth and close comparison of the Latin and English texts.

As this book will demonstrate, not only did Burke refer to the impeachment of Verres in a general sense, but he closely looked at and repeatedly referred to Cicero's orations *In Verrem*. Though Burke had frequently identified himself with Cicero throughout his career,[22] it was during the long years of the impeachment of Hastings that he most insistently encouraged and welcomed the comparison with his Roman exemplar. Cicero's relentless attack on Verres, the *propraetor* who had exploited and oppressed the province of Sicily between 73 and 71 BC, had been an undisputed success. Outwitted by the speed and forensic tactics of the orator, Verres fled Rome for exile in Massalia (Marseille) sometime after Cicero gave the speech recorded in his *Actio Prima* and when the court heard the testimony of witnesses. To the eyes of the Irish-born orator, the prosecution of Verres was not merely an auspicious antecedent. It was an illustrious model that he intended to hold up as an *exemplum* for the benefit of the Court and the whole nation.

Burke's reference to the proceedings against the *propraetor* of Sicily proved highly successful in capturing the public imagination. From January to June 1788, all major newspapers published in Britain, and British newspapers issued in India, described the trial of the Governor-General in terms of a re-enactment of the proceedings against Verres. Even satirists did not fail to notice the striking similarities between the impeachment of Verres and Hastings, and published cartoons representing Burke as a British Cicero and Hastings as a modern-day Verres.

In spite of the Anglo-Irish orator's vehemence and oratorical brilliance, however, the loss of the audience's interest and attention spelled out the defeat of his prosecution of Hastings. Certainly, the inordinate length of the trial did not favour Burke's cause. As Suleri has remarked, the impeachment of Hastings 'provided eighteenth-century England with a spectacle first of political pageantry and then of boredom'.[23] By the time a verdict was reached, eight years had passed, and very few were surprised when, on 23 April 1795, the members of the House of Lords acquitted the former Governor-General of Bengal of all charges.

The Trial of Warren Hastings falls into five chapters, each of which concentrates on a particular aspect of the impact of the Classics on the impeachment of Warren Hastings and, more broadly, on the public conversation about Britain and India. Through this structure I both provide a panorama of the social and cultural contexts in which the *cause célèbre* was conducted and commented on by contemporary observers, and maintain a rigorous focus on the influence of classical rhetoric on British parliamentary oratory – specifically, Burke's and Sheridan's speeches and performances. The first chapter of this book examines the crucial role played by the Classics in eighteenth-century British culture and education, and how and why Cicero and Verres were familiar to the aristocracy and gentry. It also provides a survey of the most eminent MPs and intellectuals who modelled their lives on, or were compared to, either the celebrated Roman lawyer or the greedy governor of Sicily. Chapter 2 looks at the two protagonists of the *cause célèbre* under examination, piecing together the significant details from their classical – particularly Roman – education that influenced their personalities and careers and were ultimately relevant to the impeachment. Chapter 3 considers the trial of the Governor-General of Bengal as a theatrical entertainment attended by the most fashionable members of society, and asks why Hastings's prosecutors – Sheridan and Burke, above all others – feigned illnesses and fainting spells at the end of their most striking speeches. This is a pivotal section of the book, because it determines how the managers' *coups de théâtre* were not only related to the eighteenth-century culture of sensibility or the contemporary vogue for melodrama, but were, in fact, influenced by classical rhetorical prescriptions, which recommended that the orator should transform legal debates into spectacles of justice. Chapter 4, then, brings us to the heart of Burke's appropriation and reuse of the *Verrines* throughout the impeachment of Hastings. To do so, it focuses on a shocking section in the oration delivered on the fifth day of the trial – namely, the narration of the Rangpur atrocities – in order to collate it with several relevant passages from Cicero's orations *In Verrem*. The final chapter explores receptions of the trial in contemporary satirical prints as well as in the major newspapers published in Britain and in India. The ultimate aim of this section is to emphasize how not only the political elite, but also a broader audience, followed and discussed the Hastings trial within a classically framed discourse in which Cicero, Verres and Rome were a constant presence.

As this summary suggests, *The Trial of Warren Hastings* weaves together a wide range of disciplinary strands: literary criticism and classical studies; parliamentary and cultural histories; journalism and fine arts. Indeed, to examine the inter-relatedness and multiple dialogues that developed between the Classics, rhetorical practices and the managers' melodramatic shows, as well as their reception in the late eighteenth century is necessarily to traverse the boundaries of discipline and expertise. And it is precisely by crossing these boundaries and using 'creative imagination' – as Frances Burney described Burke's ingenious thought[24] – that this book affords interpretative glances at the complex interactions at play in one of the most extraordinary spectacles and major theatrical events of all British parliamentary history.

1

Cicero, Verres and the Classics in Eighteenth-Century Britain

In his classic monograph on Greek studies in England, M. L. Clarke notes that, from the sixteenth century onwards, the education of the British cultural and political elite was 'based entirely on the classics. [...] Other languages and other subjects were scarcely taught at all'.[1] Throughout the eighteenth century, tutors, philosophers and scholars discussed and published extensively on the advantages or disadvantages of such an education.[2] Unsurprisingly, the established system had its critics. As early as 1693, for example, the renowned philosopher John Locke (1632–1704) admitted the necessity of Latin for a gentleman and Greek for a scholar. For a boy intended for trade or business, instead, the study of the Classics was useless.[3] In spite of Locke's and other critics' remarks, however, the education of the elite was not modified until well into the nineteenth century.[4] A significant example, in this sense, is provided by John Stuart Mill (1806–73), the celebrated philosopher and economist whose family had extensive connections with India.[5] In 1873, he wrote in his autobiography:

> He [my father] advised me to make my next exercise in composition one of the oratorical kind on which suggestion, availing myself of my familiarity with Greek history and ideas, and with the Athenian orators, I wrote two speeches, one an accusation, the other a defence of Pericles, on a supposed impeachment for not marching out to fight the Lacedemonians on their invasion of Attica.[6]

As John Stuart Mill's memoirs suggest, members of the governing class regarded the study of Greek and Latin as a means of acquiring a quick wit, precision in speech and sharpness of thinking: 'classical attainments contribute much to the refinement of the understanding, and the embellishment of the style. The utility of Grammar, Rhetoric and Logic, are known and felt by every one', the jurist John Dunning (1731–83) wrote in a letter to a gentleman of the Inner Temple in 1779.[7] With political careers depending largely on rhetorical skills, eighteenth-century gentlemen were trained in classical models, and Greek and Latin orations, as well as classical treatises on rhetoric, were at the heart of their education.[8] A quotation from the correspondence of one of the most profound scholars of the century, Sir William Jones (1746–94), will suffice for many examples. In an epistle addressed to Viscount Althorp (1758–1834), his fifteen-year-old pupil destined for a political career, Jones noted in 1773: 'I am glad you admire Tully, and his charming work *De officiis* [...]. He is the Man, whom I propose to you as your model, and whom I hope you will imitate'.[9]

The powerful influence exercised by the Classics on the eighteenth-century British aristocracy and gentry is a matter too vast to be developed here. Insightful studies, such as Philip Ayres's *Classical Culture and the Idea of Rome in Eighteenth-Century England* (1997), have demonstrated how classical antiquity, and in particular Republican Rome, represented for the English elite a source of paramount values, including political liberty and civic virtue. In this chapter, I will not repeat Ayres's observations. Confining my attention to a number of emblematic examples, I will show, instead, how classical orators and allusions to the ancient world figured prominently in eighteenth-century British parliamentary debates, as well as in the press and satirical prints. After this, I will turn to the numerous biographies of Cicero and translations of his speeches circulating in Britain at the time. In particular, I shall look at notions of character and eighteenth-century historical judgement of the great Roman orator who played a crucial role in Burke's life and rhetoric. By means of a few significant instances, I will argue that, although to a lesser extent, also Verres, the villain governor of Sicily, as well as the *Verrines*, were mentioned and referred to in a number of eighteenth-century texts. In doing so, I will make clear how, at the end of the century, it was possible for Burke to imply that he himself was Cicero and that Hastings was Verres 'without a trace of irony'.[10] In fact, the identification that the Irish-born orator was attempting to foster in his audiences was made not just by the former in his speeches but also by his contemporaries, both inside and out of the doors of Westminster Hall. As we will see in particular in Chapter 5, newspaper reporters and satirists portrayed Burke and Hastings as though they had simultaneously been eighteenth-century gentlemen discussing a grave legal case in front of the Lords and the protagonists of an ancient trial held in the Forum of Rome.

Latine loqui

Throughout the eighteenth century, debates in the Commons and the Lords echoed with quotations from classical authors in their original languages, and British politicians and orators were often compared to Cicero or Demosthenes.[11] In his *Life of Edmund Burke* (1798), the Scottish writer Robert Bisset (1758/9–1805), for example, included a 'Comparison of Burke and Cicero, in materials, disposition, language, and object of eloquence'.[12] At the time, newspapers and magazines largely commented on Bisset's comparison. *The Times* (25 August 1798), for instance, reported that:

> Dr. BISSET's life of Mr. BURKE has given much offence to the Author of the Preface to *Bellendenus*. This grave Gentleman thinks the comparative merits of Cicero and Burke have been too partially weighed, and laments that the modern orator should be deemed superior to the ancient.[13]

It is from this perspective that we should also read the *Oracle Bell's New World* celebration of the Earl of Mansfield (1705–93). On 7 November 1789, commenting on an important speech delivered at the House of Commons, the paper stressed how the Earl:

> so eminently distinguished himself, that Sir Robert Walpole declared the merit of his speech to be so great, that it almost appeared to him to have been an oration of Cicero. Mr. Pulteney in the same instant rose to complete the eulogium, by observing, that he not only could imagine the speech which had been just delivered, was the composition of Cicero, but that the Roman Orator had himself pronounced it.

These are but a few examples among the multitude of cases that could be mentioned. Indeed, references to and comparisons with the greatest orators of antiquity were so copious in parliamentary debates, literary publications and the London press, that – as David H. Solkin has noted – the leading figures of antiquity seemed to have 'miraculously returned to life, in order to participate in the most pressing political and social debates of the day'.[14]

The practice of comparing renowned Members of Parliament and orators to eminent figures of classical antiquity leads us to another consideration, which is that throughout the eighteenth century, the Classics represented a significant point of interconnection and mutual influence between different media, such as the London papers and satirical prints. Leading political figures were, in fact, often associated with Greek and Roman orators in caricatures.

One of the best examples is *Design for the New Gallery of Busts and Pictures* (17 March 1792: BM 8072) by James Gillray (1756–1815). In 1787, Catherine II of Russia (1729–96) had begun a second war against the Ottoman Empire. Owing to troubles in the north, by 1789 she was anxious to conclude a peace and entered into negotiations. A crucial point was Catherine II's unwillingness to surrender the fortress of Ochakov on the north coast of the Black Sea – the episode is known as the 'Ochakov crisis'. The Prime Minister, William Pitt the Younger (1759–1806), persuaded the King to side with the Ottomans, while Whig leader Charles James Fox mounted an effective attack on Pitt, emphasizing the economic argument for cultivating an alliance with Russia, rather than going to war with her. In Gillray's etching, the bust of Fox – very lifelike and depicted without any inscription – is portrayed between the images of 'Demosthenes against Aeschines' and 'Cicero against Catiline', suitably inscribed. Demosthenes and Cicero are depicted with intense frowns, as if upset by the presence of the British politician. Above the busts of the Greek and Roman orators, two pictures depicting the corpulent Empress of Russia are ironically titled 'Justice' and 'Moderation'.[15]

It is quite likely that Gillray drew inspiration for his satire from rumours circulating in the British papers the previous year. The *Morning Post and Daily Advertiser* reported on 8 August 1791 that:

> The Imperial Catharine [sic], it is said, has written, with her own hand, to her Ambassador, to request Mr. Fox to sit to Nollkens [sic; Joseph Nollekens (1737–1823) was the most fashionable English portrait sculptor of his time] for his bust in white marble, which she intends to place between the statues of Demosthenes and Cicero, as a mark of her esteem for the man whose eloquence and wisdom saved his own country and the Russian empire from an unprovoked and ruinous war.[16]

Gillray may have also been inspired by some ironic epigrams published in the columns of the *Public Advertiser* (8 September 1791):

ON A BUST INTENDED TO BE PLACED BETWEEN THE BUSTS
OF CICERO AND DEMOSTHENES IN A FOREIGN GALLERY.

THESE Busts – with *such a Bust* between,
Give satire all its strength, Sir;
Here *Wisdom's* on the *outside* seen,
There *Gambling* in the *center* [sic].[17]

ANOTHER IN A CONVERSATION BETWEEN CICERO
AND DEMOSTHENES

DEMOSTHENES.
Brother Tully,
What a sully
On our honours, is this BUST!
Cheeck by jowl,
'Pon my soul,
'Tis neither classical, or just.

CICERO.
Then why stand we shilly shally,
Brother, let us instant rally!
For let me say – Odzooks, 'tis
A cruel and unheard of case;
let him seek his *proper place*,
and find his nick at Brookes's.[18]

As a matter of fact, not only star orators but also less renowned Members of Parliament were associated with their celebrated Greek and Roman counterparts. Eighteenth-century readers would have found nothing strange in the idea that a certain Henry Flood (1732–91), 'a most distinguished member of the House of Commons', could be described as an emulator of Demosthenes's strength and vehemence, 'without aiming at the diffusion and brilliancy of Cicero'.[19] Indeed, so intimate was the interconnection between the Roman Senate and the British Parliament, that it did not escape the notice even of foreigners visiting London, including, notably, Voltaire. In his *Letters on the English*, the French philosopher significantly observed: 'The members of the English Parliament are fond of comparing themselves to the ancient Romans as much as they can'.[20]

Each of these examples reveals the extent to which leading Greek and Roman rhetoricians acted as inspiring and unrivalled models for the eighteenth-century elite and its parliamentary representatives. A closer analysis of the press, however, also suggests that, oratory aside, classical culture *tout court* was the object of intense interest and much discussion among the nation's readers. New translations of the Classics into English were widely publicized and articles were commonly opened with epigraphs in Latin and Greek. Each number of the *Spectator*, for instance, was prefaced by a *sententia* (maxim) either in Latin or – although less frequently – in Greek, which remained untranslated.[21] No less importantly, satirists and political reporters frequently hid their identities under *noms de plume* such as Aristophanes, Junius, Sallust, Cato, Historicus, Philologus, Decius, Marcus and Candidus. As Solkin writes, 'Latin pseudonyms, it should be pointed out, were used by writers of all shades and political opinion, from the most radical to the most reactionary'.[22] To offer but one eminent example, the pamphleteer and classical scholar Thomas Gordon (d. 1750) and the critic John Trenchard (1662–1723) co-authored *Cato's Letters*, a series of essays concerning the contemporary British political system. The essays were published under the pseudonym of Cato, the Roman aristocrat who preferred committing suicide rather than submitting to Caesar.

If we shift our attention to British papers issued in India in the period of the Hastings trial, they equally abounded in citations from the Classics and allusions to Greek and Roman cultures. A precious source of information, in this respect, is the British Library's collection of early English-language Indian newspapers. A survey of the latter shows, for instance, that on 23 October 1788 the *Calcutta Chronicle: And General Advertiser* gave over much of its front page to an article titled *On Roman Actors*. Similarly, a close examination of the *India Gazette: Or, Calcutta Public Advertiser* reveals that classical, particularly Roman, culture was a frequent topic. One may think of such articles as *Of the Head-Dresses of Roman Ladies* (20 October 1788), discussing Roman ladies' hairstyles, ornaments and fashions, including that of covering the hair 'with gold dust, to make it still more brilliant'; or *Of Roman entertainments* (10 November 1788), concerning Roman amusements before and during supper.[23] Many issues then offered imitations of classical poetic forms, particularly odes. In this respect, Horace was probably the most frequently emulated poet.[24]

Public interest was also kindled by new English versions of classical texts. The *Hircarrah*, a British newspaper issued in Madras, publicized in 1794 the 'admirable translation of the works of Tacitus' by the actor-playwright Arthur Murphy (1727–1805), a volume tellingly dedicated to Edmund Burke. It is interesting to note that the *Hircarrah* printed both Murphy's dedication to Burke (7 January 1794) and two passages taken from Murphy's translation of Tacitus's *Agricola*, namely the speech of Galgacus to his army on the Grampian Hills (12 August 1794) and the speech of Agricola to his army (2 September 1794). Published in 1793, Murphy's translation was immensely popular and continued to be reprinted until the beginning of the twentieth century. Burke found this translation extremely enjoyable. In a letter penned on 8 December 1793, he wrote to Murphy: 'You have done what hitherto, I think, has not been done in England: you have given us a translation of a Latin prose-writer which may be read with pleasure. [...] I have always thought the world much obliged to good translators, like you.'[25]

Popular perceptions of Cicero and Verres

Among the classical models that were a constant source of inspiration for the political and cultural elite, Cicero was certainly prominent. At the time, the most authoritative classical text on his life was Plutarch's *Lives*. Providing a window on the ancient world, the *Lives*, in Susanne Gippert's words, 'were most widely celebrated throughout the eighteenth century as the ideal biographical model'.[26] Plutarch had already been translated into English in the sixteenth and seventeenth centuries. For example, Shakespeare probably used Thomas North's *The Lives of the noble Grecians and Romanes [sic], compared together by that grave, learned philosopher and historiographer Plutarke [sic] of Chaeronea: translated out of Greeke [sic] into French by I. Amyot and into Englishe [sic] by T. North* (1579). A version attributed to Dryden, but in fact translated by several hands, appeared more than a century later.[27] In 1770, two brothers, John (1735–79) and William (1721–72) Langhorne, started publishing a new translation in six volumes, which soon became widely renowned and fashionable.

Plutarch's Cicero is not a monolithic figure, but presents three different facets: the orator, the statesman and – though less prominently – the philosopher. Repeatedly, the Greek biographer celebrates the power and magnificence of the orator's performances: his rhetoric is called 'victorious', his speeches displaying 'such a variety of pathos, so irresistible a charm, that his colour often changed'.[28] Along with this, the Greek writer incessantly highlights Cicero's 'diligence, justice and moderation', as well as his 'great integrity and honour'.[29] It is particularly in the description of Catiline's conspiracy – which occupies a long section of the *Life of Cicero* – that the great orator emerges as an indefatigable and capable statesman. Cicero's devotion to philosophy, conversely, is dealt with quite hastily. Plutarch remarks that Cicero preferred being called a philosopher to being called an orator 'because he had made philosophy his business, and rhetoric only the instrument of his political operations'.[30] After eulogizing the Roman statesman's undisputed merits, the Greek historian alludes to Cicero's numerous flaws and moral imperfections, including '[his] continually praising and magnifying himself' and a 'natural avidity of glory'.[31]

If we turn to the lives of Cicero composed and published in Britain throughout the eighteenth century, the orator's narcissism and insatiable craving for honour and fame were very much the focus of *Observations on the Life of Cicero* (1733) by the Whig statesman George Lyttelton (1709–73). Even though Lyttelton admits that the Roman orator's writings were 'the noblest Lessons of Publick [sic] Honesty, Disinterestedness, and the Love of Liberty, that are to be found in all Antiquity', he also frequently refers to Cicero's unlimited ambition, private interests and passions.[32] Lyttelton's criticism of Cicero increases in severity when considering the period of Caesar's ascendency in Rome, blaming Cicero for leading 'a most inglorious and dishonourable Life, courting the Usurper whom in his Heart he hated, with the most abject and servile Adulations, entirely forgetting the Dignity of his former Character'.[33]

That Lyttelton's portrait of Cicero is overall negative, and in some cases even scornful, is quite ironic. Two years after the publication of the *Observations*, Lyttelton formed a group of young politicians known as Cobham's Cubs or the Boy Patriots (all the members were less than thirty years old). According to Christine Gerrard, 'they attracted praise for their apparently disinterested patriotism as well as ridicule for the Ciceronian rhetoric which distinguished their political speeches'.[34]

Less than a decade after the appearance of Lyttelton's *Observations*, the clergyman Conyers Middleton (1683–1750) completed what was probably the most authoritative eighteenth-century biography of Cicero, the monumental *History of the Life of Marcus Tullius Cicero*.[35] First published in London in 1741, Middleton's *Life* was subscribed to by the royal family as well as the most influential members of the social, political and literary circles, including Sir Robert Walpole (1676–1745), Alexander Pope (1688–1744) and Samuel Johnson (1709–84).[36] Its hefty volumes had a vast resonance also on the Continent; it was translated into French in 1763 by the Abbé Prévost (1697–1763) and into Spanish in 1790.[37] Even in the thirteen colonies, where it was read in the original edition, Middleton's *Life* was extremely influential, particularly in the early years after the War of Independence. In this context, Yasunari Takada has suggested that 'Middleton's *Life of Cicero* had an important role to play in forming what can be termed English and American Ciceronian culture for at least a hundred years after its publication'.[38] In contrast with Plutarch's *Life* and Lyttelton's *Observations*, Middleton's blockbuster biography of 1741 may be regarded as a panegyric or a hagiography of Cicero. Indeed, in the Reverend's own words, Cicero was 'the man, who after a life spent in perpetual struggle against vice, faction and tyranny, fell a Martyr at last to the liberty of his country'.[39] Within this laudatory context, even Cicero's most renowned flaw, his vanity, was eventually justified: 'if we attend to the circumstances of the time, [...] we shall find it not only excusable, but in some degree even necessary.'[40]

Middleton's idealization of the Roman orator raised a number of criticisms.[41] Among others, *The Death of M-L-N in the Life of Cicero: Being a Proper Criticism on That Marvellous Performance* by an anonymous 'Oxford scholar' is remarkable for its witty satire. Published in London in the same year of Middleton's *Life*, *The Death of M-L-N* is ironically dedicated 'To the Right Honourable, Right Reverend, Right Worshipful, Honourable, Reverend, and Worshipful SUBSCRIBERS to Dr. M---n's Life of Cicero; as likewise TO the Mr's, Mrs's, Masters, Misses, & c., in the same Subscription-List'. Given the sarcastic title and dedication of this treatise, it comes as no surprise that Middleton is accused of 'ignorance and presumption' and his work is described as 'Much-a-do about nothing; [...] a crude, indigested, incoherent Mass'.[42] If, the anonymous writer continues, Lyttelton depicted 'the Man Cicero, of

Caesar's and Pompey's Times', the 'Reverend Author', instead, conjures up 'a faultless Monster of his own creation', 'a Patch-Work Hero [sic] of his own Imagination'.[43] After offering a number of examples testifying to Middleton's ignorance and inability to translate Latin into English, the Oxford Scholar concludes his text with an expression of utter disdain and contempt: '[Middleton] has poisoned and perverted every Part of History he has laid his Fist upon, and warped and misrepresented every Character which he has attempted with his Sign-Post Pencil'.[44]

In 1747, six years after the publication of *The Death of M-L-N*, the Poet-Laureate, actor and theatre manager Colley Cibber (1671–1757) launched another attack on Middleton's *Life* in *Character and Conduct of Cicero, Considered, From the History of his Life, by the Reverend Dr. Middleton*. Following Middleton's *Life* page by page, Cibber paints a new portrait of the ancient orator, in which he appears to be anything but perfect; repeatedly, the Poet-Laureate dwells on Cicero's want of firmness during the exile, his vanity, his political opportunism and 'his frequent changing from and to the Interests of *Pompey* and of *Caesar*'.[45] Even the episode Cicero was most famous for, Catiline's defeat, is contemptuously described as 'the work of *Fortune* not of *Cicero*'.[46]

New clouds on Middleton's success were cast again almost forty years later, in 1782, when the poet and literary critic Joseph Warton (1722–1800) accused the Reverend of plagiarism. According to Warton, Middleton had drawn largely from a seventeenth-century rare book, *De Tribus Luminibus Romanorum* (1634), by the Scottish classicist William Bellenden (c.1550–c.1633). The three 'lights' of the title referred to Cicero, Seneca and the elder Pliny; the author had intended to write a section on each 'light', but had in the end only managed to complete the first part on Cicero. Juxtaposing Middleton's *Life* with Bellenden's unfinished study, Warton came to the conclusion that:

> The life of Tully procured Dr. Middleton a great reputation, and a great sum of money. [...] It may be worth observing, that he is much indebted, without acknowledging it, to a curious book little known, entitled, G. Bellendeni, Scoti, de Tribus Luminibus Romanorum, Libri 16. Parisiis. Apud Tassanum du Bray, 1634. Folio; dedicated to King Charles. [...] In his book Middleton found every part of Cicero's own history, in his own words, and his works arranged in chronological order, without farther trouble.[47]

The criticisms did not stop there. In 1787, the accusation of appropriating Bellenden's work was once more made against Middleton by the schoolmaster and illustrious classical scholar Samuel Parr (1747–1825). In his *Prefatio ad Bellendenum* – significantly dedicated to three of the most renowned orators of the time – Edmund Burke, Frederick Lord North (1732–92) and Charles James Fox – Parr maintained that, after diligently collating Middleton's composition with *De Tribus Luminibus*, he was finally able 'to speak decisively on the subject':[48] 'to conclude the whole', the schoolmaster asserted, 'whatever Middleton ostentatiously declares it to be his wish and his duty to do, had been already done to his hands, faithfully and skilfully, by Bellendenus, from the beginning of the work to its final conclusion.'[49]

Assessing the veracity of Warton's and Parr's accusations lies beyond the purpose of this study.[50] What needs to be stressed, however, is that this animated, vehement and constant debating about Cicero occurred at a time when some of the most crucial stages of the trial against Hastings were taking place. For example, in 1782, while Warton vilified Middleton's work, Burke called for Hastings's punishment.[51] Even more significantly, in 1787 and 1788, when Parr's *Prefatio ad Bellendenum* and its translation into English appeared respectively, Burke launched the impeachment of Hastings. This context is particularly noteworthy, if we consider that Burke – as we will see in some detail in Chapter 4 – conducted the arraignment of the Governor-General of Bengal as though he were Cicero and Hastings Verres, the *propraetor* of Sicily brought to trial in Rome in 70 BC.

Our review of the most influential eighteenth-century British biographies of Cicero, and of the polemics and critical quarrels that sprang from them, would not be complete without reference to the *Encyclopaedia Britannica*. First published in Edinburgh between 1768 and 1771, the *Encyclopaedia* was soon praised as one of the century's most credited sources of information on art, science and literature. Starting from the second edition (1778–83), the name of Cicero appeared among its entries. Indeed, as its frontispiece promised, the second edition was enriched with new sections, including an 'Account of the Lives of the most Eminent Persons in every Nation, from the earliest ages, down to the present times'. Before the end of the century, a third, enlarged edition was issued in Dublin (1791–7). This time, the account of the life of Cicero – largely drawn from Middleton's eulogy – was followed by two critical commentaries, the first on the orator's character, and the second on his rhetorical style.

In both the second and third editions, the biography of the orator occupies fewer than six pages and is reconstructed around some salient events of Cicero's life. The prosecution of Verres is discussed at length and described as 'one of the most memorable transactions of his life; for which he was greatly and justly celebrated by antiquity, and for which he will, in all ages, be admired and esteemed by the friends of mankind'.[52] According to the *Encyclopaedia*, the episode shows Cicero as an outstanding rhetorician, as well as a clement and merciful man, as in the remark that, when Verres submitted to a voluntary exile, 'he is said to have been relieved in this miserable situation by the generosity of Cicero'.[53]

First and foremost, however, the *Encyclopaedia* casts Cicero as 'the celebrated Roman orator'.[54] Not only did he achieve perfection in the *ars rhetorica*, but he also attained excellence in nearly every field: ideally without flaws, he was the quintessence of *virtus*. As such, the *Encyclopaedia* variously depicts him as a great supporter of the *res publica* and an enemy to the triumvirate. For example, when Caesar defeated Pompey and Cicero retired from the public scene, 'he [Cicero] paid a constant attention to public affairs; missed no opportunities, but did every thing that human prudence could do for the recovery of the republic'.[55] In such a eulogy, Cicero's only weakness appears to have been his despondence during the exile. Conversely, his notorious *vanitas* is hinted at, and his divorce from Terentia is presented as a consequence of his wife's 'imperious and turbulent spirit'.[56]

Starting from the third edition of the *Encyclopaedia*, this laudatory biography was complemented with the critical comments of the traveller Henry Swinburne (1743–1803) and the minister and literary critic Hugh Blair (1718–1800). After the death of his parents and elder brother, the former began travelling around Europe and visited, amongst other places, an archaeological site adjacent to the putative spot where Cicero was murdered by the killers sent by Antony. The fascination and evocative power of the area inspired Swinburne's reflections, which were recorded in his *Travels in the Two Sicilies, 1777–1780* (1783–5). In evident contrast with the *Encyclopaedia*'s previous section of the biography of Cicero, Swinburne's remarks are introduced by a significant sentence which sets the tone for the traveller's negative thoughts: 'A modern writer, however, is of opinion that posterity has been too much seduced by the name of Cicero, and that better citizens were sacrificed to the jealousy of the triumvirs without exciting too much indignation'.[57] Indeed, Swinburne's observations are particularly harsh, as he suggests, for instance, that from 'an impartial survey of Cicero's conducts and principles', one would 'find more to blame than to admire' or that Mark Antony 'caused Cicero to be killed, as an angry man that has been stung, stamps on a venomous animal that comes within reach of his foot'.[58]

The second comment on Cicero's life is by the illustrious Scottish rhetorician Hugh Blair. Interested in classical rhetoric since an early age, in 1759 Blair began to deliver a course of lectures on composition. Indeed, so successful was this course that in 1762 King George III (1738–1820) appointed Blair as Regius Professor of Rhetoric and Belles Lettres at the University of Edinburgh. Like Swinburne, Blair does not hesitate to reprimand Cicero: 'this great orator [...] is not without his defects'.[59] After admitting that 'No one knew the force of words better than Cicero', Blair is quick to note that 'In most of his orations there is too much art, even carried to a degree of ostentation. He seems often desirous of obtaining admiration rather than operating conviction'.[60]

From the 1750s onwards, the large number of Ciceronian biographies and the heated discussions to which they gave rise were paralleled by a flourishing market of new editions and translations of Cicero's texts into English. Middleton himself was involved in a controversy over the authenticity of the epistles *Ad Marcum Brutum*. A convinced and relentless supporter of the authenticity of these letters, in 1743 he published an English version with parallel text, which became the object of many criticisms.[61]

One later volume, which encapsulates the eighteenth-century British fascination with Cicero, is *A view of the English Editions, Translations and Commentaries of Marcus Tullius Cicero, with Remarks* (1795), by the German chaplain to the Prussian king, Ludwig Wilhelm Brüggemann (1743–1817).[62] As the title suggests, Brüggemann's thirty-six-page compilation offers us a glimpse into the sheer range of Cicero's English versions and editions, the most recent of which are followed by a detailed critical commentary derived from either the *Monthly Review* or the *Critical Review*. According to Brüggemann, up until 1795, Cicero's works circulating in Britain were: *Rhetorica, De Oratore, Brutus, Orator, Orationes, Epistolae ad Familiares, Epistolae ad Atticum et ad*

M. Brutum, Academica, De Finibus, Tusculanae Quaestiones, De Natura Deorum, De Divinatione et de Fato, De Legibus, De Officiis, Cato Maior, Laelius, Paradoxa, Somnium Scipionis, Consolatio, Fragmenta Oeconomicorum Ciceronis.

From Brüggemann's survey, one may easily infer that Cicero's most frequently translated texts were the *Orationes* – the majority of the translations being the work of either William Guthrie (*c*.1708–70) or William Melmoth (1710–99). From this we gather that the latter was constantly eulogized in British critical reviews. For instance, his edition of *Cato; or, an Essay on Old Age* (1773) was described as 'executed by a masterly hand. The language is pure and classical and expresses the sense of the original with fidelity and spirit'.[63] Conversely, Guthrie's versions are often dismissed as inaccurate, hasty and bearing 'upon them the strongest marks of want of attention'.[64]

Interestingly enough, the first and sole eighteenth-century English version of the orations *in Verrem* – a 'version', the *Critical Review* noted, 'not only spirited but generally correct'[65] – was published in 1787, a year before the start of the trial against the Governor-General of Bengal. J. M. S. Tompkins has stressed that 'the book was no mere exercise in scholarship': its translator, James White (1759–99), 'had in mind the preparations for the impeachment of another provincial governor – Warren Hastings'.[66] In the introduction to his translation, White tellingly exhorts 'the statesman and the senator', as well as the 'patriot Englishman', to consider 'the political observations with which they [the *Verrines*] abound'.[67] Parallels between Verres's misrule of Sicily and the British presence in India radiate out from practically every page in the preface. For example, after observing that Verres 'could, for three years, act the tyrant uncontrollably', in spite of his being 'within reach of Roman justice', White significantly wonders: 'how numerous must be the temptations to an European officer for oppressing the human species beneath the Equinoctial?'[68] The preface terminates with an ominous admonition in the form of a *sententia*: 'Justice and probity are the main pillars of an empire: remove them, and, be its pride, infatuation, and insolence what they may, the speedy ruin of that empire is inevitable'.[69]

If Cicero the orator was admired and imitated, particularly by the governing elite, Verres, the tyrannous *propraetor* of Sicily persecuted by Tully, was no less renowned, as several texts penned throughout the eighteenth century demonstrate. Margaret M. Miles, for instance, notes that Verres and the *Verrines* were often evoked by 'private persons concerned with issues of plundering or extortion'.[70] Her point is supported by a few concise examples, among which is an anonymous pamphlet in verse titled *Verres and his Scribblers: A Satire in Three Cantos* (1732). In this specific case, the unknown author's irony is directed at Sir Robert Walpole, then first lord of the treasury, and his 'heavy-handed monetary policy'.[71] The text also includes 'an examen of the piece', from which we may assume that contemporary readers were well acquainted with the story of Verres: 'I have laid the Scene in *Sicily*, at the time, or soon after *Verres* govern'd there, (that *Verres* who was immortalized by *Cicero*'s Orations against him)' – the anonymous pamphleteer explained.[72] The 'key to the poem' also proves quite illuminating, as it provides a list of the main vices and misdeeds for which Verres – and his eighteenth-century alter ego 'Lawlope' (an anagram of Walpole) – were notorious. Among them, the author lists the (illegal) 'Practice or Practices' by means of which Verres/Lawlope 'has amassed prodigious Sums'. Other similarities between them include their being 'litigious, odd, avaritious squandring, vain, [...] bullying, noisy, haranguing, powerful, wealthy' and their employing 'a pert, noisy, illiterate, ignorant, impudent Sett [sic] of Fellows' to perform scandalous actions in their name.[73]

In political satire, the stratagem of portraying a powerful public figure in the guise of Verres was not new. In 1710, Jonathan Swift (1667–1745) had published an anonymous article in the *Examiner* (23–30 November 1710) juxtaposing Thomas, first Earl of Wharton (1648–1715), with the *propraetor* of Sicily. Before drawing directly on Cicero's first *Verrine*, Swift himself elucidates the expedient ('frequently practic'd with great safety and success by Satyrical [sic] Writers') he is about to use: 'That of looking into History for some Character bearing a Resemblance to the Person we would describe; and with the absolute Power of altering, adding or suppressing what Circumstances we please'. Readers are further informed that, prior to choosing Verres as the ancient counterpart to the Earl of Wharton, Swift consulted Livy and Tacitus, but, being unable to find any parallel, 'without doing Injury to a *Roman* Memory', he resolved 'to have Recourse to *Tully*'.[74] This introduction is followed by Swift's own translation of a section of the *Actio Prima*. As with the protagonist of *Verres and His Scribblers*, also in Swift's hands, the Roman governor of Sicily comes to represent the prototype of a degenerate politician, acting 'with Rashness or Wilfulness, Corruption, Ignorance or Injustice'.[75]

Cicero's orations against Verres, and Verres himself, resurfaced also in legal treatises and travel accounts. For instance, in his *Idea of the Modern Eloquence of the Bar* (1711), the Advocate to King Charles II, George Mackenzie (1636/8–1714), refers to 'the *Pleadings* of *Cicero* against *Verres*' as 'the best Models and Patterns in the World of just and natural *Narrations*': that is to say, speeches pronounced by a crafty orator, who 'makes those Things seem to be present and visible which are absent and already past'.[76]

As we have previously seen with Swinburne's example, Sicily was included among the itineraries of the Grand Tour from the 1770s onwards.[77] It goes without saying that those who could afford to travel were the members of an elite that was forged and modelled on Graeco-Roman culture and values. This thorough classical education, which included the study of oratorical treatises, as well as the speeches of the leading orators of antiquity, represented the powerful lenses through which the cities and archaeological remnants in southern Italy and Sicily were seen and understood.

Thus, one of the earliest English travellers to Sicily, John Breval (1680/1–1738), recorded in his memoirs that, during a walk 'round *Catanea*', he was 'shewn [sic] the Foundations of the old Temple of *Ceres* (mention'd by *Cicero* in one of his Orations against *Verres*)'; similarly, while describing the precious objects of art in Syracuse's most renowned shrines, he noted: 'These Rarities were all carry'd [sic] off by *Verres*'.[78] References to the *Verrines* and the *propraetor* of Sicily also filter into what Edward Chaney has described as 'the most widely read of all eighteenth-century travelogues', namely *A Tour through Sicily and Malta* (1773) by Patrick Brydone (1736–1818).[79] The visit to the temple of Hercules in Agrigentum works as a sort of *madeleine* for the author, who is suddenly reminded that 'it was here that the famous statue of Hercules stood, so much celebrated by Cicero; which the people of Agrigentum defended with such bravery, against Verres who attempted to seize it. You will find the whole story in his pleadings against that infamous praetor'.[80] Four years later, the same episode from the *Verrines* was evoked again – albeit more succinctly – by Richard Payne Knight (1751–1824), a traveller who was later to become a distinguished art collector. On the occasion of a trip to the same site, he observed: 'In this temple was the famous Statue of Hercules, which Verres attempted to carry away but was prevented by the Spirit and Activity of the Agrigentines'.[81]

From this perspective, it is far from surprising that allusions to the governor of Sicily, as well as the orations *In Verrem*, may even be found in fictitious autobiographies, such as *The Travels of Edward Brown, Esq* (1739) by the historian John Campbell (1708–75). In the section concerning the island of Malta, after dwelling on some trivial considerations, including that 'The Dogs and Cats of Malta are particularly handsome', Brown/Campbell observes that 'In ancient Times the Inhabitants of Malta were famous throughout all Europe for their Skill in maritime Affairs, their extensive Commerce, and for their refined Luxury, as appears from one of the Orations of Cicero against Verres, in which he upbraids him with being as voluptuous as a Maltese'.[82]

Campbell's *Travels* remind us that, throughout the eighteenth century, Cicero, Verres and the former's speeches against the latter were mentioned, translated and alluded to in a variety of different contexts, from political satire and manuals of law, to travelogues and fictitious works. These references to the greatest Roman orator and the villainous *propraetor* of Sicily attest to a wide-ranging interest in classical culture. Hence the propensity of MPs and orators to imitate, compete and, possibly, even surpass the star rhetoricians of antiquity. Besides constituting the basis of the political and governing elite's education, Graeco-Roman civilization, along with its languages, written texts and civic and spiritual values, was the subject of what we may imagine as a constant, lively discussion not only in the columns of newspapers but also among the reading nation, and the educated members of society at large. This Classics-saturated context constitutes the groundwork on which I begin my quest for the subtle and multiple classical presences in the trial of Warren Hastings – those of Cicero, Verres and the *Verrines*, in particular – that follows in the rest of this book. The identities of the 'classicized' protagonists of the impeachment – the British Cicero on the one hand, and the modern-day Verres on the other – comprise the theme to which we now turn.

2

A Clash of Characters

Mankind are neither so good nor so bad as they are generally represented. Human life is a stream formed and impelled by a variety of passions, and its actions seldom flow from single and unmixed sources.[1]

This quotation comes from the journal of the diplomat George Bogle (1746–81), the first British envoy to Bhutan and Tibet (1774–5), Hastings's 'deputy to the Teshu Lama, the sovereign of Bhutan'.[2] Even though Bogle's remarks are directed to the Hindus – his comments follow a description of the Hindu custom of women burning themselves alive on their deceased husband's funeral pyre – they may well be extended to the existence and actions of the two protagonists of this chapter, Edmund Burke and Warren Hastings. Both characters may, indeed, be recognized as extraordinary examples of deep respect for the Other, acute intelligence, courage and strength. At the same time, however, their lives abound in episodes that raise questions about their personal integrity.

Summarizing the career and works of Burke, a most controversial politician and orator, as well as an eclectic philosopher, is a daunting task. The same is true of Hastings, the first Governor-General of Bengal and bitter enemy of Burke: describing his adventurous life across Britain and India in a few pages can only result in a partial and rushed portrait of the man. From the nineteenth century onwards, the men's intertwined lives have been the subject of a large number of studies and monographs, including Thomas Babington Macaulay's *Memoirs of the Life of Warren Hastings, First Governor-General of Bengal* (1841) and P. J. Marshall's classic *The Impeachment of Warren Hastings* (1965).[3] In what follows, I shall concentrate on those details of the two protagonists' personalities and careers that may help to illuminate the *cause célèbre* under examination, specifically in light of their knowledge and use of classical culture.

Edmund Burke

On being asked whether Burke had 'read Cicero much', the renowned lexicographer Samuel Johnson (1709–84) replied:

> I don't believe it, Sir. Burke had great knowledge, great fluency of words, and great promptness of ideas, so that he can speak with great illustration on any subject that comes before him. He is neither like Cicero, nor like Demosthenes, nor like any one else, but speaks as well as he can.[4]

This joke attests to the tendency of Burke's contemporaries to associate the Anglo-Irish orator with the leading Graeco-Roman rhetoricians. As we saw in the previous chapter, this was a common trend in eighteenth-century Britain, but between Burke and Tully there was 'a particular affinity' (to use the words of Paddy Bullard) – a perception that Burke encouraged throughout his career.[5] 'In my long intimacy with *Edmund Burke*, [...]' – Sir Philip Francis (1740–1818) observed in his *Letter Missive to Lord Holland* in 1816 – 'it could not escape me, nor did he wish to conceal it, that Cicero was the model, on which he laboured to form his own character, in eloquence, in policy, in ethics and philosophy'.[6] Burke had, indeed, been represented as a latter-day Cicero well before the commencement of the *cause célèbre*. For example, together with an article on the life and political career of the Irish-born orator, the *London Magazine* for April 1770 published an elegant engraved portrait of Burke significantly titled 'the British Cicero'.[7] The anonymous print is not a caricature but depicts Burke as an eighteenth-century gentleman brandishing Magna Carta. At his back, behind a curtain, is a statue of Cicero. As the *London Magazine* reads, the connection between the Roman and Anglo-Irish orator was possibly to be made by virtue of Burke's 'uncommon display of oratorical powers'.[8]

The similarities between the two will be dealt with in more depth in Chapter 4. Suffice it to say here that Burke cites Cicero directly or alludes to him in nearly all his works.[9] In this respect, it is worth recalling that the Anglo-Irish orator's library included such volumes as *Ciceronis Opera Philosophica* (1642); *Ciceronis Epistulae ad Familiares* (1657); *Ciceronis Opera. Notis Gruteri et Gronovii* (1692); *Ciceronis Orationes* (1770); *Cicero de Natura Deorum* (1744) and *Ciceronis Opera, Notis Variorum et Verburgii* (1724).[10]

The son of a prosperous attorney, Burke was born in Dublin.[11] The year of his birth is uncertain, with 1730 seeming more probable than 1729.[12] In 1741, he was sent to a Quaker school at Ballitore, which provided him with a thorough academic training. In order to prepare for the law, Burke then returned to Dublin, where he attended Trinity College between 1744 and 1748. While he was a student there, he founded with six friends an 'Academy of Belles Lettres', intended to provide autodidactic training in public speaking. The Academy's main activity, as Lock has highlighted, 'was the practice of rhetoric. Members made extempore speeches on given subjects, or delivered orations carefully prepared in advance'.[13] Sometimes model speeches from ancient rhetoricians would be delivered; at other meetings a subject would be chosen and debated as in the Irish House of Commons nearby.

We have very little evidence of the Greek and Roman rhetoricians studied at Trinity College at the time, but we can conclude with Bullard that 'Burke's heart seems always to have been with the Latin authors'.[14] Tellingly, around the age of fifty, Burke himself confessed to be 'one so many years disused to Greek literature'.[15] On the other hand, the abundance of Latin quotations interspersed in his writings and speeches leads us to assume that he read Latin texts mostly in the original language. This assumption is corroborated by a confession made to Sir William Jones, the celebrated linguist, orientalist and judge to whom Burke wrote in 1779: 'I do not know how it has happened, that orators have hitherto fared worse in the hands of the translators, than even the poets; I never could bear to read a translation of Cicero'.[16] As Michael J. Franklin has significantly pointed out, the two friends and fellow members of Johnson's and Reynolds's Turk's Head Club, Burke and Jones, were to break their friendship a few years later, owing to 'their divergent estimates of the career and character of Warren Hastings, the Governor-General of Bengal, whom Jones was to invite to be President of his newly-formed Asiatick and Burke was to impeach'.[17]

By 1753, Burke had drafted his masterpiece, *A Philosophical Enquiry into the Origin of our Ideas of the Sublime and Beautiful*. Originally published in 1757 – a second revised edition followed in 1759 – this small treatise linking human psychology and aesthetic taste would have an enormous impact and far-reaching effects not only in Britain, but also on the Continent. Notably, Kant regarded Burke as 'the foremost author' in 'the empirical exposition of aesthetic judgments'.[18]

A few years earlier, in 1750, Burke had arrived in London to study law at Middle Temple. The five years he spent at the London Inns of Court maintaining a pretence of studying were profoundly unhappy, with Burke even suffering a breakdown. However, when he finally entered the Commons, in 1765, he immediately made a name for himself as an outstanding speaker. He owed his talent to an extensive knowledge of political and economic topics, as well as to an uncommon vehemence of speech. It is in a tone of stupefaction that on 25 December 1767 the English-born Charles Lee (1732–82), later a revolutionary army officer in America, wrote to Prince Czartoryski that 'An Irishman, one Mr. Burke, is sprung up in the House of Commons, who has astonished everybody with the power of his eloquence'.[19] As we will see in more detail in Chapter 3, Burke's speaking enthralled his audiences and produced strong, physical effects upon them. For the moment, it will suffice to note that most of his listeners – both his supporters and enemies – were particularly struck by two qualities: 'an uncommon extent and depth of knowledge and thought, and a remarkable prodigality of imagination'.[20]

Burke's talent for performing highly emotional speeches may also be attributed to his passion for the stage. One biographer of Burke has stressed that, as 'a regular theatre-goer while a student in Dublin', Burke continued to attend theatrical performances in England, where he made friends with star actors and actresses of the time, among whom were David Garrick (1717–79) and Sarah Siddons.[21] Including a vast repertoire of histrionic gestures, the Anglo-Irish orator's exaggerated theatricality was repeatedly the object of comments and parody in contemporary newspapers and satirical prints.[22] In this respect, Burke's most celebrated *coup de théâtre* (made famous by Gillray and other caricaturists) occurred on 28 December 1792: while denouncing France as an infectious state of atheism and revolution, the orator took a dagger from under his coat and threw it to the floor.[23]

The combination of a dramatic performance with emotional appeals to sensibility and sensational images may be traced in Burke's parliamentary pronouncements at least ten years before the trial of the Governor-General of Bengal. One may think, for instance, of the 'Speech on the Use of Indians', which Burke delivered on 6 February 1778. In 1777, during the early stages of the American War of Independence, Jane McCrea, a young American woman betrothed to an English officer, was scalped by a group of Native American scouts working for the British forces. Soon the episode became 'a media sensation' and 'headline news on both sides of the Atlantic'.[24] The details and circumstances of the incident were not entirely clear. Nonetheless, Burke seized on the tragedy and created 'a sentimental tableau' out of it.[25]

Contemporary comments on the 'Speech on the Use of Indians' and the speech on the Rangpur atrocities (18 February 1788), one of the most sensational orations pronounced throughout the impeachment of Hastings, reveal a number of significant correspondences and striking continuities between the two orations. As such, it is worth briefly touching on the oratorical strategies that Burke employed in both speeches. In what follows, I will refer in particular to the 'Speech on the Use of Indians'. A detailed analysis of the Rangpur speech, as well as its reception, will be provided in Chapters 3 and 4.

As early as 1778, the orator seized on spectacularly violent material and dwelled on those disturbing details that would shock the sensibility of the audience. According to the *Parliamentary Register*, Burke 'repeated several instances' of the Native Americans' cruelty and systematic brutality – their savage culture of warfare far exceeding 'the ferocity of all barbarians mentioned in history'.[26] The account then moved into what Ian Haywood has called 'the register of hyperbolic realism':[27]

> their [the Native Americans'] rewards were generally received in human scalps, in human flesh, and the gratifications arising from torturing, mangling, scalping, and sometimes eating their captives in war. He [Burke] then repeated several instances of this diabolical mode of war, scarcely credible, and, if true, improper to be repeated.[28]

Although the 'Speech on the Use of Indians' survives only in drafts and fragments – among other things, the numerous 'scarcely credible' examples of the Native Americans' violence have been lost – the comments we may glean from contemporary sources as well as newspaper reports attest to the Anglo-Irish orator's ability to 'paint' horrid stories 'in very strong colours' and to manipulate his auditors' feelings to the verge of tears.[29] The *Public Advertiser* (7 February 1778), for instance, recorded that Burke spoke with 'a Pathos which melted the Auditory almost to Tears, and filled them with the utmost Horror', while in his *Last Journals*, Horace Walpole (1717–97) lauded Burke's oration as a 'chef-d'oeuvre'.³⁰ Similarly, the Rangpur speech agitated the whole assembly and some ladies even fainted.

Some indications of the horror generated in 1778 by Burke's 'pathetic eloquence' – as the *Morning Chronicle and London Advertiser* (9 February 1778) described it – can be derived from the orator's draft notes for the speech. Much of interest, in this sense, is 'the horrid story of Miss Mac Ray, murdered by the savages on the day of her marriage':³¹

> that hair dressed for other purposes that morning torn from her head to decorate the infernal habitation of cruelty and barbarism and there left a naked and [foul scale] her body a mangled ghastly spectacle of blood and horrour [sic], crying through an [sic] hundred mouths to that whose image was defaced for Vengeance.³²

Arguably, the emotional power of this cameo resonates in Burke's famous account of the French mob escorting the royal family from Versailles on 6 October 1789: 'It was (unless we have been strangely deceived) a spectacle more resembling a procession of American savages, entering into Onondaga, after some of their murders called victories, and leading into hovels hung round with scalps.'³³ But, before finding an echo in the *Reflections on the Revolution in France* (1790), the gothic description of Jane McCrea's mutilated corpse anticipates the gory images conjured up by the Anglo-Irish orator in his Rangpur narrative. In particular, McCrea's undressed and violated body (as Burke chooses to suggest here, though there was no evidence that the young woman had been raped), together with the allusion to her 'infernal' murderers, are evocative of the sexually abused Indian women and their torturers in the account of the Rangpur atrocities. As we will see in more detail in Chapter 4, Burke described Indian virgins and wives as 'cruelly violated' by 'infernal villains' and 'fiends', their bodies being 'naked and exposed to the public view'.³⁴

After the 'Speech on the Use of Indians' some contemporaries, such as the diplomat James Harris (1746–1820), dismissed the Anglo-Irish orator's emotional performances as 'mock tragedy, more plausible at Drury Lane'.³⁵ Also, the newspapers criticized Burke's use of dramatic and quasi-theatrical narratives. The *Morning Chronicle and London Advertiser* (9 February 1778), for example, suggested that 'The facts alledged as proofs of the untameable and ungovernable rage of the Indians, were [...] by much exaggerated' and 'owed a great deal of their horror to the fancy of the orator'. Similarly, the *Public Advertiser* (7 February 1778) reported that: 'his [Burke's] Stile [sic] [was] in general pathetic, eloquent, and sublime: But his Colourings we hope, for the Honour of Human Nature, were too high [...]. That Crimes were committed by some of the Indians was granted; but that they were of so deep a Dye as they were represented was flatly denied'.

Apparently, Burke intended to publish his Indian speech along with his two great American speeches, known as the 'Speech on American Taxation' (19 April 1774) and the 'Speech on Conciliation with America' (22 March 1775), but what would have been, as Paul Langford has put it, 'an astonishing triptych of American orations' remains incomplete.[36] Even so, the speech on taxation probably contributed to his election on 2 November 1774 as MP for Bristol, the empire's second city. On the occasion of new elections in 1780, however, the orator was compelled to withdraw and was deprived of his seat. Burke's failure is hardly surprising, considering that during the six years of his mandate he visited Bristol only twice (once in 1775 and once in 1776) and supported such causes as the commercial concessions to Ireland, the promotion of the Catholic Church in Scotland and the abolitionist movement. It goes without saying that Burke's endorsement of the latter was not well received in one of Britain's great slaving ports.

In the next two decades, the Irish-born orator maintained an impassioned engagement with imperial politics in India. Even though Burke travelled little and, according to Carl B. Cone, 'never further than Paris',[37] he took great pains to collect information about the geography, history, religions and cultures of the Indian subcontinent. A large number of volumes listed in the catalogue of the orator's library, among which *Koran, Translated by Sale* (1734), Dow's *History of Hindostan* (1768), *History of Bombay* (1781), Rennell's *Bengal Atlas* (1781), and Crawfurd's *Sketches of the Hindoos* (1792), bear witness to his close and detailed study of India.[38] One of the foremost scholars of the Hastings impeachment has, indeed, stressed that 'Burke's study of India was probably more intensive and more prolonged than any study of a non-European people undertaken by any of his great contemporaries, Voltaire and Diderot included'.[39]

Owing to an exuberant personality, Burke often proved dogmatic and impervious to criticism. He seems always to have pursued what he believed were the interests of the Company's Indian subjects, in accordance with morality.[40] It has often been remarked that Burke's approach to the problem of reconciling moral law and particular traditions is akin to Cicero's, with Frederick G. Whelan arguing, for example, that both men sought to justify the institutions of their own country 'as embodying justice and other values of natural law, and thus as satisfactorily realizing the proper ends of social life'.[41] Peter J. Stanlis has also contended that the Anglo-Irish orator borrowed largely from Cicero 'one of the most important ideas derived from the Natural Law – that the state is an indirect emanation of God's power and goodness and rests on divine law'.[42]

Burke's conception of a transcendent origin of power is encapsulated in his 'Speech on the Opening of the Impeachment' (16 February 1788). While demolishing any claims to arbitrary power, Burke enunciated his belief in a universal law ('We are all born in subjection, all born equally, high and low, governors and governed, in subjection to one great, immutable, pre-existent law [...] by which we are knit and connected in the eternal frame of the universe') and eloquently appealed to the divine origin of the 'great gift of Government, the greatest, the best that was ever given by God to mankind'.[43] This part of the speech contains some of the most fundamental elements in Burke's political and moral thought, particularly his 'total rejection of any kind of moral relativism'.[44] For the Anglo-Irish philosopher it was not conceivable that there could exist one law for Europe and another for India, all men being bound by a universal 'code of morality, resting on the will of God'.[45]

As P. J. Marshall has highlighted in his Introduction to the sixth volume of the *Writings and Speeches of Edmund Burke*, any educated eighteenth-century gentleman would have recognized that the arguments used by Burke to prove that Indians were subject to the same 'laws of morality' as the British, were 'of great antiquity'.[46] Indeed, they were the arguments employed by Cicero also in his arraignment of Verres. Burke's renowned accusation of 'geographical morality', for example, may have been inspired by a passage in Cicero's *Verrines*.[47] The section where the Anglo-Irish orator contends that 'the laws of morality are the same every where, and [...] there is no action which would pass for an action of extortion, of peculation, of bribery and of oppression in England, that is not an act of extortion, of peculation, of bribery and of oppression in Europe, Asia, Africa, and all the world over'[48] tellingly echoes

Cicero's trenchant question to Verres 'Or is one thing fair in Rome and another in Sicily?' (*Verr*. II.1.118: *an aliud Romae aequum est, aliud in Sicilia?*).[49]

Burke's interest in India began many years before the commencement of the trial of Hastings and lasted until his death. From 1781 to 1783, the orator served on a Select Committee on Bengal, for which he drafted eleven reports on the activities of the East India Company. The reports later underpinned many of the twenty-two 'Articles of Charge of High Crimes and Misdemeanors' against Hastings that Burke presented between 4 April and 5 May 1786 before the House of Commons. It has been observed that Burke's work for the Committee 'left its mark on his thinking on Indian questions': as a matter of fact, 'insistence that Indian institutions should be preserved from alien impositions' was to become a constant presence in practically all of Burke's speeches and writings about India.[50]

Before describing in more detail the circumstances that led Burke to prosecute the ills of imperial rule in the person of Hastings, we should set India aside for a moment and turn our attention towards France, as the impeachment of the Governor-General of Bengal is inextricably intertwined with the outbreak of the French Revolution. The sensational events that followed the taking of the Bastille in the summer of 1789 were, in fact, to have an enormous repercussion on Burke's life as well as on his political career and alliances. In this respect, although Burke continued to speak in Parliament until the conclusion of the trial against Hastings, the *Reflections on the Revolution in France*, which he passionately set out to write in 1790, 'is very much a valediction to his career as an orator'.[51]

Ever since the news of the taking of the Bastille had reached England, many observers – among whom Fox, Sheridan and most of the Whigs – supported the French Revolution and applauded it as the dawn of liberty. Conversely, insisting on the Revolution's destructive nature, Burke responded furiously to the events in France and fiercely opposed any attempt to imitate them in the British Isles. In vivid and memorable language, Burke condemned the Revolution as 'a progress through Chaos and darkness',[52] the work of 'Atheistick [*sic*] Banditti' and 'systematick [*sic*] regicides'.[53] These stigmatizing expressions were charged with highly evocative power in the English collective imagination: not only were they reminiscent of literary texts dealing with transgression, such as Milton's *Paradise Lost* ('Chaos and darkness') or eighteenth-century Gothic novels (bandits populated Gothic landscapes as suggestive figures of threats), but they also alluded to bloody historical events, particularly the execution of Charles I (1600–49). It was at this point – first, with the publication of the *Reflections* (1 November 1790) and then, officially and acrimoniously, with Burke's reply to Fox at the end of the parliamentary session of 11 May 1791 – that Burke decided to separate from the latter and from his former friends in the Whig party. Eloquently, a footnote in the *Parliamentary History*'s report for 11 May reads: 'Thus ended the friendship which had lasted for more than the fourth part of a century'.[54]

F. P. Lock has acutely noted that the *Reflections* 'has proved the most enduring book on the Revolution [...] and one that remains contested and contentious'.[55] As a matter of fact, the text made an immediate impact and triggered an endless ideological debate that was to transform Burke's reputation not only among his contemporaries but also for posterity. The treatise immediately received extensive coverage in the press, with Burke and the *Reflections* being parodied in popular caricatures.[56] The controversy surrounding the text and its author was further inflamed by the appearance of at least six hundred pamphlets – very few of which were written in Burke's defence. Four weeks after the publication of the first British edition, the *Reflections* appeared in French. The translator and friend of Burke's, Pierre-Gaëton Dupont (*c.* 1759–1817), wrote enthusiastically to the orator that, in two days, the text had sold 2,500 copies.[57]

Meanwhile, the trial went on and necessitated a minimum of collaboration between Burke and his old Whig friends. After the storming of the Bastille, however, the outcome of the prosecution of Hastings ceased to interest most of the latter. Indeed, even before the first year of the impeachment was out, the Duchess of Devonshire noted in her diary that 'Sheridan, who is heartily tired of [the] Hastings trial, and fearful of Burke's impetuosity says that he wishes Hastings would run away, and Burke after him' (20 November 1788).[58] In spite of Burke's tenacity and dedication to the cause to the end, on 23 April 1795 the Governor-General of Bengal was acquitted on all charges, after the trial had dragged on for eight years and 180 changes to the peerage had taken place.[59]

Who was, then, the first Governor-General of Bengal? And how was his political and, particularly, cultural administration of India informed by classical models? In order to attempt to answer these questions, it is important to illuminate Hastings's early life and education first.

Warren Hastings

The image of Hastings that Sir Joshua Reynolds painted at some point between 1766 and 1768 encapsulates many aspects of the sitter's personality. The portrait shows a young, refined man with an ivory complexion. Even though he is not looking at the viewer, but instead glances to the left, his upright pose and slightly parted arms infuse a sense of composed self-confidence. Hastings's figure and sophisticated clothing stand out against a purple-red heavy curtain of brocade and a refined armchair of the same colour.

Thanks to the high quality of Reynolds's representation, it is also possible to make out the fabric of Hastings's expensive garments: he is wearing black velvet breeches; a silk-wool-blend dark blue coat with gold-thread buttons and buttonholes, velvet collar and frills, and an unusually long, floral waistcoat.[60] The latter, a *shakula*, is an Indian version of a British waistcoat made of a delicate muslin fabric. Hermione De Almeida and George H. Gilpin have stressed that 'Hastings' adoption of this waistcoat as the defining feature of his clothing is a mark of his ease in India and his fascination with its culture because he wears a *shakula* not only in this London portrait by Reynolds but in a 1784 portrait done in Calcutta by Arthur William Devis'.[61] As was the case with many British expatriates, Hastings enjoyed combining traditional British clothing with garments of native manufacture. The Ashmolean Museum in Oxford, for example, has a pair of crocheted short gloves in fine wool and some knitted woollen hose that he brought back from India. As we shall explore in greater detail below, in his political practice and administration of justice, Hastings constantly showed a tendency to combine British and Indian elements and traditions.

Two years before sitting for Reynolds, Hastings had returned to England after fifteen years' residence in India. Born in Oxfordshire to a clergyman of the Church of England, he found himself virtually an orphan in early infancy: his mother died soon after he was born and, within nine months of his birth, his father abandoned him, remarried and moved to Barbados, where he was to live for the rest of his life. Warren was first entrusted to his grandfather and then to an uncle, Howard Hastings, who provided him with what was probably the best education then available. In 1743 Warren was enrolled in Westminster School in London, where he was named a King's Scholar and Captain of the School.

While he showed a great promise as a schoolboy, in 1749, on his uncle's death, Hastings found himself cut off from formal education. As P. J. Marshall has suggested, 'his time at Westminster seems, however, to have been a good preparation. It left him with [...] a facility to learn languages, with a cultivated taste for literature, and above all with a quick, inquiring intelligence that absorbed new knowledge very readily' – all aptitudes and skills that, later in life, would kindle his interest in Indian culture and civilization.[62] Following the mode of the period, Hastings also relished classical studies and never lost the habit of versifying in Latin or, more frequently, in English, imitating Latin metres.[63] Hastings's early attraction to literature and his persistence in writing verse may indicate a passion that, later in his life, was to take him towards the classical languages of India.

Having to fend for himself, Hastings was granted a junior appointment as a writer in the East India Company and in January 1750, at the age of seventeen, he left for Bengal. When he arrived at Calcutta in September, the city was already a large commercial emporium, whence merchant ships loaded mostly with cotton cloth and silk sailed for London. For the early part of his career in India, Hastings worked in the East India Company's commercial business. But after 1756 the role of the Company, as well as that of its servants, underwent a series of radical changes. Between the 1750s and 1760s the Company became involved in hostilities in south India with the French and subjugated the vacillating regime of the Bengal *nawabs*. A conventional breakpoint, in this sense, was the battle of Plassey (1757): in an expedition under Robert Clive (1725–74) in which Hastings himself participated as a volunteer, the British deposed the *nawab* of Calcutta and installed a new ruler. In theory, the new *nawab* was independent; in practice, Clive secured from him a grant of new territories and their tax revenues, so much so that the Company's servants – including Hastings – were drawn more and more into Indian politics. From 1761 to 1764 Hastings succeeded to the Company's council, the body that managed its affairs in Bengal. Owing to bitter disputes within the council, however, his career was interrupted, and in January 1765 he returned to Britain.

Even though he had failed to make his fortune, Hastings lived in some luxury in England: he rented different homes in London, purchased several paintings and even a carriage, which he had ornamented with his coat of arms. It was in this period that he commissioned the striking portrait described above. It has been calculated that this picture must have cost him an enormous sum of money, Reynolds having been appointed in 1768 – the year of the completion of Hastings's portrait – first president of the Royal Academy of Arts. Jeremy Bernstein has, indeed, remarked that 'Reynolds charged twenty guineas for a head, fifty for a half length, and over a hundred pounds for a full length. The Hastings painting is somewhere between a half and a full'.[64] Throughout his life, Hastings showed a tendency to spend more than he possessed. As a result of his profusion and extravagance, he squandered most of the £220,000 which he had amassed during the period of his governorship, even before settling in England for good in 1785.[65]

During the four years of his permanent residence in Britain, Hastings tried to spread his interest in Indian civilization at home. Hence his *Proposal for Establishing a Professorship of the Persian Language in the University of Oxford* (1767), which he discussed with, among others, Samuel Johnson, the well-known man of letters and Royal Academy's Professor of Ancient Literature. It was through the latter that Hastings also became familiar with the foremost linguist at Oxford at the time, William Jones. Even though the project of establishing a chair in Persian was approved both by Johnson and the Chancellor of the University, it did not receive enough encouragement to succeed. A dedicated believer in learning Asian languages as a means of building bridges between England and India, some thirty years later Hastings vigorously argued for the introduction of Persian and Arabic in the curriculum at the College of Fort William, the institution founded in 1800 at Calcutta with the aim of providing instruction in the languages of India to the officials of the East India Company.[66] Hastings himself was a skilled linguist and had a good knowledge of Persian and Urdu. In a 1784 sketch for a painting by Johan Zoffany (1733–1810), for example, he is portrayed in the act of speaking to a Mughal prince without an interpreter.[67] During his early years in India, Hastings also became acquainted with the circle of the East India Company army officer and philanthropist, Claude Martin (1735–1800), 'whose collections of Indian watercolors and Persian and Sankrit documents' – Hermione de

Almeida and George H. Gilpin note – 'became a valuable archive for the study of Indian culture during his governorship'.[68]

Hastings's early attraction to Indian languages, laws, religions and institutions is also clearly visible in the Reynolds portrait: if we pay particular heed to the papers lying under Hastings's right hand, we notice some documents and a seal in Persian script. Possessing a monogram in one of the Oriental languages was, at the time, quite fashionable. Yet, in Hastings's case, the presence of an exotic alphabet does not simply represent a transient attempt to follow a contemporary fashion, but rather the reflex of a profound interest, as well as a political philosophy that accompanied him throughout his life.

An ambitious man short of money, Hastings sought to go back to India with an important post. Therefore, on 26 March 1769 he sailed for Madras and then returned to Calcutta, where in 1772 he was appointed Governor of Bengal. One of the most important and urgent reforms that he believed was necessary was the revision of the local judicial system. Although the latter was placed under British supervision, Hastings was vigorously opposed to the introduction and imposition of British law.[69] As Marshall observes, Hastings considered that 'it was neither practical nor desirable to tamper with traditional Hindu or Muslim law, which were "consonant to the ideas, manners and inclinations of the people for whose use it is intended"'.[70] In addition to the practical aspect of his conviction – namely, ensuring the stability of the acquisition in Bengal by securing the affection of the natives – Hastings's judicial reform also adumbrated a 'classical' approach towards Indian languages, manners and institutions, which is worth noting here.

The idea of ruling the conquered by means of their own traditions bears a striking similarity to the toleration and forbearance adopted by the Romans towards their provinces. According to Keith Feiling, for example, one may recognize 'a Roman theme' in Hastings's attempt 'To conciliate, to elevate "the British name", by fair and magnanimous dealing'.[71] In his preface to the *Code of Gentoo Laws* (1776), a translation of the Persian text of the pandits' code, the orientalist Nathaniel Brassey Halhed (1751–1830) pointed out that the Romans 'not only allowed to their foreign subjects the free exercise of their own religion, and the administration of their own civil jurisdiction, but sometimes by a Policy still more flattering, even naturalized such Parts of the Mythology of the conquered, as were in any respect compatible with their own System'.[72] As time went on, parallels between Britain's empire and that of Rome were to be drawn more persistently. For example, Sir William Jones wished that Lord Cornwallis (1738–1805), Governor-General of India from 1786 to 1793, would become the 'Justinian of India'. In Jones's view, in fact, the British government should give to the natives 'security for the due administration of justice among them, similar to that which Justinian gave to his Greek and Roman subjects'.[73] Parallels between the Graeco-Roman heritage and India were not to stop there.

Many colonial European writers compared contemporary Indians to ancient Greeks and Romans. Particularly significant here is a letter penned by Jones on 23 August 1787. Addressed to the second Earl of Spencer (Jones's former pupil Viscount Althorp), the epistle pointed to resemblances between Brahmans and 'the priests of Jupiter':

> To what shall I compare my literary pursuits in India? Suppose Greek literature to be known in modern Greece only, and there to be in the hands of priests and philosophers; and suppose them to be still worshippers of Jupiter and Apollo; suppose Greece to have been conquered successively by Goths, Huns, Vandals, Tartars, and lastly by the English; then suppose a court of judicature to be established by the British parliament, at Athens, and an inquisitive Englishman to be one of the judges; suppose him to learn Greek there, which none of his countrymen knew, and to read Homer, Pindar, Plato, which no other Europeans had ever heard of. Such am I in this country; substituting Sanscrit for Greek, the *Brahmans*, for the priests of *Jupiter*, and *Valmic, Vyasa, Calidasa*, for Homer, Plato, Pindar.[74]

Although in this 'little Anglo-Indo-Hellenic fantasy' the Greece to which Jones likens India is a place 'not yet modern (the old gods were still worshipped) but also no longer classical (it has been conquered by post-classical invaders)', references to classical Greek literature and religion figure prominently.[75]

To promote a 'conciliation' between the British and Indian cultures, the Governor-General encouraged and patronized Oriental learning to such an extent that, as has been stressed, a history of Oriental studies would be 'incomplete without a mention of Hastings'.[76] Among his many acts of patronage, the Governor founded the Calcutta *madraseh*, or college, and promoted the study of Hinduism. He attracted and surrounded himself with young men of extraordinary ability, among whom the aforementioned Nathaniel Brassey Halhed and Charles Wilkins (1749–1836), who produced in 1785 the first scholarly translation into any European language of the *Bhagavad Gītā* (a small part of the epic poem *Mahabharata*) – 'a performance of great originality; of a sublimity of conception, reasoning, and diction, almost unequalled', as Hastings himself described it.[77]

Wilkins's translation and the many others that started to appear in the 1780s, following the establishment in 1784 of the Asiatick Society in Calcutta, drew further attention to Sanskrit and its relationship with Greek and Latin. Of particular importance, in this respect, is Jones's emphasis on the common origin of what came to be known as the family of Indo-European languages.[78] One of the implications of Jones's claim was that the study of Sanskrit would help learners to understand European classical languages better.[79] In this sense, as Phiroze Vasunia reminds us, from an early date, Orientalists linked Sanskrit to Latin and Greek. The 'European "discovery" of Sanskrit' was, in fact, 'the discovery of its similarity to Latin and Greek'.[80]

As a consequence of the good reputation that Hastings had gained since his appointment as Governor of Bengal, in 1773 he was given the title of Governor-General. His undisputed power, however, came to an end or, at least, was drastically diminished in the next year. Following the East India Regulating Act – an act aimed at reducing the power of the Company's Indian administration – the British Government decreed that authority in Bengal was to be split up between the Governor-General and a Supreme Council of five. Apart from Hastings, the Council was composed of another Company servant, Richard Barwell (1741–1804), and three others all new to India, General Clavering (1722–77), Colonel Monson (1730–76) and a very ambitious clerk, Philip Francis. The effectiveness of the Supreme Council was immediately undermined by the virulent quarrels that broke out among its members, as the three newcomers were unremittingly hostile to the Governor-General's policies. Not only did they accuse Hastings and the majority of his fellow servants of personal corruption, but they also demanded an investigation into the causes behind the war against the Rohillas, a group of mercenary soldiers of Afghan origin who had settled in northern India.

Twelve years later, this conflict would be singled out by Burke as the first article of charge against Hastings to be discussed in front of the House of Commons.[81] Presenting the Rohilla war anew, on the occasion of a major speech on 1 June 1786, Burke included a reference to classical Rome. In his evocation of 'the noble character of an accuser in Rome', as well as the contrast that he delineated between the 'facility of coming at a Roman Governor with high crimes and misdemeanors, and the extreme difficulty of making out any accusation with effect against a British Governor', we may easily trace the germ of what would become a constant point of reference for Burke throughout the eight years of the trial, namely the arraignment of Verres by Cicero.[82]

As a result of the multiple accusations piled up against the Governor-General of Bengal, the British government tried to dismiss him in 1776, but the Company did not consent to this. Suddenly and unexpectedly the situation changed in favour of Hastings, for two of his opponents – Monson and Clavering – died in 1776 and 1777 respectively. Conversely, Francis's opposition to Hastings dragged on for three more years and was terminated in a pistol duel on 17 August 1780. Francis was slightly wounded and that same year, in December, he left India.[83] After this, he worked relentlessly to discredit Hastings and was in regular contact with Burke. In 1785, Hastings finally resigned and on 7 February he returned to Britain. The previous year his wife had been forced by illness to leave India – a separation that he found hard to bear. Most importantly, he was convinced that he had little to hope for from the new government directed by William Pitt the Younger.

In the meantime, with the help of Francis, Burke drew up an indictment in the form of twenty-two 'Articles of Charge of Crimes and Misdemeanors', which he presented to the Commons between April and May 1786. A string of charges – six out of twenty-two – was accepted as 'Articles of Impeachment', and against all expectations Hastings was tried before the House of Lords. Nine months later, on 13 February 1788, the trial began. How and to what extent Burke and his fellow managers successfully employed classical rhetorical techniques to transform – at least, during the first months of the prosecution – what may have been a tedious legal action into a public spectacle attended by the most fashionable members of the British and foreign elite, will be the subject of the next chapter.

3

Classical Oratory and Theatricality in the Trial against Warren Hastings

On 13 February 1788, commenting on the first day of the trial of Warren Hastings, *The Times* observed: 'From the scarcity of accommodation at every part of the West end of the town, the trial of Mr. Hastings is supposed to have drawn more people to London than have visited the metropolis at any one time for several years past'.[1] Returning to the theme in a column entitled 'Parliamentary Intelligence', *The Times* informed its readers that, on the previous day, the House of Lords had debated regulating the tickets of admission to the trial. The Duke of Norfolk, it was reported:

> thought it would be proper for the tickets to be signed by the receiver as well as the donor. His reason for suggesting this to their Lordships, was to prevent the common practice of forging them, which had been adopted on former trials of similar nature. The signatures he meant should be in their Lordships' own hand writing. The tickets, he conceived, should be signed as they were given for every day of the trial.[2]

During the first six months of 1788, British society at large was so obsessed with the impeachment of the Governor-General that designers chose to decorate everyday items, such as fan-leaves, with images of the trial Daniel O'Quinn has called 'a public sensation like no other'.[3] Among the stunning collection of fans amassed throughout the nineteenth century by the businesswoman and collector Lady Charlotte Elizabeth Schreiber (1812–95), a couple of identical fan-leaves (Figure 3.1) – unmounted and mounted with wooden sticks, respectively – are significant in this regard.[4] Produced in 1788, both items replicate Thomas Prattent's etching, *A view of the court sitting on the trial of Warren Hastings Esq.* (Figure 3.2). Prattent's image represents the galleries of Westminster Hall crowded with spectators and is reproduced in

48   *The Trial of Warren Hastings*

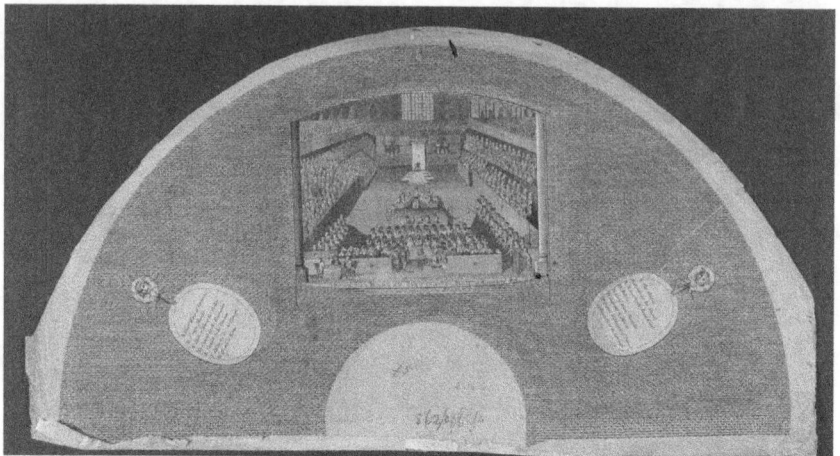

Fig. 3.1 Anon., *Print/fan*, 1788. BM 1891,0713.387. © Trustees of the British Museum.

Fig. 3.2 Thomas Prattent, *A view of the court sitting on the trial of Warren Hastings Esq.*, 1788. BM 1880,0911.1217. © Trustees of the British Museum.

brown above a grey-greenish pattern. A legend helps to identify the participants: in the work by Prattent, the inscription is placed below the image; in the fan version, it is located within two elegant medallions decorated with the head of a Medusa.

While staring at such fans as those decorated with a scene of Westminster Hall during the *cause célèbre*, ladies and gentlemen commented on the most fashionable spectacle of the moment and, possibly, showed each other where they were seated. MacIver Percival has, indeed, remarked that a fan's decoration 'beguiled a dull moment, or formed a topic of conversation'.[5] Since fans were inexpensive items, and therefore universally carried, we might venture to say that those women whose social status did not permit them to enter the courtroom eagerly looked for these collectibles, not only to celebrate but also, somehow, to participate vicariously in this sensational event.

From January to June 1788, newspapers reported and commented extensively on what had become – in the words of Nicholas B. Dirks – 'not just the trial of the century, but the most extraordinary political spectacle in Britain during the second half of the eighteenth century'.[6] Significantly, Glynis Ridley has suggested that 'The impeachment proceedings opened [...] in an atmosphere of expectation and publicity that would stand comparison with any televised celebrity trial today'.[7] Although numerous scholars have commented on the sensationalism and theatricality which permeated the event,[8] the relationship between ancient rhetorical treatises and the theatrical gestures performed at Westminster Hall deserves further exploration.

In this chapter, I will show the extent to which classical rhetorical strategies, as well as contemporary oratorical treatises, deeply influenced the managers' spectacular performances. In particular, I will focus on the orators' body language and dramatic enactments, and argue for the constant overlapping of theatre and politics. As will be discussed below, classical – especially Roman – rhetorical treatises exhorted orators to utilize their body as an eloquent visual medium, an expressive vehicle of passions, apt to manipulate their audience's feelings. Similarly, the prosecutors fully exploited the theatrical atmosphere and staged a sentimental drama in a legal arena, hence constructing and conducting the imperial discourse with the magic of histrionic rhetoric. As with classical *oratores* and professional *actores*, their flamboyant performances comprised heightened physical reactions, such as swooning, painful fits, and indispositions.

Since the arraignment of Hastings stopped being a sensation after a few months, I have chosen to analyse the most intense and exciting performances given at Westminster Hall between February and June 1788, namely Burke's account of the Rangpur horrors and Sheridan's orations in defence of the Begums of Oudh. Before turning to the magic of Burke's and Sheridan's extraordinary shows, however, some further thought should be given to the spectacular context in which the two orators performed.

Turning a legal conflict into a theatrical show

Conceived from the outset as a dramatic setting, the location of the trial, Westminster Hall, was extensively modified between December 1787 and February 1788, as temporary stands were erected on four sides to accommodate a vast public.[9] The Hall was impressive not only for its symbolic resonances – it had been the setting of some of the most celebrated events of English history, such as the trials of Sir Thomas More (1478–1535) and Charles I – but also for its visual display; its magnificent decoration having a profound impact on those who entered it. With its stunning hammerbeam roof, its walls draped in scarlet, and the crowd of refined gentlemen and ladies assembling there, the hall was permeated by an atmosphere of grandeur. Reporting on the first day of the trial, Sir Gilbert Elliot (1751–1814) told his wife: 'it is difficult to conceive anything more grand or imposing than this scene [...]. Everything that England possesses of greatness or ability is there assembled, in the utmost splendor [sic] and solemnity'.[10]

A mid-nineteenth-century illustration to *London Interiors* (*Westminster Hall, Trial of Warren Hastings*), gives us a taste of what a spectator might have experienced at the time (1841–4: BM 1948,0217.83). The engraving shows the hall as seen from the north end. In the foreground, the grave members of the Committee of the House of Lords, recognizable in their wigs and black robes, talk animatedly, while some notables move around. The three magnificent boxes with a golden canopy that appear at the far end of the hall were built for the Lord Chancellor, the King (although he never attended the trial), and the

Princes. On the left- and right-hand sides, as well as at the end of the hall, one sees the temporary stands crowded with ladies and gentlemen.

Those who attended the trial belonged to the *crème de la crème* of British society and foreign representatives in England. The brightly coloured, elegant clothes and the wigs, along with the dignified, upright position of most of the spectators depicted, bear witness to their high social status. The fourth side of the seating is not shown, but can be identified in an anonymous print, *Plan of the High Court of Parliament, Erected in Westminster Hall for the Trial of Warren Hastings, Esq. Late Governor-General of Bengal, for High Crimes and Misdemeanors* [sic], *on Wednesday, February 13, 1788* (c.1788: BM 1978, U.1960). A legend shows the layout of the areas reserved to the participants: the fourth side was assigned to the 'Honorable [sic] House of Commons' and peeresses; the Lord Great Chamberlain's Box for Ladies was also located there.

Not only was Westminster Hall transformed into a theatre in the round, but even the auditors and the prosecutors seemed to have turned into the fashionable audience of a theatrical entertainment and the actors of a sentimental drama, respectively. References to theatre in contemporary comments of the impeachment are legion. The pages of the diary of Lady Sophia Fitzgerald (1762–1845), for example, record the impressions of a casual frivolous audience for whom the trial was a public spectacle and Burke a 'charming' performer:

> [15 February 1788] Sophia was obliged to get up very early, which she did not much like: breakfasted, then went to call upon Lady Talbot and they both went to the Trial, where they stayed till four o'clock. Mr Burke spoke, and they were delighted with him. It really was very fine. [...]
> [16 February 1788] Sophia persuaded her mother to go to the Trial to-day, as she knew it would entertain her to hear Mr Burke. He was charming again, and Mother very well pleased at having gone. [...]
> [18 February 1788] We went again to the Trial to hear Mr Burke, who really made one's blood run cold with the account of all the tortures and cruelties in the East Indies. [...] We all went in the Evening to see the play at Richmond House. Henry [an amateur actor] was charming. Mrs Siddons [the renowned tragic actresses] was there.[11]

That the impeachment of Hastings was conceived on a par with the theatre is further suggested by contemporary newspapers. Eddy Kent has noticed that the *London Chronicle* published a description of the opening day's procession from the House of Lords to the High Court of Parliament in Westminster Hall 'in a format not dissimilar from conventional contemporary theatre notices':[12]

> The Lords were then called over by the Clerk, and arranged by Sir Isaac Heard, Principal King at Arms, when upwards of two hundred proceeded in order to Westminster Hall. The Peers were preceded by
> The Lord Chancellor's attendants, two and two.
> The Clerk of the House of Lords.
> The Masters in Chancery, two and two.
> The Judges.
> Serjeants Adair and Hill.
> The Yeoman Usher of the Black Rod.
> Two Heralds.
> The Lords Barons, two and two.
> The Lords Bishops, two and two.
> The Lords Viscounts, two and two.
> The Lords Marquesses, two and two.
> The Lords Dukes, two and two.
> The Mace Bearer.
> The Lord Chancellor with his train borne.
> (All in their Parliamentary Robes)
> The Lords Spiritual seated themselves on their Bench, which was on the side on which they entered; as they passed the throne, they bowed to it, as if the King was seated in it. The Temporal Lords crossed over the house, and each made a respectful bow to the seat of Majesty.[13]

It should also be recalled that eighteenth-century accounts of private theatricals often included comments on ladies' dresses. A 1799 article describing a private invitation to attend 'two pretty little Dramatic Pieces' at Lord Shaftesbury's house, for example, recorded that Lady Barbara Ashley Cooper 'was neatly dressed in a beautiful tartan jacket and philibeg, made of silk, and a blue bonnet. The young ladies were dressed in tartan silk bodices, and white muslin petticoats ornamented with tartan: the dresses were very beautiful and elegant'.[14]

Similarly, the newspapers reporting on the impeachment of Warren Hastings offered detailed descriptions of the stylish clothes and jewels that could be admired in Westminster Hall. Commenting on the first day of the trial, *The Times* noted that: 'There were few feathers, and these very low – but a profusion of artificial flowers ornamented the ladies heads – Many wore chains, and strings of pearl, or of beads of various colours from their ears – [...] The gowns were full and flowing, with long trains – the fabric mostly of sattin – the colours dark or white'.[15]

The contrast between what ought to have been the austere atmosphere of a courtroom and the improper sensual ostentation of female grace can be gleaned from several newspapers. The *Morning Post and Daily Advertiser*, for instance, recorded that:

> It was impossible [...] not to be struck with the symmetry of the building erected for the trial, the convenient disposition of its parts, and the appearance of awful grandeur through the whole. But all these vanished, or were absorbed in the contemplation of the beauteous females that graced the benches, and dispelled the awe we felt, when we consider that this was the seat of VINDICATIVE JUSTICE. Rich in beauty as in dress – they could not be viewed without admiration and emotion – their jewels darted light, but their eyes shot fire.[16]

In the above excerpt, the abundance of terms referring to the semantic field of sight ('appearance', 'contemplation', 'viewed', 'eyes') amplifies the effect of a theatrical show. In this respect it might be worth recalling that the word 'theatre' is related to the Greek verb θεᾶσθαι, 'to behold'. In a similar way, as a number of records indicate, we can assess to what extent visual details played a key role in the impeachment of Hastings.

One of the most vivid descriptions of the opening sessions of the trial was provided by the then Keeper of the Robes to Queen Charlotte, the novelist Frances Burney. According to Elizabeth Samet, Burney's journal 'accurately captures the trial's theatrical atmosphere and the conception of courtroom-as-stage so crucial to an understanding of Burke's rhetoric'.[17] As if depicting an evening at the theatre, Burney's pages are interspersed with a myriad visual details and, especially, a complex interplay of glances. On the first day of the impeachment, for example, she observes how, throughout the reading of the general charges against the defendant:

> Mr. Hastings [...] began to cast his eyes around the House, and having taken a survey of all in front and at the sides, he turned about and looked up; pale

looked his face – pale, ill, and altered. I was much affected by the sight of that dreadful harass which was written on his countenance. Had I looked at him without restraint, it could not have been without tears. I felt shocked, too, and ashamed, to be seen by him in that place. I had wished to be present from an earnest interest in the business, joined to a firm confidence in his powers of defence; but *his* eyes were not those I wished to meet in Westminster Hall. I called upon Miss Gomme and Charles to assist me in looking another way, and in conversing to me as I turned aside.[18]

This scene depicts a triangular exchange of looks which, besides Hastings and the diarist herself, involves the latter's brother, Charles (1757–1817), and Miss Gomme. The abundance of verbs referring to the semantic field of sight ('to cast his eyes around', 'looked up', 'looked at', 'be seen', 'looking another way') conveys the sense of the incessant movement of restless eyes, both horizontally ('around', 'in front and at the sides', 'about', 'aside') and vertically ('up').

Inside this theatrical frame, Hastings resembles the suffering hero of a sentimental drama: so visibly altered are his features that not only does Burney feel emotionally shaken ('I felt shocked, too, and ashamed') but she experiences physical symptoms as well, verging on tears as she responds to the pathos of the scene. Being profoundly touched by the suffering of a distressed character was very common among eighteenth-century theatre-goers, who were expected to show palpable signs of sympathy, 'specifically' – as Jean Marsden reminds us – 'through highly visible tears'.[19]

In her lively account of the trial, Burney further records that both the general public and Burke's colleagues made use of opera glasses, and I would suggest that, as in the theatre, the spectators of the trial watched and admired ladies and gentlemen in other parts of the hall, as much as they observed the orators' performances. As a contemporary playwright, James Boaden (1762–1839), contended, theatres 'are made glittering and gaudy, because our spectators love to be an exhibition themselves'.[20] Attending a play at Drury Lane or Covent Garden at the end of the eighteenth century was in fact quite different from our experience of the theatre. Jeffrey N. Cox has noted that, while we are used to 'a solemn theatrical experience' in a dark, quiet place, at the time audiences 'would have gone to large, noisy, constantly illuminated spaces', where they spent time in social conversation, laughed, looked around and were looked at.[21]

Similarly, when the proceedings at Westminster Hall were particularly technical and tedious, spectators rose to greet an acquaintance or gossip with a friend. The unorthodox, careless attitude of a Member of the House of Commons is quite emblematic in this respect:

> In the midst of the opening of a trial such as this, so important to the country as well as to the individual who is tried, what will you say to a man – a member of the House of Commons – who kept exclaiming almost perpetually, just at my side, 'What a bore! – when will it be over? – Must one come any more? – I had a great mind not to have come at all. – Who's that? – Lady Hawkesbury and the Copes? – Yes. – A pretty girl Kitty. – Well, when will they have done? – I wish they'd call the question – I should vote it a bore at once!'[22]

Interestingly, even members of the foreign elite remarked on the similarity between the courtroom and the theatre: 'A Spanish gentleman enquired on Friday last of the person who sat next to him, whether the Peeresses were privileged to laugh as loud in Westminster-hall, as they do at a playhouse?', *The Times* reported on 5 March 1788.

Not only literary sources but also contemporary illustrations of the trial offer us glimpses of a distracted audience. The watercolours of James Nixon (c.1741–1812), for example, crystallize spectators in the act of talking to each other, rising, yawning, dozing and looking around through opera glasses.[23] Among the variety of contemporary ephemera that add to our impression of a restless, inattentive audience treating the impeachment as an evening at the theatre or a fashionable social event, Sarah Sophia Banks's collection of tickets from the trial deserves special attention.

Souvenirs from a trial

Despite being a precious source of information for Romantic-period social history, Sarah Sophia Banks's collection of 'Tickets for Warren Hastings Trial' has received little attention. This is scarcely surprising, considering that Miss Banks (1744–1818) gathered more than 30,000 objects, including coins, medals, cards, prints and bookplates.[24] Immediately after her death, her collections of printed and engraved ephemera were donated to the British

Museum, and there they have remained since 1818. The majority of her Hastings memorabilia and some additional rare and curious items probably reached Sarah Sophia via her brother's contacts: Sir Joseph Banks was a renowned naturalist and the longest-serving president of the Royal Society, as well as a well-connected member of several clubs, such as the Spalding Gentlemen's Club.[25]

Thanks to the large number of important guests who visited Sir Joseph, Sarah Sophia could satisfy her keen interest in the social world of elite society. In 1779, a few months after her brother's marriage to Dorothea Hugessen (1758–1828), Miss Banks moved in with them. The three of them were thereafter inseparable, and invitations would customarily come for Sir Joseph Banks, Lady Banks, and Miss Banks. As we will see below, few of the letters included in Sarah Sophia's collection of 'Tickets for Warren Hastings Trial' bear witness to their close relationship.

Comprising 110 items (BM J,9.1–110), the 'Tickets for Warren Hastings Trial' collection is primarily composed of admission tickets. Ladies and gentlemen wishing to attend Burke's and Sheridan's spectacular speeches and, more generally, to gain access to Westminster Hall, had to produce a ticket. The pass was presented to a receiver who, as if at the entrance of a theatre, 'tears off a Corner of it, and returns it'.[26] Miss Banks's ephemera testify to this practice – as shown in Figure 3.3, Admission-ticket for day 28 of the trial of Warren Hastings – and also of the changes that admission tickets to the trial underwent over time.

As we noted at the beginning of this chapter, the Duke of Norfolk's apprehension that passes might be forged was well founded: notwithstanding the precautions taken, as early as the first day of the trial, the engraved tickets (featuring the Great Chamberlain's coats of arms and the motto '*sub liberate quietem*') were counterfeited. According to the *London Chronicle*, in order to prevent falsification, the Duke of Norfolk ordered 'That all the tickets issued from the Great Chamberlain's Office on Thursday the 14th, and on every succeeding day of the trial of Warren Hastings, Esq. be signed and sealed by the respective Peers' to whom they had to be delivered, 'with an exception to those of the Royal Family'.[27] The tickets collected by Miss Banks prove that this measure came into effect. As can be seen, for instance, in Figure 3.3, the passes were signed and sealed not only (as in the case of Figures 3.4 and 3.7) by the Deputy Great Chamberlain, Sir Peter Burrell (1754–1820), but also by the

Fig. 3.3 Admission-ticket for day 28 of the trial of Warren Hastings, 1787. BM J,9.46. © Trustees of the British Museum.

Peers for whom the tickets were intended. Thanks to the order of the Duke of Norfolk, more than 200 years later, we still know the names of some of the fashionable spectators who attended the trial.[28]

In order to prevent forgery, each day the passes were changed in colour as well as in the design.[29] These modifications are evident in Sarah Sophia's collection:

the tickets are signed and printed in a variety of colours (ochre yellow, emerald green, olive green, orange, red, blue, sepia, dark brown) and the engravings differ. So, for instance, 'Esquire' is differently abbreviated 'Esq'. or 'Esq.'.'. Besides being printed in different colours, some tickets (such as Figure 3.3) also show the specific day of the trial for which they were intended. That the design of the tickets frequently varied is further proved by Miss Banks's annotation. Indeed, as well as collecting the items themselves, Sarah Sophia recorded information about them. On the back of one of the passes (Figure 3.4), for example, she wrote: 'May 6. 1788 Suppose this would have been the same since April 10. but did not send for it till May 6. (believe it has been changed once since April 10.)'. Again, on the verso of another (c.1787, BM J,9.30), she commented: 'between May 6. 1788. and Feb. 15. 1790. (or certainly before Feb. 15. 1790.)'. As it is evident from this, the design was printed anew after 15 February 1790.

For sessions that were expected to be particularly interesting, such as when Burke and Sheridan were scheduled to perform, passes were in great demand.[30] As with contemporary performers, who were asked for tickets by members of their families and friends, so were the managers of the trial against Hastings. In the early weeks of the trial, for example, Edmund Burke begged Sir Peter Burrell to dispense him a supernumerary ticket for a gentleman of his acquaintance (Mr Baker). As the orator wittily put it, 'I have hunted you, whilst Mr Baker was hunting me, through Westminster Hall last Night, and we all missed each other'.[31] The Great Chamberlain must have been very strict about the distribution of tickets, if the *Gazetteer* reported, not without a vein of irony:

> Though there is so much room in the hall, particularly in the box and gallery of the Great Chamberlaim [sic], Sir Peter Burrell is most rigid in the disposal of tickets; so much so, that Mr Hastings has a ticket for his admission. Were he to lose his ticket upon any one day, he might send an answer to the Court, when called upon to come forward, that they would not let him enter.[32]

From the opening of the impeachment until the close of the parliamentary session in June 1788, the trial of Hastings dominated political satires, and the tickets for Westminster Hall were not spared. Indeed, they became so familiar that they were soon parodied by two of the most celebrated caricaturists of the time, James Sayers (1748–1823) and James Gillray. In their cartoons, *For the Trial of Warren Has[tings]/Seventh Day* (Figure 3.5) and *Impeachment ticket.*

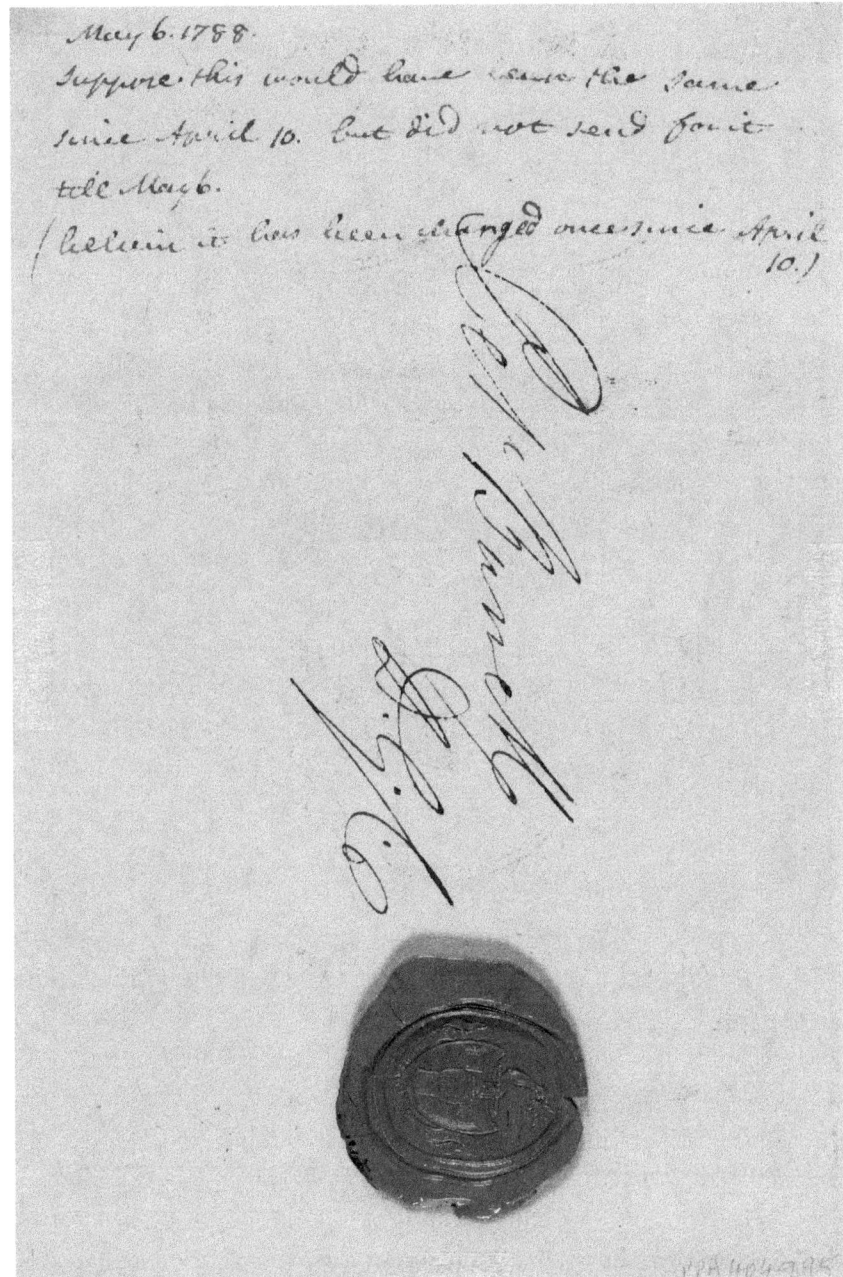

Fig. 3.4 Admission-ticket, 1787. BM J,9.21. © Trustees of the British Museum.

Fig. 3.5 James Sayers, *For the Trial of Warren Has[tings]/Seventh Day*, 1788. BM 1868,0808.5692. © Trustees of the British Museum.

For the Trial of W-RR-N H-ST-NGS Esqr (c.1788, BM 1851,0901.391), the three rams' heads of Sir Peter Burrell's coat of arms are replaced by those of Burke, Fox and Francis; the embowed arm above the Great Chamberlain's crest no longer holds an olive branch: in Sayers's print, it brandishes a scourge; in Gillray's, a bludgeon. Also the motto '*sub libertate quietem*' is deformed and replaced with the slogan '*sub libertate tyranni*'.[33] Miss Banks's collection of satirical prints includes a copy of both prints.

Even though her collection of 'Tickets for Warren Hastings Trial' is composed mostly of Sir Peter Burrell's passes, Sarah Sophia gathered other printed ephemera, including a list of 'Refreshments to be had in the Hall' (Figure 3.6). A genuine collector, on the verso she recorded the date – 19 February 1788 – in which these 'curious Bills of *Sandwiches*', as a newspaper described them, were handed about Westminster Hall.[34] This advertisement is particularly significant, as it reinforces our impression of a trial perceived as a theatrical spectacle. As the impeachment sessions normally started late in the morning and lasted for many hours, food and drink could be brought in or purchased in the hall itself.

It should be recalled that most tickets did not permit the bearer exit and readmission.[35] In this sense, Sir Joseph certainly belonged to an inner circle of a privileged few, as one of his passes proves (Figure 3.7). This 'not transferable' ticket, which allowed the bearer 'to pass and repass', must have been part of a limited, special edition. In fact, besides being numbered (No. 16), the pass bears the name and title of the person it was issued to – Sir Joseph Banks B[t] (Baronet). That these tickets were particularly rare is further suggested by a letter from Edmund Burke to Sir Peter Burrell. In February 1788, the former asked the Great Chamberlain for a 'pass and repass' ticket for a gentleman whose 'health is so bad that he cannot attend very long at a time or in any fixed place; at the same time he is extremely anxious to hear the Trial'.[36] Significantly, the orator reassured Burrell that this gentleman was 'incapable of abusing it' and promised to 'keep this favour a secret'.[37]

The rarity of 'pass and repass' tickets, along with Burke's promised secrecy, seem to suggest that, had the auditors been given permission to come and go, Westminster Hall – as was the case with most theatres at the time – would have turned into a chaotic and noisy place. We should not forget that eighteenth-century spectators would sit, stand up, enter and leave, with theatres as sites of an endless flow of people moving and settling. Some spectators, for example,

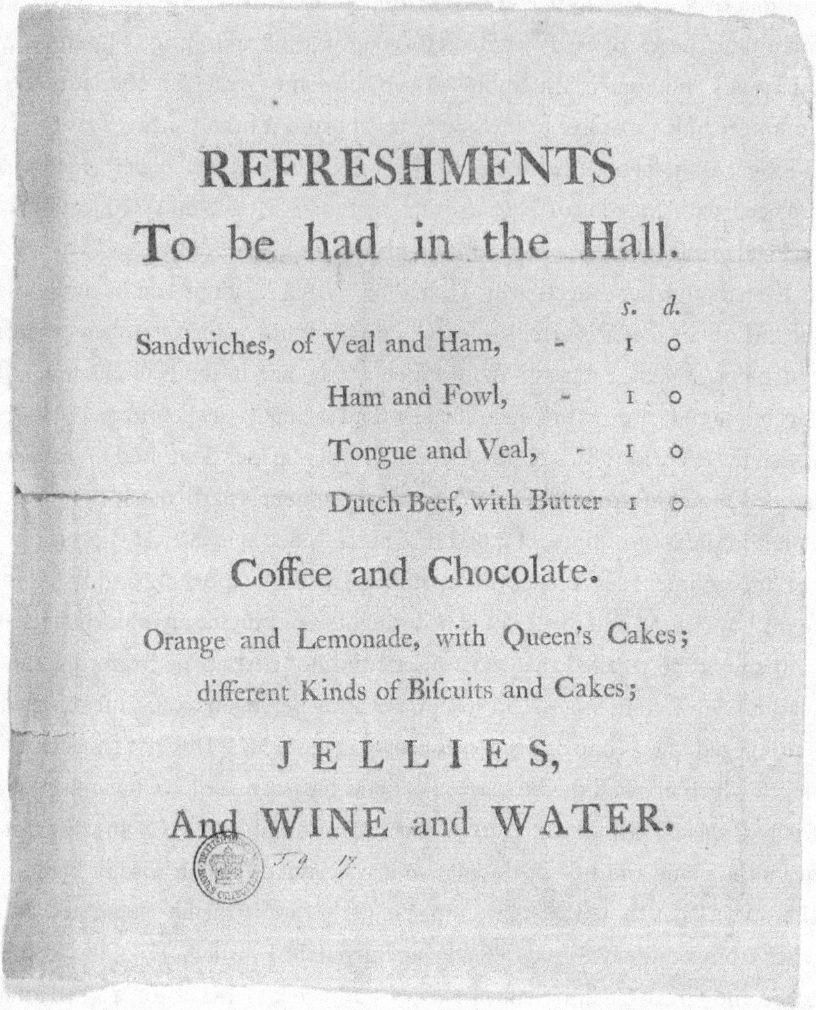

REFRESHMENTS
To be had in the Hall.

	s.	d.
Sandwiches, of Veal and Ham, -	1	0
Ham and Fowl, -	1	0
Tongue and Veal, -	1	0
Dutch Beef, with Butter	1	0

Coffee and Chocolate.

Orange and Lemonade, with Queen's Cakes;
different Kinds of Biscuits and Cakes;

JELLIES,
And WINE and WATER.

Fig. 3.6 *Refreshments to be had in the Hall*, 1788. BM J,9.17. © Trustees of the British Museum.

wishing to dine first or attending to some business, might send their servants to hold their seats and arrive at the end of the first act, others, instead, wishing to save money, 'might enter for half price after the third act of the mainpiece'.[38]

According to the leaflet collected by Miss Banks, refreshments sold inside Westminster Hall included different kinds of sandwiches (veal and ham, ham and fowl, tongue and veal, Dutch beef with butter), at the cost of one shilling each; (unpriced) delicacies, such as coffee and chocolate; orange and

Fig. 3.7 Admission-ticket, 1788. BM J,9.8. © Trustees of the British Museum.

lemonade with Queen's cakes; different kinds of biscuits and cakes; jellies, wine and water. Those who bought this refined food must have been gourmands; as if they had been enjoying a spectacle at the theatre, the frivolous audience at the impeachment was more interested in consuming food – we can imagine them eating, gossiping, and looking around with spy glasses – than in paying close attention to the grave debate taking place in front of them.

The practice of eating and drinking while watching a theatrical performance was common in the late eighteenth century. On a visit to London's Sadler's Wells Theatre in 1786, the German novelist and traveller Sophie von la Roche (1731–1807), for instance, observed:

> The scenes in the pit and boxes we found as strange as the ten-fold comedy itself. In the pit there is a shelf running along the back of the seats on which the occupants order bottles of wine, glasses, ham, cold chops and pasties to be placed, which they consume with their wives and children, partaking while they watch the same play. The front seats of the boxes are just the same.[39]

Complete with a distracted audience consuming food and wine, the atmosphere at Sadler's Wells Theatre resembled that of Westminster Hall during the Hastings trial.

Besides a vast array of printed ephemera, Miss Banks's collection also includes a few peculiar tickets.[40] As shown in Figure 3.8, they appear to be passes to enter the box of Sir William Chambers (1722–96), the eclectic architect under whose direction the Office of Works built the wooden stands inside Westminster Hall. These five items feature a coat of arms, presumably Sir William's, the Cross and motto – *nescit occasum*, 'it knows no decline' – of the Swedish order of the Polar Star, as well as the inscription: 'William Chambers, Surveyor General of his Majesties [sic] Works'.[41]

Sir William and the Banks must have been closely acquainted, as a couple of letters inserted in Sarah Sophia's collection further suggests. One of them, addressed to Lady and Miss Banks, reads:

> S William Chambers presents his Compliments to Lady and Miss Banks and has sent them three tickets they need not have the trouble of going sooner than Eleven o'clock as the under written note will Secure them a front row in Lady Chambers's box. (BM J,9.6)

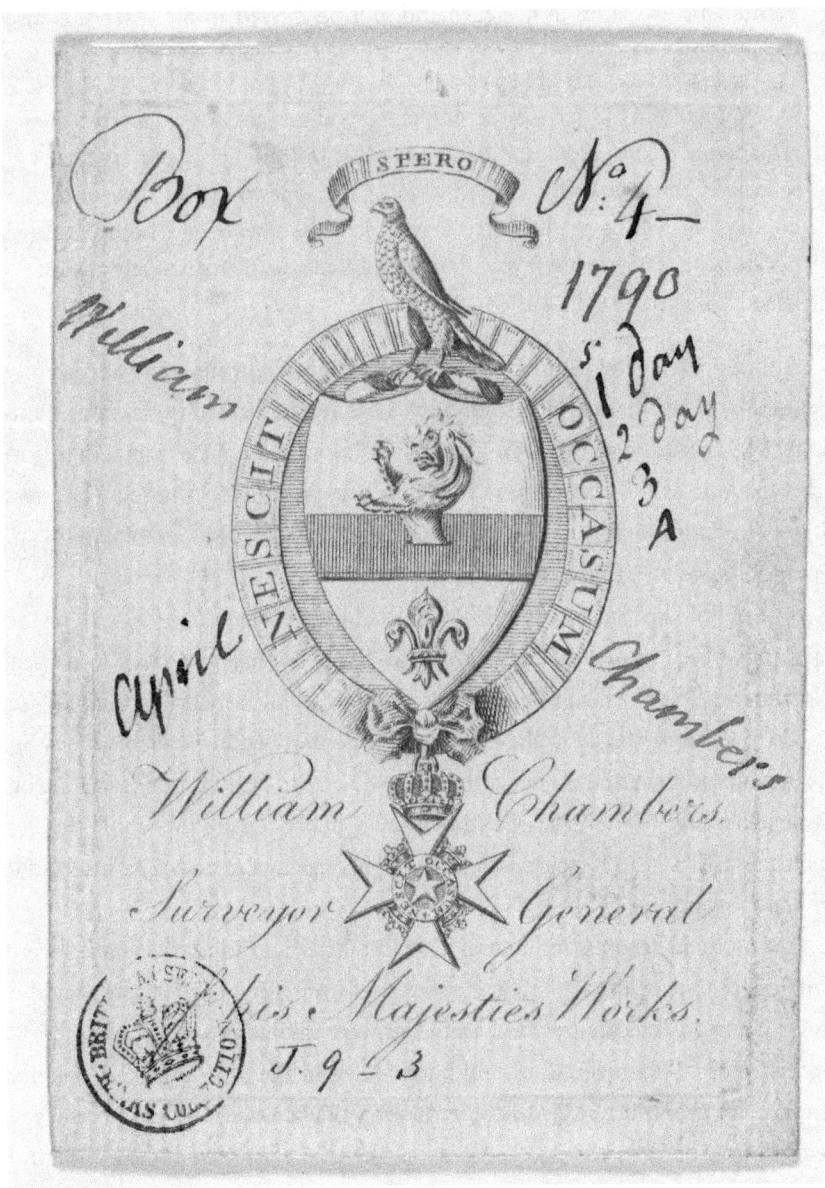

Fig. 3.8 Admission-ticket, 1787 c. BM J,9.3. © Trustees of the British Museum.

Written in the same thin, neat hand, but addressed to Sir Joseph, is also another epistle:

> Dr Sir I am Glad to have three tickets to send you the way in, used to be remarkably commodious and flatter myself it will still be so, and my box is so placed that the Ladys [sic] may go in and out whenever they please, hoping you will be of the party. Have taken the liberty of sending three tickets instead of two but if you do not want it please to give it to any of your friends. Berners St Feb 12 1788. (BM J,9.7)

Although this letter is unsigned and the seal is broken, the note was certainly penned by Sir William. Indeed, not only is the epistle written in the same hand as BM J,9.6 but it also bears an important clue to solve the enigma, that is to say the name of the street where the letter was presumably drafted – Berners Street (north of Oxford Street). In 1766, Sir William Chambers moved from Poland Street to 13 Berners Street.

So well known was Sir Joseph Banks that on the same day (the eve of the opening of the impeachment) not only was Sarah Sophia offered a seat in Lady Chambers's Box, but also in the Great Chamberlain's.[42] Especially designed for ladies, the latter was centrally located and guaranteed an enviable view. Sir Joseph himself was given a ticket that allowed him to be admitted (as a note on the back reads) 'to the Great Chamberlain's Gallery during the whole time of the trial' (BM J,9.25).[43] He gave this pass to his sister, who promptly inserted it in her collection.

Owing to Sir Joseph's influential acquaintances, Lady and Miss Banks were thus offered special tickets that granted them numerous privileges: they did not need to rush to secure good seats, but were invited into Lady Chambers's exclusive box. Moreover, they could arrive late in the morning. This was not the case for everybody: as with contemporary playhouses, a system of reserved seats did not exist, as admission tickets for the trial permitted entrance, but did not guarantee a specific seat. For example, in the description of her third time at Westminster Hall, Frances Burney confessed: 'We went early, yet did not get very good places'.[44]

People queued for hours outside Westminster, especially when renowned orators were due to speak. The correspondence of the British elite for the early months of 1788 is scattered with references to the audience's rush to the courtroom. In a letter addressed on 22 February 1788 to the diplomat William Eden (1744–1814), the politician and collector of books and prints, Anthony Morris Storer (1746–99), noted for example: 'Everybody is up by nine o'clock, the ladies have finished their toilette by that time, and are at the door of Westminster Hall, pressing and squeezing to get good places within'.[45]

Among the vivid images evoked in Sir Gilbert Elliot's letters to his wife, the portrait of the crowd gathering round Westminster Hall becomes sinister: outside the courtroom, the polite and sociable elite metamorphoses into a violent and impatient mass of people who do not hesitate to press and crush those around them. Aware of the wild rush and injuries that entering Westminster Hall might produce, Elliot offered to accompany a lady, Mrs Morrice, to 'save some of her bones at the door getting in'.[46] As Sir Gilbert himself wrote to Lady Elliot:

> It is not yet seven o'clock in the morning, and I expect Mrs. Morrice to call every moment on her way to Westminster Hall, where I am to accompany her, by way of saving some of her bones at the door getting in. She will have to mob it at the door till nine, when the doors open, and then there will be a rush as there is at the pit of the playhouse when Garrick plays King Lear. This will give you some notion of the expectation raised on this occasion. The ladies are dressed and mobbing it in Palace Yard by six or half after six, and they sit from nine to twelve before business begins.[47]

This passage refers to 3 June 1788, the thirty-second day of the trial and the first of Sheridan's four-day-long speech. As we shall see, so high was the expectation of the public that the price of the tickets, as well as the eagerness to secure good seats, had no precedent. For this reason, ladies who normally assembled in front of the courtroom by nine o'clock arrived, instead, by six.

While referencing different sessions, both Anthony Morris Storer's and Sir Gilbert Elliot's comments are littered with allusions to the theatre. For a start, the audience faced a few hours' wait – during the winter months, 'shivering, without either fires or beaux to warm them' – before the legal spectacle had even begun.[48] Commenting on the eighteenth-century London stage, Allardyce Nicoll has noted that 'when any special attractions were announced it was necessary to reach the playhouse doors at least an hour and a half before the scheduled time of the performance'.[49]

Secondly, entering Westminster Hall – as with most theatres at the time – was a traumatic process. Those who were not wealthy enough to buy a ticket for the boxes could risk life and limb in their struggle to gain admission to the playhouse. In his lively survey of eighteenth-century London, Jerry White has observed that 'Popular actors and plays could produce a great crush at the doors that sometimes proved dangerous and worse'.[50] In this sense, it is certainly not coincidental that Sir Gilbert compared Sheridan to one of the most celebrated theatre stars of the time, David Garrick. Although on 3 June no grievous accident was reported, the *London Chronicle* stressed that 'very great difficulties occurred, and several ladies in the crowd had their habiliments stripped from them'.[51] Despite these discomforts and 'difficulties', Londoners had a fascination with the theatre. It is in this light that we should read Sir Gilbert's vibrant account:

> We stood an hour and a half in the street in the mob, and at last the press was so terrible, that I think it possible I may have saved, if not her [Mrs Morrice's] life, at least a limb or two. I could not, however, save her cap, which perished in the attempt. Shoes were, however, the principal and most general loss. Several ladies went in barefoot; others, after losing their own, got the stray shoes of other people, and went in with one red and one yellow shoe.[52]

For the fashionable members of society who entered Westminster Hall in 1788, therefore, the trial of Warren Hastings was akin to a theatrical spectacle. In this context, Sarah Sophia Banks's collection of 'Tickets for Warren Hastings Trial' is a precious source of information for the social history of her age. It offers a portrait of the elite which is not static and lifeless, a faded image crystallized into a remote past; on the contrary, it conjures up a dynamic tableau of knights and baronets writing letters, sending tickets; people crowding outside Westminster Hall; the Banks trio arriving late in the morning; gentlemen presenting counterfeited tickets; ladies wearing gorgeous dresses and jewels; peers leaning out of boxes, peeresses looking around with their opera glasses; auditors sipping chocolate; gentlemen requiring an 'exit and readmission ticket' – and so on. As these vignettes show, the spectators who attended the impeachment against the former Governor-General of Bengal behaved as if they were at Drury Lane or Covent Garden, their frivolity being more attuned to the variegated spectacle of a theatrical evening than to a parliamentary debate questioning the moral integrity of the Empire.

Aware of the theatrical atmosphere in the court, Hastings's prosecutors acted accordingly and performed like the actors of a melodrama. Significantly, classical rhetoricians – above all Cicero – had attached much importance to acting techniques. In point of fact, effective body language was fundamental to making a 'strong push at the passions' of the audience.[53] As we shall see in a moment, Burke and his fellow managers followed Cicero's prescriptions: they excited the attention and engaged the emotions of their hearers, shaping their rhetoric in less technical and instead in more emotional terms.

Actio in performance

In a recent study on eighteenth-century British eloquence, Paddy Bullard has suggested that, although the art of rhetoric was firmly rooted in national contexts, 'commentators on rhetoric from England, Ireland, and Scotland shared a classical and humanistic inheritance as the basis of their criticism, and they also felt that they were involved in a common conversation'.[54] As early as 1712, for example, the writer and politician Joseph Addison (1672–1719) argued over the importance of 'Gestures' and 'Voice' for a successful public speaker. Published in the *Spectator*, the article opens with a Latin epigraph from Ovid's *Metamorphoses* – *abest facundis Gratia dictis* (No Charm does his eloquence adorn) – which encapsulates and foreshadows the writer's thought.[55] Throughout the piece, Addison repeatedly asserts that English speakers are dull and vapid. Comparing British orators to 'cold and dead' figures, or 'speaking Statues', Addison laments the lack of 'those Strainings of the Voice, Motions of the Body, and Majesty of the Hand, which are so much celebrated in the Orators of *Greece* and *Rome*'.[56]

Thirty years later, in Scotland, ancient and modern public speaking were juxtaposed and contrasted anew. In an essay entitled *Of Eloquence* (1742), the philosopher David Hume (1711–76) highlighted how eighteenth-century British oratory – 'argumentative and rational; [...] calm, elegant, and subtile' – paled when compared to the 'pathetic and sublime' elocution of classical orators.⁵⁷ 'Even a person, unacquainted with the noble remains of ancient orators' – he pungently remarked – 'may judge, from a few strokes, that the stile [sic] or species of their eloquence was infinitely more sublime than that which modern orators aspire to'.⁵⁸

Addison's article and Hume's essay testify to the rich and lively debate on rhetoric that flourished in Britain – notably in Scotland – during the second half of the century. The copious number of studies penned at that time include, among others, *Lectures on Rhetoric and Belles Lettres* (1748–51), by the renowned moral philosopher and political economist Adam Smith (1723–90); *The Philosophy of Rhetoric* (1776), by the Church of Scotland minister George Campbell (1719–96); *A Course of Lectures on Oratory and Criticism* (1777), by the natural philosopher Joseph Priestley (1733–1804); and *Lectures on Rhetoric and Belles Lettres* (1783), by the literary critic Hugh Blair, to give just a few of the famous names. In 1748 Adam Smith began delivering a course of public lectures on rhetoric and *belles lettres* in Edinburgh, and he continued to give them as 'private classes' after he was offered regular employment as professor of logic at Glasgow University in 1751.

Within this dynamic context, elocutionists promoted new methods of pronouncing and performing speeches, focusing on what Paul Goring has called '*emotionally affecting* modes of delivery'.⁵⁹ In order to mould British orators into persuasive performers who appealed to the emotions of the audience, importance was particularly attached to the body, as a medium to express and transmit feelings. For example, in *The Art of Speaking* (1761) – one of the most influential manuals on elocution published in the 1760s – the educationist and author James Burgh (1714–75) argued that the most important part of oratory was '*delivery*, comprehending what every gentleman ought to be master of respecting *gesture*, *looks*, and command of *voice*'.⁶⁰

An eloquent body was thus essential to raise and manipulate the passions of the audience. In this sense, the orator's voice was also an important tool that might enable the orator to influence the minds of an audience. Among his many classically informed reflections on composition and delivery was the antiquary and biographer John Ward's (1678/9–1758) observation that 'the orator's province is not barely to apply to the mind, but likewise to the passions, which require a great variety of the voice, high or low, vehement or languid, according to the nature of the passion he designs to affect'.⁶¹

Certainly, delivery was the key to persuasion through the emotions. From this perspective, classical canons of rhetoric retained a good deal of currency in the eighteenth century, particularly in parliamentary oratory. Although some of the managers performed very successful speeches, the most affecting orations delivered throughout the eight years of the trial were Burke's account of the Rangpur atrocities (18 February 1788) and Sheridan's four-day oration on the Begums of Oudh (3, 6, 10, and 13 June 1788). In recent years, these striking speeches have been approached from various perspectives, including the historical, political, artistic, literary and postcolonial. And yet, they have never been systematically surveyed in light of Graeco-Roman rhetorical treatises. What I wish to argue here is that Burke's and Sheridan's *coups de théâtre* were not only related to eighteenth-century modes of delivery or the contemporary vogue for sentimental drama, but that they were also influenced by classical rhetorical prescriptions, which recommended that the orator should transform legal debates into spectacles of justice.[62] My reading of Burke's and Sheridan's dramatic performances will be conducted with reference to Cicero's and Quintilian's theoretical works on oratory (respectively, *De Oratore*, *Orator*, *Brutus*, and *Institutio Oratoria*) and, specifically, through the lens of *De Oratore*.[63]

In June 1788, when he delivered his four-day speech before the Lords, Richard Brinsley Sheridan was already widely known as a brilliant orator. The previous year, on 7 February 1787, he had opened the Begums of Oudh charge (the fourth Article of Charge against Hastings) in an 'epic' speech of five hours and forty minutes, which was followed by the first burst of applause ever heard in the Commons.[64] Unanimously praised in London as one of the finest orations ever performed there, the echo of the Begum speech reached as far as India, where the *Calcutta Gazette* lauded it in the most enthusiastic terms:

> A speech fraught with argument, so detailed, yet so compact, illumined with flashes of eloquence so sublime, and fraught in such a degree with all the powers that tend to conviction, we speak from the highest authority, when we say, was never heard within the walls of St. Stephen's chapel'.[65]

So successful was Sheridan's speech that, in 1813, while commenting on Sheridan 'and other *hommes marquants*', Lord Byron (1788–1824) still described it as 'the very best Oration [...] ever conceived or heard in this country'.[66]

As a consequence of Sheridan's extraordinary performance in 1787, the request for tickets in June 1788 was unprecedented and entrance passes were 'sold for as much as fifty guineas'.[67] 'You have no conception of the rage and clamour for tickets for to-morrow's trial'; – Sir Gilbert Elliot wrote to his wife on the eve of the great orator's performance – 'at Mrs. Legge's people were almost putting their hands into one's pocket for them'.[68] Not unexpectedly, the 'ticket-hunting' had started a few months earlier, no doubt since April 1788, as a letter published in *The World* clearly suggests. Addressing an unspecified 'Sir', the author of the epistle asks for as many as eleven tickets for 'the day that Mr. *Sheridan* is to display his powers, not only as a Manager but as a Performer'.[69] Significantly, Sheridan is referred to both as an orator ('a Manager') and as an actor ('a Performer').

As this example demonstrates, borders between politics and theatre were often blurred and easily crossed over. Christopher Reid has shown how eighteenth-century parliamentary debate should, in effect, be understood as a form of dramatic action: both 'drama and oratory address themselves to a collective audience' and 'indeed develop their full potential, in the process of performance'.[70] Even where a verbatim record preserves a parliamentary speech in a written form, Reid continues, 'certain important details of the performance – intonation, delivery, gesture, reception, and so on – will inevitably be lost'.[71] With this in mind, we might perhaps understand why Sheridan himself, conscious of the crucial importance of acting, never published the great speech he delivered in February 1787. Commenting on the orator's decision to leave the magic of his performance to pure imagination, his biographer, Thomas Moore (1779–1830), emphasized how 'We may now indulge in dreams of the eloquence [...], as we do of the music of the ancients and the miraculous powers attributed to it'.[72]

Analogies between political and theatrical characters had repeatedly been pointed out in the classical world, particularly in Rome.[73] Cicero, for example, frequently recommended that orators should receive a theatrical training: 'we must carefully observe not only orators but also actors' (*Intuendi nobis sunt non solum oratores, sed etiam actores*).[74] Interestingly, in Latin, both actors and lawyers were referred to by the same term, *actores*.[75] This accident of language highlights similarities: as William Batstone has put it, actors and lawyers 'are the ones who hide behind the mask, manipulate the mask, make you see what you do not see'.[76] In this respect, in his renowned treatise on the orator's education, Quintilian significantly observed:

> I have frequently seen tragic actors, having taken off their masks at the end of some emotional scene, leave the stage still in tears. And if the mere delivery of the written words of another can so kindle them with imagined emotions, what shall *we* be capable of doing, we who have to imagine the facts in such a way that we can feel vicariously the emotions of our endangered clients?[77]

It was not by chance that Cicero not only defined orators as *veritatis ipsius actores* (players that act real life) and actors as *imitatores autem veritatis* ([those] who only mimic reality),[78] but even likened his ideal orator to Roscius, Rome's most famous actor.[79]

It is against this background of dramatized politics – with the courtroom turned into a stage, and orators into actors – that we should read Ralph Broome's vitriolic attack on the managers' exasperated theatricality. In *Letters from Simpkin the Second to his Dear Brother in Wales*, a popular verse narration of the trial of Hastings, Broome (d. 1805) repeatedly provides evidence of what Julie Stone Peters has defined as 'misconstrual of law as entertainment'.[80] In one of his lampoons, Broome depicts Sheridan as a playwright:

> As SHERRY in speaking is fond of Precision,
> He adopts the *Theatrical mode of Division:*—
> That is, he arranges the *Plot* and the *Facts*,
> And the Play will consist of a *Number of Acts*.[81]

In another, he shows how Sheridan was taken ill after describing slaughters and tortures allegedly committed in India. The pamphleteer's comment is full of keen irony: Sherry's fainting is not the expression of a sensitive soul but, rather, 'a trick, which stage orators use in their need':

> Such horrors presented themselves to his view,
> That SHERRY took fright at the picture he drew;
> He had something, 'twas thought, still more horrid to say,
> When his tongue lost its powers, and he fainted away.

> Some say, 'twas his Conscience that gave him a stroke,
> But those who best know him, treat that as a joke;
> 'Tis a trick, which *Stage Orators* use in their need,
> The Passions to raise, and the Judgment mislead.[82]

As the final line of this passage intimates, one of the crucial questions lying at the heart both of classical treatises on oratory and of contemporary works on theatre was that of 'feeling the part'. Indeed, as Jay Fliegelman remarks, 'the oratorical manuals of the period were often indistinguishable from acting manuals'.[83] Thus, for example, in *The Actor* (1750) – the first English acting treatise to examine the emotional attributes of a performer – John Hill (1714–75), a physician and actor himself, observed:

> It is a maxim as old as the days of *Horace*; *if you wou'd have me shed tears, you must weep your self* [sic] *first*. That excellent author address'd this doctrine to orators; but it is still more applicable to actors. [...] in order to his [the tragedian's] utmost success, it is necessary that he imagine [sic] himself to be, nay that he for the first time really is, the person he represents.[84]

Orators were encouraged to appeal to the emotions of the audience also in eighteenth-century rhetorical treatises. 'The most virtuous man, in treating of the most virtuous subject, seeks to touch the heart of him to whom he speaks', Hugh Blair noted.[85] In particular – Blair continued – 'The internal emotion of the Speaker adds a pathos to his words, his looks, his gestures, and his whole manner, which exerts a power almost irresistible over those who hear him'.[86]

This view was shared by, among others, Burke, Sheridan and Elliot. The year before the beginning of the trial, on 12 December 1787, the latter had opened proceedings against Sir Elijah Impey (1732–1809), a school friend of Hastings's from Westminster, who had been the Chief Justice of the Supreme Court at Calcutta for most of Hastings's administration. The most important charge against Sir Elijah was the execution of Maharaja Nandakumar (d. 1775), a Hindu Brahaman official in Bengal who was tried by the newly constituted Supreme Court. After accusing the Governor-General of accepting bribes, Nandakumar was in turn accused of forgery allegedly committed in 1769 and sentenced to death. The death penalty for such a crime appeared inordinately harsh and the execution of Nandakumar inevitably aroused suspicion that Hastings 'had taken an active part in bringing it about'.[87]

Elliot's speech was extraordinarily well received and the following day Burke wrote a letter to Lady Elliot to congratulate her on her husband's exceptional delivery:

> It was an opening of wonderful Splendour and Beauty; a magnificent Portico full of Chaste Grandeur, and perfectly suitable to the Temple of Justice which it leads to. [...] This well combined piece was so very affecting, that it drew Tears from some of his auditory, and those not the most favourable to his Cause. In Truth the whole came from the heart, and went to the heart.[88]

As Burke noted, Sir Gilbert's great success was due to the display of an emotional body language, enhanced by an appropriate 'Tone and modulation of Voice'. In accordance with the Ciceronian theories that encouraged the orator to stamp on himself the same feelings he wished to arouse in the audience, Elliot's oration 'came from the heart and went to the heart'. Similarly, Sir Gilbert's own comment on his performance – 'what a powerful ingredient in eloquence a *sincere feeling* in the speaker is' – shows how he himself had introjected classical rhetorical prescriptions.[89]

In classical Rome, Cicero had, indeed, stressed the importance of persuasive appeals based on emotions that might be transferable from the orator to the audience. This principle, known as *ipse ardere*, to be oneself aflame, is explored at length in *De Oratore*. Antonius, one of the characters in the treatise, utilizes this phrase in reference to Crassus's rhetorical ability: 'to me you seem to be not merely inflaming the arbitrator, but actually on fire yourself' (*non solum incendere iudicem, sed ipse ardere videaris*).[90] The imagery of fire – the fire of passion that consumes the orator and spreads among the auditors – is recurrent throughout Cicero's dialogue. For instance, it is Antonius again who explains:

> For just as there is no substance so ready to take fire, as to be capable of generating flame without the application of a spark, so also there is no mind so ready to absorb an orator's influence, as to be inflammable when the assailing speaker is not himself aglow with passion.[91]

Perhaps Elliot had this passage in mind when he described Sheridan's June orations on the tragedy of Oudh; his letters to his wife abound with references to the semantic fields of fire and cold.[92] According to Sir Gilbert, Sheridan's opening speech on 3 June was disappointing, in part, because it was too contrived and lacked 'the luxuriance and grace of spontaneous nature'. 'His exordium' – Elliot continued – 'was [...] colder and less effective than I expected from him'.[93] Elliot's portrait of a distant, unemotional speech is further conveyed by a vivid metaphor: Sheridan's eloquence is compared to 'flowers, which are produced by great pains, skill, and preparation, and are delivered in perfect order, ready tied up in regular though *beautiful bouquets*'.[94] A good example, in this sense, is Sheridan's description of the Indian zenana (the area of the household reserved for women):

> Women there *are not as in Turkey*. They *neither* go to the mosque *nor* to the bath. It is *not* the thin veil alone that hides them; *but*, in the inmost recesses of their zanana [sic], they are kept from public view by those reverenced and protected walls which, as Mr. Hastings and Sir Elijah Impey admit, are held sacred even by the ruffian hand of war or by the more uncourteous hand of the law. *But*, in this situation, *they are not confined* from a mean and selfish policy of man – not from a coarse and sensual jealousy. *Enshrined rather than immured*, their habitation and retreat is a sanctuary, *not a prison*. Their jealousy is their own jealousy – a jealousy of their own honour, that leads them to regard liberty as degradation, and the gaze even of admiring eyes as inexpiable pollution to the purity of their fame and of their honour.[95]

Sheridan's key point here is the harem/zenana, Turk/Indian dichotomy.[96] While the harem, evoked metonymically by an allusion to the Ottoman Empire ('Turkey'), its religion and culture ('the mosque' and 'the bath'), was associated, among other things, with sexual slavery and perversion, the Indian women's wilful withdrawal from public life is tinged with a quasi-religious aura ('reverenced and protected walls, which [...] are held sacred'; 'enshrined rather than immured'; 'their retreat is a sanctuary'). In terms of style, the stark contrast between harem and zenana is structured with litotes and antitheses, as well as with a triple, almost-chiasmatic repetition of 'jealousy' ('Their jealousy is their own jealousy – a jealousy of their own honour'). Undoubtedly, this speech was 'the work of a man of very extraordinary genius'. Yet its 'artificial execution' – we can picture Sheridan here as a cold, authoritative speaker in perfect control of his material – left the audience's 'passion' and 'judgment unaffected'.[97]

On 6 June, again, Sheridan appeared distant and detached, so much so that Elliot confessed: 'I object to it [...] as bearing too evidently the marks of deliberate and cold-blood preparation just where the utmost degree of real passion and fire is to be represented'.[98] From the outset, Sheridan's second-day speech was pervaded by an 'artificial fire'.[99] For instance, arguing for the improbability of an attempt of the Begums on the East India Company, the orator observed:

> The next circumstance which I wish your Lordships to advert to is what is admitted through the whole of this testimony – I mean the *infinite improbability* at least that the Begums should have made this attempt, and the *absolute impossibility* of their succeeding. But I don't ask you then to say that because a crime is *improbable* to have been *attempted*, and the success is *impossible*, therefore the *attempt* is not made. No, my Lords; but I think again I have a right to claim this; because I am ready to admit that it is *impossible* to look into the history of these transactions – it is *impossible* to trace the conduct of the wild and irregular mind of the man whom we accuse – without admitting that there is such a thing as a *perverse propensity* to *evil* that leads the mind of a man to *evil* acts, even where the perpetrator has no obvious motive, either of interest or opposition, to answer.[100]

Such highly structured passages were based on parallelisms with homoteleuton ('the infinite improbability' and 'absolute impossibility'), repetitions ('improbability'/'improbable'; 'impossibility'/'impossible'/'impossible'; 'attempted'/'attempt'; 'evil'/'evil') and alliteration ('perverse propensity'), making them readily memorable, but devoid of emotive appeal.

Where his first two orations were only marginally successful, Sheridan's final speech on 13 June was universally praised as triumphant.[101] Although, upon this occasion, Sir Gilbert did not comment on the orator's general style of speaking, he praised his performance as 'finer [...] than ever'.[102] According to *The Times*, the orator's elocution 'surpassed every thing that was ever heard or imagined'. 'Mr. Sheridan' – the reporter continued – 'broke out in a strain of the most pathetic and beautiful language that can be conceived, and we lament our insufficiency to do it the justice it is so highly entitled to'.[103] This time we can imagine Sheridan being himself aglow – or, as Cicero would have put it, *ipse inflammatus* – to the point that 'he once or twice had nearly fainted away'.[104]

According to Sheridan's account, Hastings had incited the Wazir, Asaf al-Daula, to seize his mother's and grandmother's treasure. Although, as Julie Carson has noted, indicting Hastings for crimes against the family presented 'nothing remotely resembling evidence',[105] Sheridan's great speech still vibrates with the magic of his extraordinary performance:

> Good God! my Lords, what a cause is this we are maintaining! What! when I feel it a part of my duty, as it were, when I feel it an instruction in my brief to support the claim of age to reverence, of maternal feebleness to filial protection and support, can I recollect before whom I am pleading? I look round on this various assembly that surrounds me, seeing in every countenance a breathing testimony to this general principle, and yet for a moment think it necessary to enforce the bitter aggravation which attends the crimes of those who violate this universal duty.[106]

The numerous exclamations of this passage bear witness to the pathos of the orator. The appeal to all the auditors ('this various assembly that surrounds me') and the advocation of a 'universal duty' – filial pity – were part of a rhetorical strategy, enabling Sheridan not only to form a close bond between himself and his audience, but also, even more importantly, to 'generate sentimental identification' with the distant and alien Begums.[107] Indeed, it was this very sentimental identification that paved the way for one of Sheridan's most moving sections on filial love:

> My Lords, how can I support the claim of filial love by argument, much less the affection of a son to a mother, where love loses its awe, and veneration is mixed with tenderness? What can I say upon such a subject? What can I do but repeat the ready truths which with the quick impulse of the mind must spring to the lips of every man on such a theme? Filial love – the morality, the instinct, the sacrament of nature – a duty; or rather let me say it is miscalled a duty, for it flows from the heart without effort – its delight – its indulgence – its enjoyment.[108]

It is not difficult to imagine Sheridan inflamed with the all-consuming passion that enthralled the ladies and gentlemen sitting in Westminster Hall. Through the oratorical symbiosis of body and language, Sheridan successfully utilized what his father, the actor and orthoepist Thomas Sheridan (1719?–88), had called 'the language of emotions'.[109] Like Cicero, Sheridan's father had argued for the importance of a body language 'composed of tones, looks, and gesture', by means of which 'the [speaker's] passions, affections, and all manner of feelings, are not only made known, but communicated to others'.[110]

Just as Sheridan seemed to be suffering, the audience was spectacularly seized by a fit of tears: 'there were few dry eyes in the assembly' – Elliot informs us – 'and as for myself, I never remember to have cried so heartily and so copiously on any public occasion'.[111] This highly emotional drama reached its climax when Sheridan collapsed into Burke's arms, seemingly overwhelmed with physical pain and intense feelings. Among the audience who assisted at this *coup de théâtre*, the historian Edward Gibbon commented: 'Sheridan, on the close of his speech, sunk into Burke's arms, but I called this morning, he is perfectly well. A good actor'.[112] Sheridan's final act was commented on by Warren Hastings himself, who lamented that the managers had turned 'the Court into a theatre'.[113] Once again, politics and theatre overlapped.

With his pathetic performance culminating in a swoon, there is, indeed, little doubt that Sheridan's 'prosecuting theatrics' were profoundly influenced by the contemporary vogue for sentimental drama.[114] Between 1740 and 1780, theatre was dominated by the acting style of the celebrated actor David Garrick, who emphasized the importance of actors themselves feeling the emotions they portrayed.[115] Drawing on Cicero's and Quintilian's exhortations to orators to emulate actors, Burke himself remarked how Garrick was:

> a man to whom were all obliged; one who was the great master of eloquence; in whose school they had all imbibed the art of speaking, and been taught the elements of rhetoric. For his part, he owned that he had been greatly indebted to his instruction.[116]

As a result, it is not surprising that the theatre-going, fashionable audience who attended the trial in 1788 responded to the orators' performances as if they were at a playhouse. In the eighteenth and early nineteenth centuries, the discourse of sensibility powerfully shaped the spectators' responses to theatrical spectacles. For example, as Jim Davis has pointed out, the intense tragic performances of Sarah Siddons caused both men and women to cry and 'some of her female supporters even succumbed to hysteria and fainting fits'.[117] Similarly, as we have seen above, spectators reacted to Sheridan's highly emotional delivery on 13 June with copious tears. This was also the case with Elliot's affecting speech against Sir Elijah Impey on 9 May 1788: as he himself put it, he achieved a success 'beyond my most sanguine expectations'.[118] Again, the reasons for this triumph are to be traced in the emotional intensity of the orator's performance. In a letter penned to his wife on 10 May 1788, Sir Gilbert explained:

> I was fortunate enough to conclude with an affecting passage. I had tears and violent emotions all round me as before, and my powers certainly went very far beyond any idea I could have formed of myself. Dudley Long was one of the weepers, Adam another, and indeed the whole House and gallery were worked up to an extraordinary degree of feeling and emotion.[119]

Given the overpowering impressions that both Sheridan and Elliot made on their audience and given the sympathetic response that they inspired in their spectators, it is tempting to speculate that, just as the orators' histrionic performances were influenced by the contemporary style of acting characterized by an intense emotional delivery,[120] so were they also informed by classical rhetorical models. Indeed, classical scholars such as James M. May have shown that every Ciceronian oration is rich in passages full of pathos, 'several even ending with the orator in tears, barely able to continue'.[121] In a passage from *De Oratore*, for example, Antonius observes how:

> (Moreover) it is impossible for the listener to feel indignation, hatred or ill-will, to be terrified of anything, or reduced to tears of compassion, unless all these emotions, which the advocate would inspire in the arbitrator, are visibly stamped or rather branded on the advocate himself.[122]

Repeatedly, Cicero highlights the importance of stirring up the audience's emotion as the most important means for winning lawsuits.[123] In *Brutus* 89, for instance, the Latin orator makes it clear that *inflammare iudicem* (inflaming the court) is far more important than *docere* (instructing):

> of the two chief qualities which the orator must possess, accurate argument looking to proof, and impressive appeal to the emotions of the listener, the orator who inflames the court accomplishes far more than the one who merely instructs it.[124]

It is within this perspective of *inflammare* rather than *docere* that we should undoubtedly read Burke's peroration on the Rangpur horrors. On 18 February 1788, seizing on the reports of atrocities allegedly perpetrated by revenue collectors in Rangpur, a district in northern Bengal, the Anglo-Irish orator provided the audience with gruesome details. The gravamen of Burke's charge was that a certain Devi Singh (d. 1805) had bribed Hastings in order to be awarded the revenue farms of Rangpur. As a consequence of the Governor-General's corruption – Burke thundered – Devi Singh's agents had inflicted tremendous tortures on the local population.[125]

As P. J. Marshall has shown, these reports caught Burke's attention too late to be incorporated in the charges. However, when the orator perused the list of horrid and nefarious cruelties purportedly inflicted in the most ferocious manner, he 'was obviously much moved by what he read and fully recognized that others would be so moved'.[126] Despite the unreliability of these events and their irrelevance to the charges brought against Hastings, Burke dilated upon the episode 'for' – he wrote to Philip Francis – 'it has stuff in it, that will, if anything, work upon the popular Sense'.[127] Affecting popular sentiment was, in fact, 'essential to Burke's purpose' (to steal a phrase from Richard Bourke).[128] Believing the Lords to be biased in favour of Hastings, Burke thought that the most likely means of putting pressure on them to condemn the accused was to inflame the audience.[129]

Willingly sacrificing accuracy for the sake of sensationalism, the prosecutor dwelled on shocking scenes of torments, the instruments of torture and maiming, as well as mutilated and bleeding bodies.[130] 'In the process' – Marshall contends – 'he [Burke] produced some memorable rhetoric, such as his description of how torturers "crushed and maimed those poor, honest, laborious hands"'.[131] As will be shown in some detail in the following chapter, the whole section of the Rangpur speech is interspersed with frequent references to brutal corporal punishments – one of the most notorious and often cited episodes is that of the nipples of the women being put 'into the sharp edges of split bambooes' and torn from their bodies.[132] This long and lurid catalogue of atrocities is, indeed, structured through a sequence of disturbing vignettes, which include scourging with rods made of 'a poisonous plant called Bechettea plant, a plant, which is deadly caustic, which inflames the parts that are cut, and leaves the body a crust of leprous sores and often causes death itself'.[133] As with his shocking account of Jane McCrea's death analysed in Chapter 2, Burke's speech on the Rangpur horrors slips into a register of hyperbolic realism.

Burke's vivid account of abominations had its effects. 'It is impossible for us to give the public any idea of the influence of his description', the *London Chronicle* claimed. According to the reporter:

The cruelties practiced on helpless people, so shocking to humanity, to modesty, and to every tender and manly feeling, convulsed and agitated the whole Assembly. The ladies were, throughout the whole Hall, in agony of grief, and the tear of compassion stood in the eye of the most veteran soldier present.[134]

So greatly did Burke stir the feelings of his auditors that many ladies, among whom were the most acclaimed tragic actress of the time, Sarah Siddons, and Sheridan's wife, the celebrated soprano Elizabeth Ann Linley, fainted away. With a simile drawn from the classical world, the aforementioned politician and collector, Anthony Morris Storer, likened Sarah Siddons to Niobe, the mythological figure who cried unceasingly in grief: 'even she who has drawn tears from so many others has shed them on hearing Mr. Burke's description of India. Mrs. Siddons, they say, was like Niobe, all tears, and Mrs. Sheridan fainted away.'[135]

In this theatrical setting, quite interestingly, roles are reversed, with Mrs. Siddons and Mrs. Sheridan transforming from objects of the audience's glances to members of the audience themselves. Edmund Burke, in turn, appeared to be no longer the spectator of a tragedy starring Sarah Siddons – in a celebrated passage from his *Reflections* he would recall 'the tears that Garrick formerly, or that Siddons not long since, have extorted from me' – but metamorphosed into a supreme actor.[136] Commenting on the Rangpur speech, the *Gazetter and New Daily Advertiser* reporter concluded: 'Certainly such a tragedy was never exhibited on any stage.'[137]

To amplify the drama, after dwelling on the goriest details, the orator himself was taken ill with a sudden pain in his side. Burke's sickness was said to have been caused by 'his drinking cold water and eating oranges during the time he was speaking'.[138] Oranges were commonly reputed to soothe a dry and sore throat. Sir Gilbert Elliot, for instance, was much annoyed at his mouth being 'as dry as parchment, in spite of an orange which I kept sucking'.[139] Apparently, it was not uncommon for orators to feel indisposed after eating cold oranges. For example, on 5 March 1788, *The Times* reported that an orator, a certain Mr. Erskine, was taken ill while pleading at the bar of the House of Commons: 'His indisposition' – noted the newspaper – 'was occasioned by eating an orange, which was too cold for his stomach, and brought on a shivering'.[140] According to Burke, however, his sudden malaise was not produced by 'a draught of cold water which he drank in the midst of the heat of his oration' – as he seemingly told Frances Burney – but was, instead, caused by the revolting tortures he was describing:[141]

> My Lords, I am sorry to break the attention of your Lordships in such a way. It is a subject that agitates me. It is a long, difficult, and arduous; but with the blessing of God, if I can, to save you any further trouble, I will go through it this day.[142]

Burke tried to resume, but was in no state to continue and the session had to be adjourned. Although the account of the Rangpur horrors probably took no more than half an hour, its importance is much greater than its length would suggest. Undoubtedly, this was one of the most sensational speeches ever pronounced during the trial, and was regarded by Burke's contemporaries as a masterpiece of rhetoric. 'We may venture to say a more perfect piece of oratory was never delivered to an English audience', observed the *London Chronicle* on 19 February 1788. Even newspapers normally hostile to Edmund Burke, such as *The World*, lauded the power of the images that, by the magic of his eloquence, the orator was capable of evoking: 'his descriptions were more vivid – more harrowing – and more horrific – than human utterance on either fact or fancy, perhaps, ever formed before'.[143]

Within this narrative of pain, Burke's body language acquired possibly greater importance than his verbal language. By fainting, he transformed distant, impalpable torments into visible and tangible sufferings. His body became a decisive medium to direct the feelings of his spectators against Hastings. By means of the technique of *aposiopesis* – that is, when an orator breaks off the speech to suggest overwhelming emotion – Burke provided his audience with a powerful example of emotional response to imperial atrocities. According to Ahmed, the Irish-born orator's performance – along with the very theatricality of the trial – seems to suggest that the basis of civil society lies in 'social mimicry'.[144] Similarly, Stone Peters has noted that the detailed description of tortured body parts, made visible through Burke's pain and indisposition, 'would communicate itself somatically to the listeners, whose tears (mixing pathos and pathology) would both realize this bodily transmission and offer visible proof of their sympathy'.[145]

Burke's histrionic style, with its emotional insistence, combined a variety of different features and cultural influences, among which were personal temperament, classical oratory, contemporary sentimental drama and the omnipresent eighteenth-century obsession with sympathy. It is difficult to define how far each of these components affected him, not least because by overlapping and intertwining, they all informed the Anglo-Irish orator's vivid rhetoric or 'painted orations', as Horace Walpole called them.[146] Undoubtedly, as with Sheridan and Elliot, eighteenth-century theatre and its emphasis on pathetic performances influenced Burke considerably. The fact that the trial of Warren Hastings was performed in an atmosphere of extensive theatricality, then, added to the managers' tendency to turn to the irresistible natural force of theatre which classical rhetoricians had employed.

4

Spectacles of Passion: Cicero's *In Verrem* and Burke's 'Speech on the Opening of the Impeachment'

As early as 1914, the American classicist H. V. Canter published an article significantly titled 'The impeachment of Verres and Hastings: Cicero and Burke'.[1] Despite dating back more than a hundred years, Canter's study represents to this day a starting point for those interested in the relationship between the arraignment of Verres and the impeachment of Warren Hastings. The essay by Canter is especially illuminating because it explores references to nineteenth- and early twentieth-century scholars and politicians, such as Macaulay and Lord Erskine (1750–1823), who discussed general resemblances and differences between the two illustrious cases. No less importantly, Canter also offers a more personal analysis, providing some examples of textual comparison between Cicero's *In Verrem* and Burke's speeches against the former Governor-General of Bengal.

More recently, on the occasion of the bicentenary commemoration of the impeachment of Hastings organized by the University of Edinburgh, the discussion was resumed by Geoffrey Carnall, who described in broad terms the importance of Cicero as a model for Burke.[2] Since then, though a number of scholars from different backgrounds (including Marshall, Whelan and Ayres) have variously remarked on this fascinating relationship, hitherto no full-length study has been devoted to an analysis contrasting the Latin and English texts.[3]

In this chapter, I address this gap and, by attempting to fill it, I indicate some fruitful lines of enquiry for further research. Inevitably, a problem arises with any discussion of Burke's orations, particularly those against Hastings: the text is so extensive as to render commentary on it rather diffuse.[4] To meet this difficulty, I have deliberately chosen to restrict my attention to the so-called 'Speech on the Opening of the Impeachment'.[5] Pronounced on 15, 16, 18 and 19 February 1788, this was 'by far' – as F. P. Lock has put it – '[Burke's] most ambitious effort to date'.[6] It has been calculated that, with its written text running to over 80,000 words, this four-day performance lasted about eleven hours.[7] Owing to its extensive length and importance (in substance, if not formally, this oration opened the trial), the speech may be regarded as a significant example with a general application.

It is not surprising that many contemporaries considered this oration 'as one of the greatest rhetorical achievements' of their time.[8] Indeed, Burke's harangue received eloquent accolades: even those who were extremely sympathetic to the accused, such as Frances Burney and Hannah More (1745–1833), paid tribute to its power.[9] Just as importantly, newspapers commented extensively on this speech. The *Gazetteer and New Daily Advertiser* (19 February 1788), for example, praised the tirade of 16 February as a 'Philippic against arbitrary power', one that was 'altogether without parallel'. Similarly, *The Times* (18 February 1788) praised the orator's second-day speech as 'perhaps the most eloquent oration ever delivered in a Court of Judicature'.

It goes without saying that Burke's 'Speech on the Opening of the Impeachment' and Cicero's *In Verrem* may be juxtaposed and analysed within numerous discursive frameworks and from different perspectives. Some may be concerned, for instance, with matters of form or style, while others would rather emphasize political issues, such as the administration of justice in the Roman provinces and the British colonies, and in India in particular. Inevitably, pressures of space restrict what can be discussed here, so I have decided to concentrate on resemblances, rather than evident and more widely recognized differences. Among others, I will focus on the semantic fields utilized by Cicero and Burke to describe the defendants, as well as on 'vivid description'.

Because my analysis is mostly based upon a philological comparison, before I turn to the Latin and English texts, it is important to add a note on the written version of Burke's orations.[10] Critics, such as Paddy Bullard, have stressed that only a small proportion of the myriad speeches that Burke made in Parliament was, in fact, recorded with accuracy.[11] This is why the task of assessing the authority of the transcriptions often presents formidable difficulties. Luckily enough, the long and complex 'Speech on the Opening of the Impeachment' was transcribed by the most esteemed shorthand writer of the time, Joseph Gurney (1744–1815), who, in most cases, managed to record the proceedings of the trial almost verbatim.[12] As a matter of fact, Gurney's 'impeccable' transcriptions constitute a fuller and more reliable basis than any of the newspapers' records, which are normally the principal source for parliamentary debates.[13]

While borrowings from and allusions to Cicero are noticeable in the 'Speech on the Opening of the Impeachment', neither the *Verrine Orations* nor their villain protagonist are ever referred to directly. In fact, throughout the eight years of the trial, Burke alluded to the *propraetor* of Sicily and the orations *In Verrem* only twice. In the first instance, the Anglo-Irish orator compared Hastings to Verres, while discussing the Governor's illegal receipt of presents from the Indians (21 April 1789): 'He [Hastings] has just got the same character as Caius Verres got in another cause'.[14] The equation of Hastings–Verres was restated several years later in the 'Speech in Reply', on 16 June 1794. This time, not only did Burke allude to the governor of Sicily, but he also referenced Cicero's orations against Verres: 'We have all in our early education read the Verronean [sic] orations. [...] In these orations you see almost every instance of rapacity and peculation which we charge upon Mr. Hastings'.[15]

On a more general level, echoes of the *Verrines* are apparent from the very first sentences pronounced on 15 February 1788. In this respect, the *incipit* of the 'Speech on the Opening of the Impeachment' constitutes a distillation of Burke's strategic appropriations and adaptations of his Roman counterpart:[16] as we shall see, Burke modelled after the *Actio Prima*, imitating Cicero's oration in order and arguments.

Money and corruption

In her study of *In Verrem*, Ann Vasaly has noted that 'the beginning of the exordium (1–10) immediately turns to the thematic crux of the oration: that in this case it is not just Verres who is on trial, but the senatorial *ordo* itself'.[17] In 82 BC, some ten years before the arraignment of the *propraetor* of Sicily, the Senate had in fact been granted by Sulla the monopoly of jury-membership (*lex Cornelia iudiciaria*).[18] According to Cicero, it was rumoured not only at

Rome, but also abroad (*Verr.* I.1: *Inveteravit enim iam opinio* [...] *non modo apud nos sed apud exteras nationes*) that a rich man, though guilty, could not be condemned (I.1: *pecuniosum hominem, quamvis sit nocens, neminem posse damnari*). If Verres were acquitted – Cicero continued – the evident guilt of the defendant, as well as his renowned wealth, would lead everyone to assume that the ex-governor of Sicily had successfully corrupted the judges.[19]

Within this context, the orator presents the prosecution of Verres as a heaven-sent opportunity (I.1: *prope divinitus datum*) for the senatorial jurors:[20] a conviction will allow them to recover the favour of the Roman people and give satisfaction to foreign nations (I.2: *redire in gratiam cum populo Romano, satis facere exteris nationibus*). The *exterae nationes* are a constant presence throughout the *Verrines*: Cicero repeatedly highlights how the trial is enacted not only in the presence of the Roman people, but also *usque ad ultimas terras* (II.4.64).[21]

In parallel with Cicero's exhortations to the Senate to prove incorruptible, on the first day of the 'Speech on the Opening of the Impeachment' Burke warns the Lords against 'narrow partiality, so destructive of justice' (p. 278). Like his ancient counterpart, the Anglo-Irish orator urges the Lords to be beyond reproach, for 'the credit and the honour of the British nation will itself be decided by this decision' (p. 271). Both the Roman Senate and the Lords appear to be characterized, in Frederick G. Whelan's words, 'as embodying justice and the other values of natural law, and thus as satisfactorily realizing the proper ends of social life'.[22] As a latter-day Rome, Britain is responsible for administering justice over different peoples and cultures, and it is from this perspective of 'Imperial justice' that we should read Burke's obsessive repetitions of the word 'justice', particularly in the exordium of his speech: 'What the greatest Inquest of the Nation has begun, its highest Tribunal will accomplish. *Justice* will be done to India' (p. 270); 'your Lordships always had a boundless power; I mean always within the limits of *justice*' (p. 277); 'they ['tribes of suffering nations'] are come here to supplicate *justice* at your Lordships' Bar; and I hope and trust that there will be no rule, formed upon municipal maxims, which will prevent the Imperial *justice* which you owe to the people that call to you from all parts of a great disjointed empire' (p. 277).[23]

Echoing Cicero's allusions to the *exterae nationes* and *ultimae terrae*, Burke reminds the Lords that they 'try the Cause of Asia in the presence of Europe' (p. 278) and argues vigorously that the conduct of the British Empire 'in that very elevated situation to which it has arisen, will undoubtedly be scrutinized' (p. 277). In this sense, the Lords are encouraged to uphold Roman conceptions of virtue and law, but are also alerted to the risk 'of being corrupted'. Once again, the British Empire in India is identified with Rome in the first century BC: from the start of the prosecution Burke makes the Roman point that the sudden influx of wealth from the East may infect and corrupt the ruling class:

> It is well known that great wealth has poured into this country from India; and it is no derogation to us to suppose the possibility of being corrupted by that by which great Empires have been corrupted, and by which assemblies almost as respectable and as venerable as your Lordships' have been known to be indirectly shaken. My Lords, when I say that forty millions of money have come from India to England, we ought to take great care that corruption does not follow, and we may venture to say that the best way to secure a man's reputation is, not by a proud defiance of public opinion, but by guiding one's actions in such a way as that public opinion may afterwards and not previously be defied (pp. 277–8).

The attack on luxury as the source of vice was a commonplace in Cicero's days. Roman historians of the late Republic 'pointed to the flow of luxury goods into Rome following its foreign conquests as the reason for the distruction of the morally upright city of the *maiores* and for its subsequent corruption'.[24] Notably, Polybius noted a growing corruption among the Roman youth, stemming from their encounter with oriental and, particularly, Greek vices. As Cicero – particularly in the *Actio Prima* – associates corruption (*corruptio*) with money (*pecunia*),[25] so does Burke relate 'great wealth' and 'money' to dishonesty. In the above passage, bribery appears so concrete a threat that the words 'corrupted' and 'corruption' are reiterated three times ('it is no derogation to us to suppose the possibility of being corrupted'; 'great Empires have been corrupted'; 'we ought to take great care that corruption does not follow').[26]

If Burke had Rome in mind when he alluded to 'great Empires', this was not the first time that he had associated the collapse of the Roman Empire with 'the mal-administration of its provinces'. In his 'Speech on Motion for Papers on Hastings' (20 February 1786), for example, he remarked:

> The downfall of the greatest empire this world ever saw, has been, on all hands agreed upon to have originated in the mal-administration of its

provinces. Rome never felt within herself the seeds of decline, till corruption from foreign misconduct impaired her vitals, and as an elegant commentator upon the orations of Cicero – Midianus says, *prevaricatione testimonii*, (by prevarication of testimony) the inroads of corruption destroyed the political frame, then were all things at stake (p. 63).[27]

If we are to believe the reporter of the *General Advertiser*, who is the source of this speech, Burke's reflection on the downfall of Rome was significantly complemented by an allusion to the arraignment of Verres ('*Verres* the Governor of Sicily was accused by *Cicero*, for the mal-administration of the province committed to his care' (p. 63)).[28]

The preoccupation that Britain might experience what had befallen Rome – namely, that oriental vices might infect her and bring about the demise of her imperial power – was not new. A sense of decadence and corruption 'imported from the East' appears very clearly, for example, in a passage from David Hume's 1752 essay *Of Refinement in the Arts*:

> Ancient Rome, [...] having learned from its conquered provinces the Asiatic luxury, fell into every kind of corruption; whence arose sedition and civil wars, attended at last with the total loss of liberty. All the Latin classics, whom we peruse in our infancy, are full of these sentiments, and universally ascribe the ruin of their state to the art and riches imported from the East.[29]

As the end of the century approached, anxieties about Britain's Empire intensified, with many fearing an irreversible descent into vice through exposure to the corrupting East. In this respect, it is important to note that the East India Company's employees who came to be known as 'nabobs' became, across the last half of the eighteenth century, the centre of attention of public concern. 'Rich as Croesus and hungry for power', to use Tillman W. Nechtman's expression, nabobs had been acquiring enormous fortunes in India through illegal private trade since the time of Robert Clive.[30] Among the numerous examples that may be drawn from British literature or theatre, particularly in the last quarter of the eighteenth century, *The nabob* (1772) by Samuel Foote (1720–77) proves how the term nabob grew to be a commonly used negative epithet.[31] Besides being perceived to corrupt British society through what Andrew Rudd calls 'debauched Oriental habits', such as 'smoking hookahs and arranging erotic *nautch* dances',[32] nabobs were regarded as a danger to Britain's political establishment, as the words of William Pitt the Elder, the Earl of Chatham (1708–78), notably suggest:

> The riches of Asia have been poured in upon us, and have brought with them not only Asiatic Luxury, but, I fear, Asiatic principle of government. Without connections, without any natural interest in the soil, the importers of foreign gold have forced their way into Parliament by such a torrent of private corruption as no hereditary fortune could resist.[33]

In 1783, long before the beginning of the trial, Burke had similarly warned the Commons of the dangers arising from 'Young [English]men (boys almost)' sent to India who, like rapacious 'birds of prey', had made 'a sudden fortune'.[34] 'Arrived in England' – Burke vehemently continued – 'They marry into your families; they enter into your senate; they ease your estates by loans; they raise their value by demands; they cherish and protect your relations which lie heavy on your patronage'.[35] Commenting on this passage from the 'Speech on Fox's India Bill', Iain Hampsher-Monk has emphasized how 'The nabobs were to Burke the modern equivalents of Roman provincial governors, returning home glutted with spoils, which they will spend inflating prices and corrupting domestic politics'.[36] Seen from this angle, the *princeps* of nabobs was, of course, Hastings.

'You do not decide the Case only; you fix the rule'

It is possibly not coincidental that in 1788, the year of the opening of the impeachment, Edward Gibbon published the last volume of his *Decline and Fall* (1776–88). If we locate the history of the Roman Empire, as Phiroze Vasunia suggests, within the eighteenth-century British imperial context, then 'the implication of Gibbon's work must be that the future of the British Empire, too, lies in its colonies and that its longevity, or collapse, turns on the way in which Britain manages its relationship with its overseas possessions'.[37]

In this respect, Burke's admonition to the Lords acquires particular importance: 'The question is, not solely whether the prisoner at the Bar be found innocent or be found guilty, but whether millions of mankind shall be miserable or happy. You do not decide the Case only; you fix the rule' (pp. 270–1). Likewise, the outcome of the 'Verres affair' is crucial not just for Sicily but to the whole Empire.[38] In the third section of the *Actio Secunda* Cicero emphasizes that, in case of Verres's acquittal, other *improbi* will act without fear of conviction: 'Rome will find herself without hope of escaping doom, if the precedents set by one scoundrel are to secure the acquittal and impunity of another' (*Verr.* II.3.207: *rei publicae salus deerit, si improborum exemplis improbi iudicio ac periculo liberabuntur*).[39]

A few years before the opening of the trial, a similar view was also expressed by the philosopher William Godwin (1756–1836). Between August 1785 and December 1786, he published a series of letters in *The Political and Herald Review* under the pseudonym of Mucius. The choice of this pseudonym 'is of particular interest'.[40] According to Roman legend, Gaius Mucius Scaevola was a young Roman who, when the king of Clusium, Lars Porsenna, threatened to restore the tyrannical rule of Tarquinius Superbus, volunteered to assassinate him. Instead, he killed by mistake his victim's secretary. Brought before the king, he thrust his right hand over a blazing fire and declared that he was one of three hundred Roman youths willing to make the same sacrifice as himself. Deeply impressed by Mucius's courage, Porsenna ordered him to be freed. As Jonathan Sachs explains, 'Mucius's actions can be seen as a quintessential example of the virtuous patriotism that Godwin was anxious to uphold'.[41]

Most significant for our discussion here is the fifth letter. Addressed to Henry Dundas (1742–1811), one of the politicians who voted for the impeachment of the Governor-General, this letter draws a close analogy between the prosecution of Hastings and that of Verres. After an initial ominous prediction of the interminable length into which the impeachment 'must inevitably run, and lose in its continual recurrence the honesty of inquiry and the value of the subject', Godwin notes that Cicero was the first to 'openly and fearlessly' face one of the most notorious criminals.[42] As a result of the common practice of bribing tribunals, most 'peculators and oppressors of the distant provinces' were, in fact, acquitted.[43] Moved by his love for the Roman name, as well as by 'the sufferings of the defenceless dependents of the state', Cicero undertook the cause of the Sicilians and 'in theirs [...] he undertook the cause of every province of the empire, and the character of Rome'.[44] The outcomes of Cicero's irresistible eloquence are subsequently highlighted by Mucius/Godwin: 'From this moment the government of the provinces was moderated; the guilty became timid, cautious and silent'.[45] Cicero's orations against Verres are thus interpreted by the British philosopher as a turning point in the Roman administration of justice.

Similarly, Burke's warning to the Lords, 'You do not decide the Case only; you fix the rule' (pp. 270–1), alludes to the crucial consequences that the decision of the House of Lords will have on the administration of justice within the British Empire. Godwin concludes his remarks with what may be regarded as a *sententia* which, *mutatis mutandis*, may have been applicable to Britain as well: 'It is perhaps from the sentence against Verres that we are to account for the protracted duration of the Roman Empire'.[46] If we compare this consideration with the previous assertion that 'the utility of history is to enable us to discover from former examples, the clue that may guide us through the intricacies of those which are present', we may conclude that if Britain is keen on maintaining the 'protracted duration' of her Empire – as Godwin seems to suggest – she should take the Roman example and convict Hastings.[47]

While the repercussions of both final verdicts may be similar, Cicero and Burke differ widely in their modes of addressing the jury. Besides utilizing the exhortative subjunctive,[48] Cicero often directs his remarks to the Senate in the imperative form.[49] As a matter of fact, the orator's position as a *novus homo* permits him to play the role of senator among senators and, at the same time, to be a critic of the hereditary senatorial *ordo*. Conversely, Burke suggests that the Lords are *summae auctoritates* and represent the 'Supreme power' (p. 272).[50] As a result, rather than employing the imperative, the Anglo-Irish orator chooses to direct his remarks to the Lords by means of exhortative expressions, including 'we ought to take great care'; 'we may venture to say' (p. 277). Other times – mostly when he intends to dissuade or prevent the jury from what he considers a wrong decision or action – Burke makes use of indirect formulas, such as 'God forbid that'.[51]

As I mentioned earlier, it is not my aim here to dwell on general differences between the two trials.[52] Nonetheless, we are not to lose sight of the many contrasts that one may readily detect in Cicero's and Burke's speeches. For example, we can examine the representations of the oppressed Sicilians and Indians respectively, since one of the most striking moments of divergence is how Cicero and Burke portray the wronged and the oppressed. Unlike the Roman lawyer who refers to the provincials as *socii* – that is to say, loyal allies who were not yet equal to the *cives Romani* – Burke describes the Indians as 'mankind', thus bringing into prominence the equal conditions existing between colonizers and colonized. Within this perspective, the crimes committed in India appear to be more serious than those perpetrated in Sicily. As we will see below, it is certainly not coincidental that the protagonist of one of the most pathetic scenes described in the *Verrines*, Publius Gavius, was not a *socius* but a *civis Romanus*.

Vicious villains

In a number of cases, it is evident that Burke has Cicero in mind and wants his audience to picture the Governor-General of Bengal as a latter-day Verres. Indeed, not only are Hastings's tyrannical and corrupt methods of governing very similar to those employed by Verres, but both men are portrayed as the quintessential incarnations of all sorts of evils and cruelties. In the opening of the first *Verrine*, the *propraetor* of Sicily is variously described as someone who 'has robbed the Treasury, and plundered Asia and Pamphylia; he has behaved like a pirate in his city of praetorship, and like a destroying pestilence in his province of Sicily' (*Verr.* I.2: *depeculatorem aerarii, vexatorem Asiae atque Pamphyliae, praedonem iuris urbani, labem atque perniciem provinciae Siciliae*).[53] Among Verres's plethora of vices, Cicero persistently highlights the governor's thirst for riches: *furta atque flagitia* (I.7); *se cupidum pecuniae fuisse* (I.8); *avarissimi hominis cupiditati* (I.41); *Deinde est eius modi reus in quo homine nihil sit praeter summa peccata maximamque pecuniam* (I.47).

No less importantly, the Roman orator discredits the defendant by means of adjectives that denote audacity, lack of good sense, corruption and dissolution. In short, the governor's life – *tot vitiis flagitiisque convictam* (I.10) – appears to be entirely consecrated to *avaritia, scelere, periurio* (I.42). In the *Actio Prima*, for instance, Verres is variously referred to as *audax* (I.5), *homo audacissimus atque amentissimus* (I.7); *homo amens ac perditus* (I.15); *hominem perditissimum atque alienissimum* (I.28); *homo nocentissimus pecuniosissimusque* (I.47). As these examples suggest, the *propraetor* of Sicily is not termed *vir* but *homo*. This lexical choice may not be coincidental: whereas *vir* points to those qualities that constitute the man (and, hence, it often designates 'a hero'), *homo* is applicable to any of the human species indiscriminately and does not imply any peculiar merit or excellence.

Similarly, Hastings is portrayed as a vicious villain: couching the defendant in his rhetoric of evil, Burke argues vigorously that the misdeeds committed by 'the most daring criminal that ever existed' (p. 295) are the results of a wicked and corrupt soul. Right from the beginning of the 'Speech on the Opening of the Impeachment', the Anglo-Irish orator depicts the Governor-General of Bengal as a cruel oriental despot, 'the first man in rank, authority and station; [...] the head, the chief, the captain-general in iniquity; one in whom all the frauds, all the peculations, all the violence, all the tyranny in India are embodied, disciplined and arrayed' (pp. 275–6). In this respect, Anna Clark has significantly stressed that, with his representation of the Governor-General's crimes in 'hyperbolic racial terms', Burke implies that Hastings 'became too Indian, an oriental despot himself':[54]

> They are crimes that have their rise in avarice, rapacity, pride, cruelty, ferocity, malignity of temper, haughtiness, insolence. In short, my Lords, in everything that manifests *a heart blackened to the very blackest, a heart dyed deep in blackness*, a heart corrupted, vitiated and gangrened to the very core (p. 275).[55]

This sample attests to Burke's verbal richness and rhetorical skill: besides giving memorable form to the passage, the triple repetition of terms derived from the same root ('blackened', 'blackest' and 'blackness') emphasizes the pathos of the image. Owing to his extraordinary skill to use rhetoric at once to portray Hastings in morally unambiguous terms and to fill his speech with emotive appeal, Burke presents his audience here with the instantly recognizable black-hearted villain of contemporary melodrama and Gothic romance.

Like the two faces of the coin, both the *propraetor* of Sicily and the Governor-General represent the quintessence of *omnia vitia*/'all the frauds'. Indeed, Burke's hyperbolic description of Hastings as 'one in whom all the frauds, all the peculations, all the violence, all the tyranny in India are embodied, disciplined and arrayed' may well have been modelled after Verres's description: 'Now I am denouncing a single man for all the offences of which an abandoned scoundrel can be guilty; I assert that in this one man's life you may discern all the possible signs of licentious and unscrupulous wickedness' (*Verr.* II.3.5: *Ego in uno homine omnia vitia quae possunt in homine perdito nefarioque esse reprehendo; nullum esse dico indicium libidinis, sceleris, audaciae, quod non in istius unius vita perspicere possitis*).

Interestingly enough, most terms referring to Hastings's 'high crimes and misdemeanors' are formed from a Latin root and, what is more, echo Verres's misdeeds. So, for instance, Burke's charges of 'avarice, rapacity, pride, cruelty, ferocity, malignity of temper, haughtiness, insolence' parallel Cicero's accusations of *furta, rapinas, cupiditatem, crudelitatem, superbiam, scelus, audaciam* (II.5.32). In particular, while Hastings's 'rapacity' mirrors Verres's *furta* and *rapinas*, the latter's *crudelitatem* and *superbiam* reverberate in the former's 'cruelty', 'haughtiness' and 'insolence'. Often, the Roman orator focuses on Verres's *audacia*, associating it with other vices.[56] In the same vein, Burke repeatedly brings into prominence Hastings's 'audacity': 'Mr. Hastings had the audacity, [...] he had the audacity' (p. 444).

As much as Verres and Hastings embody every sort of wickedness, so are their accomplices – Apronius and Timarchides on the one hand, and Gunga Govin Sing (Ganga Govind Singh) and Debi Sing (Devi Singh) on the other – the quintessence of cruelty, audacity and corruption. Quintus Apronius, the most notorious among the tithe collectors of Sicily, is first introduced as 'the man whom Verres [...] adjudged most like himself in villany, profligacy and reckless wickedness'.[57] Cicero repeatedly refers to his 'unique rascality' (*Verr.* II.3.22: *improbitate singulari*), as well as to his 'impudent depravity and cruelty' (*Verr.* II.3.24: *audaciae, nequitiae, crudelitati*), and variously calls him 'dirty scoundrel', 'filthy scoundrel' and 'a filthy immoral brute whose mind was as inevitably unwholesome as the very breath of his mouth was inevitably foul'.[58] The same is true of Timarchides, 'his [Apronius's] twin and his double in immorality and rascality and effrontery' (*Verr.* II.3.155: *Consorti quidem in lucris atque furtis, gemino et simillimo nequitia, improbitate, audacia*). Catherine Steel acutely notes that Cicero's discussion of Verres's henchmen serves a number of functions.[59] One effect is to reinforce the characterization of Verres as an inadequate magistrate: he has surrounded himself with, and put in positions of power, individuals who are patently wicked and vicious. Moreover, the prominence given to Verres's *cohors* and their wrongdoing 'enables Cicero to structure his characterization of Verres as a gradual revelation of his vices'.[60]

As for the Governor-General's partners in crime, Ganga Govind Singh – a revenue administrator in Bengal who, according to P. J. Marshall, enjoyed Hastings's 'confidence to an unusual degree' and was 'looked upon by the natives as the second person in the government if not the first'[61] – is portrayed as 'the most wicked, the most atrocious, the boldest, the most dexterous villain that ever the rank servitude of that country has produced' (p. 400); 'the basest, the wickedest, the corruptest, the most audacious and atrocious, villain ever heard of' (p. 401); 'a tool in the hands of Mr Hastings', 'employed in taking corrupt bribes and corrupt presents for Mr Hastings' (p. 403). Ganga Govind Singh's conduct is later described as 'licentious and unwarrantable, oppressive and extortionary' (p. 441), inspired by 'fraud', 'profit', 'heavy iniquity', 'wickedness' and 'atrocious iniquity' (p. 446). Not surprisingly, even 'his public services' are associated with 'scenes of wickedness, barbarity and corruption' (p. 443).

Equally, Devi Singh – the revenue administrator under whom the so-called 'Rangpur atrocities' were allegedly committed – is turned into a 'consummate villain', an 'insolent criminal' (p. 431). Ganga Govind Singh and Devi Singh are then sarcastically associated by Burke, who maintains that 'they had been rivals in virtue'. In order to amplify the irony of his statement, the Irish-born orator quotes two lines from Virgil's *Eclogues: Arcades ambo,| Et cantare pares et respondere parat* (*Ecl.* 7, 4–5).[62]

Focusing on Ganga Govind Singh's iniquities, Burke narrates that the former had been appointed by Hastings as guardian of a minor rajah. Not unexpectedly, instead of protecting the nine-year-old child's interest, he appropriated his lands 'by a fraudulent and probably a forged deed. [...] But whether it was forged or not' – Burke adds with a tinge of pathos – 'this miserable minor was obliged to give the lands to him. He did not dare to quarrel with him upon such a matter' (p. 446).

Episodes of orphans defrauded of their legacy can also be found in Cicero's *Verrines*, particularly in the first book of the *Actio Secunda*. Among the long list of the *propraetor*'s illegal appropriation of inheritances (*Verr.* II.1.104–54), Cicero narrates the story of young Malleolus. Following the death of his father (Gaius Malleolus), the child was made a ward of Verres, who did not hesitate to launch 'an attack upon his [young Malleolus's] property' (*Verr.* II.1.90: *cum pupilli Malleoli tutor esset, in bona eius impetum fecit*). The tone of Cicero's discourse is both indignant – not only was young Malleolus an orphan, but also the son of a colleague[63] – and full of pathos. The Roman orator, in fact, imagines that the child, along with his mother and grandmother, is present in the court. By means of highly evocative words, the figures of Malleolus and the two women suddenly appear in front of our eyes: 'it is young Malleolus whom I have brought into court, it is his mother and grandmother, who testify with tears in their eyes, poor creatures, that you have cheated the boy out of his patrimony'.[64]

Among the Governor-General's ruling passions, Burke emphasizes his avarice and rapacity: 'Mr. Hastings's crimes had root in that which is the root of all evil, I mean avarice; that avarice and rapacity were the groundwork and foundation of all his other vicious system' (p. 371). In the speech delivered on 18 February, Burke remarkably transforms Hastings into a monster of 'avarice' and 'ferocious and unrelenting rapacity' (p. 374):

> I proposed, first of all, to show your Lordships that those crimes had their root in that which is the origin of all evil, avarice and rapacity [...]. My Lords, I have to state to day the root of all these Misdemeanors, namely, the pecuniary corruption and avarice (which is a material head) which gave rise and primary motion to all the rest of the delinquincies [sic] which we charge to have been committed by the Governor General. [...] I will venture to say there is no one in which tyranny, malice, cruelty and oppression can be charged, that does not at the same time carry evident marks of pecuniary corruption (p. 374).

Not unexpectedly, the orator concludes his tirade by claiming that 'money is the beginning, the middle and the end of every kind of act done by Mr Hastings, pretendedly for the Company, but really for himself' (p. 377). Whether the audience sitting in Westminster Hall – or, at least, part of it – found this remark true or plausible can only be guessed. Nonetheless, it may be worth noting that between May and June 1786 *The Morning Chronicle*, *The London Chronicle* and *The General Evening Post* published a list of eleven East India Company employees who had amassed vast fortunes while serving in South Asia. Warren Hastings was named first.[65] Even though raising a large personal fortune was never the Governor-General's primary aim, F. P. Lock has argued that Burke was genuinely convinced that avarice was 'the leading feature of Hastings's character'. Lock goes on to suggest that, since avarice is a more degrading vice than ambition, Burke exploited this in order 'to strip him [Hastings] of his heroic pretensions'.[66]

The Latin equivalent of avarice, *avaritia*, is also singled out by Cicero as one of the most distinctive traits of Verres's personality. The Roman orator refers to the *propraetor* as to a *homo avarissimus* (*Verr.* II.5.87) and argues that numerous outrages committed against the Sicilians were caused by his *avaritia*.[67] Indeed, as much as *improbitas, acerbitas, iniuria* and *nequitia* – to name but a few of the governor's leading features – constitute the pillars of Verres's government,[68] so is Hastings's dominion over India purportedly founded on corruption and iniquity. In Burke's words, the Governor-General of Bengal adopted a 'system of corruption', making use of 'wicked, villanous [*sic*], perfidious means' (p. 372). Hastings's regime is hence stigmatized as 'an Evil System'; 'so wild, absurd, irrational and wicked a system'; 'vicious system, which clearly leads to Evil Consequences' (p. 375). Burke's implacable attack is reinforced further through several hyperbolic comments: 'such a body [...] of corruption and peculation, in every walk, in every department, in every situation of life, in the sale of the most sacred Trusts, in the destruction of the most ancient families of the Country, as I believe in so short a time never was unveiled since the World began. [...] all departments were corrupted and vitiated' (p. 387); 'it is the most daring bribery and peculation that ever was' (p. 399).[69]

Beasts, monsters and cruel tyrants

The degradation of Verres and Hastings does not stop with their depiction as vicious villains. Both Cicero and Burke choose to characterize their adversaries by identifying them with wild beasts and inhuman monsters. We may note that the *propraetor* of Sicily – at first an 'enemy, and [...] a most savage and inhuman enemy' (*Verr.* II.2.51: *hostis, et hostis* [...] *nimis ferus et immanis*) – turns into a *belua*, with Cicero wondering whether the defendant is just a cruel human being (*homine crudeli*) or a monstrous wild beast (*fera atque immani belua*).[70] Ann Vasaly has, indeed, noted that the turning point in the *propraetor*'s career 'is usually an act of great criminality after which point he is depicted as a bestial figure, hated by all and devoid of redeeming characteristics'.[71]

Similarly, the Anglo-Irish orator equates the Governor-General to 'a wild beast'. In the speech delivered on 25 April 1789, for example, Burke claimed:

Mr. Hastings feasts in the dark; Mr. Hastings feasts alone; Mr. Hastings feasts like a wild beast; he growls in the corner over the dying and the dead, like the tigers of that country, who drag their pray into the jungles. Nobody knows of it, till he is brought into judgment for the flock he has destroyed.[72]

Philip Ayres has notably commented on this passage, highlighting its close relationship with the Virgilian underworld: 'We have entered a world of myth and monstrosity. The imagery is from the sixth book of the *Aeneid*, the phrasing and rhythms from the Gothic novel'.[73] A good sense of how Hastings is portrayed as an animal – in fact, an Indian animal – may be derived from a small appendix contained in Hastings's own account of the trial, *The History of the Trial of Warren Hastings, Esq. Late Governor General of Bengal, . . .* (1796). Significantly entitled *Curious Collection of Mr. BURKE'S Abuse of Mr. HASTINGS*, this section is composed of 'extracts from Mr. Burke's Speeches in several years'.[74] Here, owing to his voracity and mortiferous instincts, Hastings is first associated with a rapacious and pitiless vulture: he is 'not like the generous eagle' – Burke observed in 1789 – 'who feeds upon a *living, reluctant, equal prey*: No; he is like the *ravenous vulture*, who feeds on the *dead*, and the *enfeebled*'.[75] It comes as no surprise, then, that the Governor-General is also compared to a ferocious tiger: '*like a wild beast he* [Hastings] *groans in a corner over the dead and dying*; and like the tyger [*sic*] of that country, he wishes to withdraw into a cavern, to indulge with unobserved enjoyment in all the wanton caprices of his appetite'.[76] 'I ask and scrutinize' – Burke thundered in 1794 – 'what was latent in a tyger [*sic*]'s heart – what was in a tyger [*sic*]'s breast to do – and he [Hastings] did'.[77]

Not only wild beasts, but also monsters appear in the gallery of dehumanized portraits of the Governor-General. According to the *Curious Collection*, for example, in 1789 Burke compared Hastings to a vampire, who 'is not satisfied *without sucking the blood of* 1400 nobles'.[78] In the official transcription of Burke's 'Speech on the Opening of the Impeachment', the adjective 'monstrous' occurs several times and is always associated with acts of cruelty, bribery and corruption.[79] It is tempting to speculate that Burke's copious use of this term inspired political satirists, including William Dent (1746–1821). In his satirical cartoon entitled *The Raree Show* (25 February 1788: BM 7273), for instance, Dent portrays Hastings as a gigantic figure in the act of devouring a woman whom he holds in his arms. He is 'the prodigious monster arrived from the East', as the caption reads.[80]

If we look further into the corpus of Burke's political writings, the noun and adjective 'monster' and 'monstrous' appear to be particularly relevant in connection to the French revolutionary context.[81] Mary Fairclough, for example, argues that Burke employs a 'rhetoric of demonology [...] in order to decry the "monstrosity" of the new French state'.[82] Similarly, Paul Youngquist has noted that 'when Burke speaks of monstrosity, he [...] means deviant parts of a social body, Jacobins for instance, ill adapted to function healthfully within the whole organism'.[83] Although these remarks are aimed at the *Reflections*, they may be extended to the orations against Hastings. What emerges clearly in the 'Speech on the Opening of the Impeachment', in fact, is that not only did the former Governor-General of Bengal constitute a threat to British order, but also – and above all – represented a menace to 'the eternal laws of justice' (p. 275).

Significantly, this was not the first time that the label of 'monster' was attached to a British statesman. As J. G. A. Pocock has notably shown, some sixty years before the commencement of the trial of Warren Hastings, Robert Walpole was frequently cast as a 'monster of corruption'. According to his enemies, Walpole's unscrupulous politics and corrupt personalities were 'undermining the moral structure of human society'.[84] *The Craftsman*, in particular, used to criticize the Prime Minister's voracity by means of images of monsters and giants. And such was the vitriol of the *The Craftsman*'s attack on Walpole that he was variously described as a 'monstrous Leviathan' (15 March 1728–9); 'the greatest Monster of Power and wickedness that ever infested the Face of the Earth' (18 May 1728); and a 'noxious Caterpillar' (19 June 1731).[85]

The practice of comparing one's chief adversaries to beasts and monsters is a traditional strategy, already utilized by Cicero throughout his oratorical career. We should note – as James M. May has highlighted – that 'in attacking his enemies by portraying them as inhuman, Cicero employs terms that are both generic (e.g. *animal, monstrum, portentum, bestia, belua*) and particular (e.g., *Verres, Scylla, Charybdis*)'.[86] Cicero's deliberate use of specific monsters aims 'to illustrate a particular trait of his enemy'.[87] In the *Verrines*, not only is the *propraetor* of Sicily repeatedly called *monstrum* but he is also ultimately identified with the dreadful monsters that populated the island in the mythical imagination.[88] Indeed, Verres is *infestior* ('more pitiless') than Scylla and Charybdis and even *importunior* ('more brutal') than the Cyclops Polyphemus.[89]

I conceive that neither Charybdis nor Scylla was as dangerous as he was to the mariners navigating those straits; he was more dangerous, because he had girt himself about with more numerous and savage hounds. He was a second Cyclops, but far more frightful, for he infested the whole island, while the Cyclops only occupied Aetna and the adjoining regions.[90]

Closely connected to the imagery of monstrosity is that of tyranny: while the governor of Sicily is repeatedly referred to as a *tyrannus*, his government is labelled as an *imperium tyranni* (II.3.25).[91] Thus, Cicero strategically alludes to the numerous cruel despots, including Dionysius and Phalaris, who had notoriously ruled Sicily before the Romans, and opines that the *propraetor* was 'one of the many cruel tyrants the island once produced' (II.5.145: *tulit enim illa quondam insula multos et crudeles tyrannos*).[92] Cicero's portrait of Verres as tyrant has long attracted the attention of critics – Ann Vasaly noting, for example, that Verres possesses 'the stereotypical traits of the tyrant – greed, lust, cruelty, and impiety'.[93] Given the Hellenized environment of the island – wealthy and sophisticated, Sicily was envisaged as an extension of Greece – Catherine Steel has argued that Verres 'is in some sense Greek' and that Cicero 'does exploit the *political* side of easterness at one point, where he likens Verres to a tyrant (II.3.76)'.[94] More recently, Kathryn Tempest has shown how the character of the *propraetor*, as Cicero describes him, 'ultimately derives from a range of *topoi* that are originally Greek'.[95]

As for Hastings, Burke variously refers to the Governor-General's misdemeanours as 'an act of tyranny' (p. 382) and as 'tyrannous exactions' (p. 383). 'My Lords,' he solemnly declared on 18 February 1788, 'when Mr Hastings first went into Bengal, the first of his acts was the most bold and extraordinary that I believe ever entered into the head of any man; I will say, of any tyrant' (p. 381). Interestingly, the term 'tyrant' appears several times also in the *Curious Collection*. According to this appendix, in the year 1794 Burke referred to Warren Hastings as to 'a tyrant, an oppressor, and murderer'; a 'cruel and bloody tyrant'; 'the captain general of iniquity – thief – tyrant – robber – cheat – sharper – swindler' (p. 154).

In such a dark scenario, unsurprisingly, both Cicero and Burke place great emphasis on their enemy's cruelty. Again and again, particularly in the second part of *In Verrem* II.5, the Roman orator addresses the *propraetor*'s *crudelitas*, highlighting the brutal, pitiless nature of Verres's misdeeds.[96] Similarly, Burke focuses on Hastings's tendency to inflict pain and suffering to others, reiterating the terms 'cruelty', 'cruel' and 'cruelly'.[97]

Examples of the tragic consequences resulting from the Roman governor's ferocity abound everywhere in the *Actio Secunda*. Cicero attempts to rouse strong emotions in his audience: pity for Verres's victims and anger at his arrogance and brutality. Among the charges that are piled up against him, in the third oration (*frumentaria* or *de frumento*), Verres is repeatedly accused of *expilatio* (plunder), *vexatio* (oppression), and *squalor* (mourning).[98] Similarly, in the fourth (*de signis*) and fifth (*de suppliciis*) orations, Cicero conjures up vivid images of the Sicilians' distress and grief, and accordingly, one of the terms most frequently repeated in *de signis* is *dolor*.[99] Another strategy Cicero employs to engage the emotions of the audience on the side of the Sicilians is eulogizing the island's loyalty to Rome and its inhabitants' sense of duty to men and the gods.[100] Sicily is variously praised as 'the first province to be acquired', the 'jewel of the empire', the 'storehouse of the Republic', a source of profit both to those who exploited it from afar and to those Romans who had settled there.[101]

Just as Cicero highlights the importance of Sicily and the Sicilians to Rome's economy, so does Burke emphasize how the Indians' 'laborious hands' proved crucial to the British trade system:

> These are the hands [...] which have for fifteen years furnished the investment for China from which your Lordships and all this auditory and all this Country have every day for these fifteen years made that luxurious meal with which we all commence the day (p. 419).

Here, Burke is referring to tea. At the time, the East India Company had developed a flourishing trade between India and China and most Chinese tea consumed in Britain was purchased with the opium cultivated in India. Rhetorically, this passage serves a number of purposes. First, it exemplifies Burke's ability to appeal to his spectators through the full force of immediacy: the reference to investments in remote and exotic countries, such as India and China, is aptly followed by an allusion to the everyday ritual of drinking tea. Secondly, it shows how the sympathetic response to the horrors that Burke is about to disclose – 'the return that the British Government made to those laborious hands' was, in fact, 'Cords, hammers, wedges, tortures and maimings'

(p. 419) – involves not only all the spectators ('your Lordship and all this auditory') and the entire nation ('all this Country'), but even the orator himself ('that luxurious meal with which *we all* commence the day').[102] In the previous chapter I have emphasized how Burke's description of the tortures perpetrated at Rangpur aroused crying and fainting among the audience and eventually caused Burke's indisposition. Likewise, as we shall see, the picture of the effects of Verres's impious actions on the inhabitants of Henna prompted an emotional response in Cicero himself (hence, we might speculate, in his imagined auditory).[103]

Vivid descriptions

The question of playing with the emotions of the audience, as another way of identifiying with the speaker's (feigned) malaise, leads us a step further. So far, I have commented on general resemblances between the *Verrines* and the 'Speech on the Opening of the Impeachment', concentrating particularly on arguments. In what follows I intend to turn to a specific stylistic feature utilized by both orators to enliven their narrative, namely 'vivid description'. I use this expression to denote – as Beth Innocenti has put it – 'several related techniques [. . .], all of which involve primarily literal uses of language designed to promote visualization of a scene'.[104] Specifically, I shall dwell on one of the most patently emotional moments of the *Verrines*, the story of Publius Gavius, and shall juxtapose it with the most pathetic, spectacular and successful section of Burke's 'Speech on the Opening of the Impeachment', the account of the Rangpur episode. In order to attempt a methodical analysis, I will follow chiefly Beth Innocenti's study of vivid description and will extend it both to the Latin and the English texts.[105]

In antiquity Cicero was considered a master of vivid description. He 'is outstanding' (*eminet*) declared Quintilian, commenting on a passage from the *Verrines*.[106] As a matter of fact, the orations against Verres offer an ample catalogue of examples of Cicero's able use of this rhetorical technique, as can be easily seen in the episodes of Haluntium and Henna. The anguish and cries following Verres' request to hand him over all the Corinthian vases and other precious objects possessed by the *Haluntini* is efficaciously associated with the commotion and grief notoriously aroused by the Trojan horse:[107]

Picture to yourselves the hurrying to and fro in the town, the cries of grief, and the wailing of the women, too; anyone looking on would have thought that the Trojan horse had been admitted, and that the city was in its enemies' hands. Here vessels, stripped of their coverings, were being brought out of doors, there they were being torn from women's resisting hands; in many houses the locks were being wrenched off and the doors burst open.[108]

Though this description is rather concise, Cicero's account turns out to be exceptionally intense and dramatic: besides enlivening the narrative by dwelling on general auditory details, such as women's weeping, the orator arouses pity for the Sicilians and indignation at Verres's cruelty by interspersing the story with verbs indicating to take away by force, to extort, to wrench off, to open violently (*efferri, extorqueri, ecfringi, revelli*).

The vividness and emotional narrative power of this episode is paralleled by another 'miniature drama', that of Ceres of Henna.[109] Cicero is keen to note that so devoted to the cult of Ceres were the citizens of Henna, that they all seemed to be 'the priests, [...] the servants and ministers of Ceres' (II.4.111: *omnes sacerdotes, omnes accolae atque antistites Cereris*). The city itself did not look like a simple *urbs* (town), but rather a *fanum Cereris* (Ceres's sanctuary). In such a sacred place, not only did Verres take away the 'most ancient and sacred' (II.4.109: *antiquissimam, religiosissimam*) sculpture of Ceres, but he also seized an exquisite statue of the goddess Victoria, placed on the hand of a gigantic (and as such immovable) statue of Ceres. In order to impress on his audience the misery and sorrow of the *Hennenses*, Cicero suggests that the whole city seemed to be in mourning (II.4.110: *acerbissimus tota urbe luctus versari videretur*).[110] As in the previous passage, the pathos of the scene is strategically amplified by means of numerous visual and auditory particulars: the orator evokes his arriving in Henna, the gathering of the goddess's priests (*sacerdotes*) 'wearing their fillets and carrying their sacred boughs' (*cum infulis ac verbenis*), the people of Henna assembling, crying and moaning.[111] Indeed, so animated and detailed is this description that the action seems to unfold before our eyes.

This passage is particularly illuminating for two reasons: first, auditors have the impression of participating in the making of the narration; secondly, the speaker himself explicitly calls attention to his own feelings and reactions. In order to manipulate his audience and win their sympathy, the impassioned orator appears emotionally moved (*non solum animo commovear*), as well as physically shaken (*verum etiam corpore perhorrescam*). As the verb *perhorrescere* demonstrates, the recollection of the inhabitants' *acerbissimus luctus* brings about an overwhelming reaction in Cicero's body. In this respect, it is important to note that the prefix *per* is an intensifier that strengthens the meaning of the simple verb *horrescere*, thus suggesting uncontrollable trembling. In a similar way, as I have shown in the previous chapter, Burke was seized by a violent pain in his side after describing the horrors perpetrated at Rangpur.

If Haluntium and Henna are two eminent examples, the most egregious instance of vivid description is represented by the story of Gavius of Consa, a Roman citizen who was crucified in Messana under Verres. Although references to crucifixion in Cicero's works are legion, John Granger Cook has noticed that the capital punishment inflicted on Gavius is 'one of the few "nominal" Roman crucifixions [...] that have survived in the tradition'.[112] Cicero introduces this dramatic episode by confessing that he is unsure whether his oratorical resources will equal the sorrow that Verres's *crimen* provokes in his heart. After concluding that no power of language could appropriately describe such an appalling event, the orator decides to avoid *eloquentia* and to let the bare facts speak for themselves.[113] There follows a narration of Gavius's miserable story: his flight from the *Latumiae* (Stone Quarries) at Syracuse; his attempt to escape Verres's jurisdiction by gaining the Italian peninsula; his incautious criticism of the *propraetor*; his arrest; Verres's arrival in the Messanan *forum*; and, finally, the beating, torture and death of Gavius, despite his dramatically repeated cry, *civis Romanus sum*. The gravity of Gavius's cruel sentence is a point worth emphasizing. As has been observed, flogging Roman citizens in the first century BC was arguably prohibited – the *lex Porcia* probably also including 'the right of appeal against a magistrate's decision'.[114] Throughout his harangue, Cicero forcefully stresses that meting out capital punishment to a Roman citizen is similar to a parricide (*prope parricidium*).[115] In this sense, the *propraetor's* cruelty is presented as an attack on Roman security, as is borne out by a number of references, such as in II.5.170: 'It was not Gavius, not one obscure man, whom you nailed upon that cross of agony: it was the universal principle that Romans are free men' (*Non tu hoc loco Gavium, non unum hominem nescio quem, sed communem libertatis et civitatis causam in illum cruciatum et crucem egisti*).[116]

In Cicero's hands, the passage dealing with Gavius becomes a powerful cameo, capable of eliciting an emotional response from the audience.[117] Significantly, Ann Vasaly has noted that the dramatic strength of this narration is amplified by the orator's 'liberal use of all those stylistic features that enliven narrative, especially vivid description'.[118] In this sense, it comes as no surprise that Quintilian and Aulus Gellius quote the same passage from the story of Gavius (Verres's enraged appearance in the Messanan *forum*)[119] as a remarkable example of what Cicero himself called 'ocular demonstration' (*sub oculos subiectio*).[120] 'This' – Quintilian explains – 'happens when, instead of stating *that* an event took place, we show *how* it took place, and that not as a whole, but in detail'.[121] Similarly, Aulus Gellius attests to the Roman orator's ability to exhibit a scene with such extreme vividness that 'you do not seem to hear the act described, but to see it acted before your face'.[122]

Much in the same way, as I have observed in Chapter 3, Burke evokes the horrors purportedly committed at Rangpur with extraordinary particularity. Aiming to conjure up appalling scenes of suffering in front of the assembled peerage and his sophisticated audience, the Anglo-Irish orator dwells on shocking visual details, such as the tormentors' furious beatings of their victims with bamboo canes or the victims' blood running 'out of their mouths, eyes and noses':

> The Heads of villages, the parochial Magistrates, the leading Yeomen of the country, respectable for their situation, and their age, were taken and tied together by the feet, two and two, thrown over a bar, and there beaten with bamboo canes upon the sole of their feet until their nails started from their toes. And then, falling upon them, while their heads hung down as their feet were above, with sticks and cudgels, their tormentators attacked them with such blind fury that the blood ran out of their mouths, eyes and noses. (p. 419).

This passage is especially significant because the scene it evokes is rendered with graphic clarity and the full force of immediacy, as if it were unfolding before the eyes of an observer.

Although the visual nature of the horrific scenes in the Rangpur speech drew on classical rhetorical features, it was also profoundly indebted to the spectacular tendencies of the contemporary representation of violence. As Ian Haywood reminds us, 'spectacular violence was a vital and indelible component of those two foundational discourses of Romanticism: sensibility and the sublime'.[123] In a period when 'spectacular violence brought the excesses of imperial violence and suffering into the heart of British culture' – Haywood continues – 'Romantic readers were prodigious consumers of spectacular violence'.[124] Examples of what Haywood calls 'spectacular violence' can also be traced in the extraordinary mass of representations of tortures and violence perpetrated against the slaves, such as, notably, William Blake's engravings for John Gabriel Stedman's *Narrative of a Five Years' Expedition against the Negroes of Suriname* (1796).[125] Indeed, the whole section of the Rangpur speech is fraught with detailed descriptions of tortures or – in Kate Teltscher's words – 'scenes of extreme horrors',[126] including hands and feet beaten and maimed; nipples ripped from breasts; and bodies whipped, scourged and plunged into cold water in winter time.

As these examples indicate, vivid descriptions may also insist on movement – in the aforementioned passage, the victims are bound together, thrown over a bar and beaten ferociously (not to mention their nails starting from their feet and their copious bleeding). If we take the story of Gavius, movement is present when Verres orders the *civis Romanus* 'to be flung down, stripped naked and tied up in the open market-place, and rods to be got ready' (*Verr.* II.5.161: *repente hominem proripi atque in foro medio nudari ac deligari et virgas expediri iubet*), or when the Roman citizen 'was beaten with rods' (II.5.162: *Caedebatur virgis*).[127]

In addition to sight and movement, vivid descriptions rely also on auditory details: sounds, such as weeping and moaning (as in the cases of Haluntium and Henna) can be used effectively to arouse sentiments of pity and indignation.[128] Cicero's strategic handling of Gavius's story includes at least two passages where specific auditory details stir strong emotions in the audience, sympathy for the unfortunate protagonist and indignation at Verres's cruelty. In the first case, Gavius's beating is accompanied by the 'crack of the falling blows' and the protagonist's agonized, repeated cry *Civis Romanus sum*;[129] in the second instance, Cicero accuses Verres of indifference both to the 'pitiful cries' (II.5.163: *imploratio et vox miserabilis*) and to 'the tears and the loud groans of the Roman citizens who then stood by' (II.5.163: *civium quidem Romanorum qui tum aderant fletu et gemitu maximo*).

The same is true of Burke. In his brief account of the violation of Indian virgins, the Anglo-Irish orator concentrates on perturbing sounds, such as 'shrieks', 'cries' and 'groans':

There in the presence of day, in the public Court, vainly invoking its justice, while their shrieks were mingled with the cries and groans of an indignant people, those virgins were cruelly violated by the basest and wickedest of mankind (pp. 420-1).[130]

This passage appears to be important for at least two other reasons. First, Burke explicitly sets the scene in broad daylight ('in the presence of day'), in a public place ('the public Court'), in front of the public gaze.[131] In this respect, it conforms to Innocenti's claim that 'Virtually all vivid descriptions include the presence of a crowd of people'. Indeed, not only does the presence of a large number of people lend 'credibility and plausibility to the scene being vividly described', but it also 'may be designed to arouse indignation by signifying the public nature of an act'.[132] This is also the case with the beating of Gavius, which is set *in medio foro Messanae*, in the presence of Roman citizens (*Verr.* II.5.162-3).

Secondly, we may also note that, in order to summon sympathy for, or to promote identification with, the actors in a scene, both orators emphasize crimes perpetrated against parents and children, husbands and wives. The Indian women violated at Rangpur were either 'Virgins whose fathers kept them from the sight of the sun' (p. 420) or 'the wives of the people of the country' (p. 421). Further examples include 'innocent children' who 'were cruelly scourged, both male and female, in the presence of their parents' (p. 420), or sons and fathers bound and whipped together.[133]

Similarly, throughout the *Verrines* Cicero attempts to amplify the emotional impact of his narration by referring to the violations of married women (*matres familias violatas*, *Verr.* II.4.116) and the executions of innocent sons and fathers. The most notorious instance of such mistreatment is perhaps the unjust death sentence inflicted on Philodamus and his son:

> In the forum of Laodicea a cruel scene was enacted, which caused all the province of Asia profound unhappiness and distress: here the aged father led forth to execution, and there his son: the one for defending the purity of his children, the other for saving his father's life and sister's honour. Both wept, but neither for his own doom: the father for his son's fate, the son for his father's.[134]

Indeed, since antiquity Cicero was renowned as a creator of narratives that elicited empathic feelings by means of vivifying words. Quintilian refers to this scene as an example of the orator's ability to 'fan the flame of indignation throughout his account, and fill our eyes with tears' when he 'describes, or rather sets before our eyes, the father weeping for his son's death and the son for his father's'.[135] 'What more pitiful effect' – the author of the *Institutio Oratoria* concludes – 'could any Epilogue produce?'[136]

In spite of the undoubted similarities between Cicero's and Burke's recourse to sympathy, Burke's 'appealing to his audience's native impulse to sympathize with affliction', to use Richard Bourke's expression, had a further aim, that is to say making Indian victims and remote suffering seem somehow familiar to the audience sitting in Westminster Hall.[137] While Sicily was, in fact, relatively close to Rome – in order to collect evidence against Verres, Cicero went to the island and made (or so he claims) an almost complete tour of it in fifty days[138] – to a British audience, India was a far away, exotic land. This should not be surprising, considering that at the end of the eighteenth century it took several months to reach Indian shores from England.

From this perspective, Cicero and Burke appear to differ significantly. On the one hand, the Roman orator must have devoted a considerable amount of energy and physical effort to his condensed tour of Sicily, as he incessantly stresses in the *Actio Prima*, through the repetition of the personal pronoun *ego*, 'I' (normally omitted in Latin) and the possessive adjective *meus*, 'my'.[139] On the other, as I mentioned in Chapter 2, the Anglo-Irish orator never visited the Indian subcontinent. And yet he is very keen on emphasizing his capacity to gather a body of evidence 'such as cannot leave the least doubt [...] of the facts' (p. 276). As much as Cicero draws attention to his own *persona*, so does Burke highlight his personal ability to collect substantial evidence against Hastings, in spite of the latter's influence and powerful position:

> My Lords, when we consider the late enormous power of the prisoner; when we consider the criminal and indefatigable assiduity in the destruction of evidence; when we consider the power that he had over all testimony, I believe your Lordships, and I believe the world, will be astonished that so much, so clear, so solid, and so conclusive a body of evidence has been obtained against him (p. 276).

No less importantly, Cicero informs his audience that he will prosecute the *propraetor* of Sicily 'by means of documents and witnesses, the written statements and official pronouncements of private persons and public bodies'.[140] In Burke's own words, the documentary proofs against the Governor-General include 'evidence of record, of weighty official, authentic record, and signed by the hand of the criminal himself in many instances', as well as Hastings's 'own letters, authenticated by his own hand' (p. 276). These written documents are complemented by 'numbers of oral living witnesses, competent to speak to the points to which they are brought' (p. 276).[141]

Though there are certainly many more similarities between Cicero's *In Verrem* and Burke's 'Speech on the Opening of the Impeachment', what we have seen so far is ample evidence of the relationship between the Roman and the Anglo-Irish orator, as well as of their use of shared rhetorical strategies. Cicero and his *Verrines* certainly inspired Burke in many ways, including the latter's arguments and stylistic features. The Anglo-Irish orator was also influenced by classical rhetorical practices which recommended that the speaker should *exhibit* rather than stylize and *present* rather than represent.

5

The Reception of the Hastings Trial in the Newspapers and Satirical Prints

From the beginning of the impeachment, both Hastings and his accusers realized that the trial would take place before a tribunal of newspaper readers, as much as before the audience in Westminster Hall. It was thanks largely to the expansion of newspaper reporting and parliamentary printing from the 1770s that – as Christopher Reid has put it – 'oratory had also come to matter outside the House [of Commons]'.[1] Tellingly, in the course of the trial John Scott-Waring (1747–1819), agent and principal director of propaganda of the Governor-General, invested a sum of nearly £6,500 on articles and cartoons in the press.[2]

The impeachment of Hastings was, in fact, debated and commented on not only in the newspapers, but also in periodicals and reviews, such as *The Gentleman's Magazine* and the *London Magazine*, or the *Monthly Review* and the *Critical Review* respectively. However, a quick survey of the latter (which usually came out monthly or yearly) shows that comments tended to be less detailed than those newspapers published on a daily basis; and more importantly, unlike daily newspapers, in the monthly publications allusions to Cicero's impeachment of Verres were sporadic, and often without reference to either Burke or Hastings. A significant example, in this sense, is the *Annual Register*. Edited originally by Burke, this periodical 'quickly became' – to borrow the words of Paul Langford – 'the standard reference work of contemporary events'.[3] Throughout the duration of the trial (1788–95), the *Register* referred to the greatest Roman orator and the *propraetor* of Sicily only once, on the occasion of Fox's speech to add Francis to the committee of managers for the impeachment (11 December 1787).[4]

As argued in the previous chapter, Burke repeatedly implied that he was Cicero and Hastings was Verres and allusions to the prosecution of the *propraetor* of Sicily were made not just by the Irish-born orator, but also by contemporary observers of the trial. From 1786 onwards, newspapers and, in smaller numbers, satirical prints represented Burke as a British Cicero and Hastings as a modern-day Verres. Concentrating on the major newspapers published in Britain and British newspapers issued in India, as well as on satirical cartoons, I will show how the arraignment of Verres and the Hastings impeachment inextricably intertwined in the imagination of the educated eighteenth-century Englishman.[5] Despite this, however, the novelty of the *cause célèbre* began to fade after a few months, and the initial surge of public interest was replaced by a sense of increasing boredom. Therefore, I shall particularly direct my attention to the press and caricatures issued between 1786 and 1788, as the period in which interest in the trial was at its peak.

Tullius Indianus

As early as 1781 India's first printed newspaper, the *Hicky's Bengal Gazette; or the Original Calcutta General Advertiser*, published two issues with an English translation of 'CICERO's famous Oration before the Senate of ROME against VERRES, who had been Governor in ASIA Minor'.[6] Despite belonging to different parts of the extant corpus of the Verrine orations, both translations share similarities. For instance, both articles are given considerable prominence, as they are strategically displayed in the first two columns of the front page. Also, in both cases the original text is not reproduced, nor is the identity of the translator revealed. As a result, the English version is rather loose and, what is more, a number of sections of Cicero's orations are omitted without any indications to the reader.

Although not directly related to the trial of the Governor-General of Bengal, both articles constitute clear evidence that, well before the impeachment of Hastings, the arraignment of Verres was associated with the British presence in India. Of particular interest in this respect is a trenchant note inserted in the conclusion to the second article:

> After Reading and duly pondering the afore recited Speech of the immortal CICERO [...] let us *shift the Scene in* immagination [*sic*] and by the powers of Fancy Conceive SICILY (as described by Cicero) to be the CARNATIC. –

The PEOPLE OF ROME the INDIA PROPRIETORS, or the ENGLISH NATION at large. – The CONSCRIPT SENATORS – the ENGLISH PARLIAMENT. – CICERO in the Person of Ed. Bourke [sic], the E. of SHELBURNE Mr. T. PITT, Mr. Dunning. And CAIUS VERRES as a xxxx Type of SIR THOMAS PILLAGE. –
The native honest powers of Sympathy confirm the horrid Picture. –[7]

Not unexpectedly, as India (the Carnatic) is equated to Sicily and the British Parliament to the Roman Senate, so is Edmund Burke named as the British counterpart to Cicero. Conversely – and perhaps surprisingly – Verres is related to a certain Sir Thomas Pillage. It would be tempting to speculate that the person cast in the role of this arcane character is Warren Hastings. However, as P. J. Marshall has acutely observed, 'During 1781 Burke had become increasingly critical of Hastings, but he could still refer to him as a "respectable" person'.[8] Therefore, the mysterious Sir Thomas may be, instead, Sir Thomas Rumbold (1736–91), first Baronet. During his service as Governor of Madras (1778–81), Rumbold was, in fact, held responsible for Haidar Ali's victories over the Madras army in 1780 and as such was 'recalled by the Court of Directors to answer charges of negligence and corruption' (whence probably the nickname 'Pillage').[9] It is also worth noting that Madras is situated in the province known as the Carnatic – hence the exhortation to 'conceive Sicily (as described by Cicero) to be the Carnatic'.

The two articles published in 1781 by the *Hicky's Bengal Gazette* are important also for another reason. A vast number of key words and expressions, including 'cruel oppressor', 'rapacious Insolence', 'Avarice', 'clearly convicted', 'Iniquitous Administration', 'Oppressed, plunder'd and Ruined by those who are sett [sic] over them', are emphasized by means of different types, either italics or capital letters.[10] As I demonstrated in Chapter 4, seven years later most of these terms would be used by Burke in his 'Speech on the Opening of the Impeachment'.

If we move forward in time, we find that the Hastings trial runs in parallel with the impeachment proceedings against Verres in various English-language Indian newspapers. On 7 January 1788, for example, the *India Gazette: or, Calcutta Public Advertiser* gave over much of its front page to the 'report of the secret committee, containing articles of Impeachment against Warren Hastings'. This piece is a distillation of the speeches delivered by two

Hastings supporters, Lord Hood (1724–1816) and the Alderman John Wilkes (1725–97), respectively. These orations were pronounced in the House of Commons on 9 May 1787, a full eight months before being published in the *India Gazette*.[11] John Wilkes's discourse appears to be particularly significant, as:

> in the course of the proceedings he had [...] more than once heard Mr. *Hastings* compared to *Verres*; but the House would recollect that when the Governor General of Sicily was called to an account before the Roman Senate, there scarcely was an inhabitant of that Island who did not exhibit a complaint against him; whereas in the present case, though the prosecution or persecution of Mr. Hastings had been in progress above three years, not a single complaint had come from India against the Governor General of Bengal. On the contrary every letter that had been sent home, was full of expressions of gratitude and applause of the conduct of Mr. Hastings while he held the Government of India.[12]

If we are to believe the Alderman's speech, in 1787 Hastings had already been compared to Verres several times. Acting as a partisan of the former Governor-General of Bengal, Wilkes firmly rejected the parallel with the *propraetor* of Sicily, but did not make any reference either to Cicero or Burke. Ten days later, on 17 January 1788, the *Calcutta Gazette; or, Oriental Advertiser* published a long article summarizing the conclusion of the same parliamentary session (9 May 1787).[13] Also in this case, the names of Cicero and Burke do not appear. Conversely, we are informed that John Courtenay (1738–1816), one of the managers of the impeachment:

> took notice that Mr. Hastings had in the course of the preceding debates, been compared to Verres, to Alexander, to Scipio, and to Epaminondas. He said, he thought the first the comparison most in point; but he would not refer to the Romans and Grecians for a comparison. It was so long since he had read books relative to them, that he had almost forgotten their contents. He would look to more modern history for a comparison, and he recollected an apt and a close one. It was Ferdinando Cortez, to whom he alluded. Ferdinando Cortez, had been sent out by Charles the fifth, to make discoveries in South America, to instruct to *murder*, and to *baptize* the uninformed Indians. He pursued his object, and his footsteps were marked with blood and cruelty; insomuch that the news of his brutality reached Madrid, and

was thought so much a national disgrace, that an enquiry into his conduct was deemed due to the national character [...].[14]

This passage offers us a valuable insight into the long series of historical Greek and Roman characters with whom the Governor-General of Bengal was compared. Besides being associated with Verres, Hastings was, in fact, repeatedly mentioned alongside great statesmen and generals, such as Alexander, Scipio and Epaminondas.[15] If we consider, for example, the parallel with Alexander the Great, Hastings himself recounts that, on the seventh day of the trial (22 February 1788 – a month after the publication of the above issue of the *Calcutta Gazette*), Charles James Fox observed:

> Mr. Hastings had lately been compared to a conqueror, whose fame filled the universe: [...] Alexander the Great. But if any resemblance were found, it could not be to Alexander when his mercies and his victories kept an equal pace; – it could not be to the generous or forgiving conqueror; – the likeness must be meant to Alexander maddened after a debauch; to Alexander in petulant wantonness setting temples on fire – to Alexander when his follies and his crimes had excited horror and contempt sufficient to obscure the radiance of his former glories. – In the first points of the comparison there was not a shade of resemblance; in the latter part of the parallel there was all the justice that could be required.[16]

In his own account of the impeachment, Hastings reports further that on the eighth day of the trial (25 February 1788) the king of Macedonia was invoked again by Charles Grey (1764–1845), the youngest member of the managers. According to Grey's allegations, the Governor-General of Bengal had exhorted Major Popham's soldiers to plunder the fortress where the wife and the mother of the Rajah resided:

> These females of dignified rank were, therefore, stripped of every resource in their want, and of every solace to their eye! – Those who had compared Hastings to Alexander the Great, would here find their parallel was greatly deficient. Alexander had so comported himself to the wife and mother of Darius, that they scarcely felt their loss; – Mr. Hastings on the contrary, had so demeaned himself to the wife and mother of Cheyt Sing, that the unfortunate Rajah felt their sufferings as the keenest aggravation of his own.[17]

Both Charles James Fox's and Charles Grey's references to Alexander exemplify how eighteenth-century British politicians freely selected episodes from the life of classical figures and adapted them for their own purposes. It is, then, not surprising that from time to time Alexander was either invoked as a merciful and generous conqueror, or, conversely, as a debauched general. Unlike Fox and Grey, however, Courtenay sarcastically refused any parallel with 'the Romans and Grecians', opting instead for a historical figure taken from 'more modern history', that is to say Hernán Cortés (1485–1547), the Spanish conquistador who overthrew the Aztec empire.[18] The reference to Cortés appears even more significant if we put it in relation with Richard Brinsley Sheridan's later *Pizarro* (1799). This play, a dramatization of the Peruvian struggle against the Spanish conquest, also alludes to Sheridan's speeches at the Hastings impeachment. Among the multiple allegorizations that habitually accompany the interpretations of this tragedy, Sara Suleri has read its villain protagonist, 'the implacable Pizarro', as Hastings.[19]

If we turn our attention to Burke, we note that he is significantly associated with Cicero in a letter published in the issue of *The World* for 4 January 1794.[20] This date is remarkable if we consider that, by then, the trial of the Governor-General of Bengal (which would conclude the following year) had long ceased being a sensation. The epistle is interwoven with witticism and it is certainly no coincidence that the identity of its author is hidden under the *nom de plume* of Aristophanes, the Greek comic playwright renowned for his subtle irony and political parodies. Significantly addressed to 'a Friend of Mr. Hastings', the letter opens with Aristophanes' reaction to what we may assume was another letter: 'Great was my surprise' – the writer observes – 'on perusing the World of the 7th instant, to perceive that any one, tho' anonymously, would stand forth as a vindicator, much less a panegyrist, of that celebrated man Mr. H'.[21]

From the opening lines, the tone of the epistle is overtly sarcastic: not only does Aristophanes note that 'any one would praise such a character at the expence [sic] of his own', but he also wittily describes the supporter of the Governor-General of Bengal as a modern-day Don Quixote:

> I always imagined quixotism was only the tale of romance, and little expected to find it realized in the enlightened era of the 18th century – the attempt to rescue a fair damsel from the chains of inchantment [sic] is as vain as to remove a fallen here from the weight of his crimes.

Just as the mysterious 'friend of Hastings' is vilified (Aristophanes suggests that he may have opted for obscurity, owing to 'gratitude for favors [*sic*] received, or the vanity of being singular') so is the Governor-General of Bengal variously described as either 'a character who will be fortunate if he sinks into oblivion', or, by contrast, as someone who 'ought for the benefit of humanity, be transmitted to posterity, as a monitor to future men in similar situations, to warn them against the temptations of avarice'.

Subsequently, Aristophanes comments sharply on the anonymous writer's accusations against Burke: 'you exclaim against Tullius Indianus, for depressing Mr. H – to raise Lord C – and do you really think, Sir, there is a latitude for comparison in the two characters?' Like Aristophanes, Burke is not named directly but concealed behind a witty pseudonym that conflates a reference to *Marcus Tullius Cicero* with the trial of the Governor-General of Bengal. Along with 'Mr. H' – a clear reference to Hastings – the author of the letter, then, mentions a more obscure 'Lord C', possibly Charles Cornwallis, Governor-General of India from 1786 to 1793, whom Aristophanes praises as someone 'whose career in India, has been marked neither by a spark of avarice, nor malice, but a noble disinterestedness'.

In order to savour fully the irony implied in the phrase 'latitude for comparison', readers are expected to be acquainted with Burke's orations against Hastings, particularly with the 'Speech on the Opening of the Impeachment'. Indeed, on 16 February 1788, the fourth day of the trial, Burke had accused Hastings of 'geographical morality':

> he [Hastings] has told your Lordships in his defence that actions in Asia do not bear the same moral qualities as the same actions would bear in Europe. [...] we are to let your Lordships know that these Gentlemen have formed a plan of Geographical morality, by which the duties of men in public and in private situations are not to be governed by their relations to the Great Governor of the Universe, or by their relations to men, but by climates, degrees of longitude and latitude, parallels not of life but of latitudes.[22]

As this passage suggests, Burke made it clear that the Governor-General of Bengal and his entourage did not 'extend universally' – as Jennifer Pitts has put it – 'the fundamental standards of respect, lawfulness, and humanity that applied at home'.[23] Rather, they cynically excluded and discriminated against the Indians on the basis of different 'climates', 'longitude and latitude'.

At this point, Aristophanes dismisses any possible accusations of bias against Hastings on his part. We are thus told that, despite a residence of many years in India, he never saw the Governor-General of Bengal but once. Aristophanes' subsequent comments are poured forth with his usual caustic irony: he calls Hastings 'the hero', and even refers to him as a 'subject for the anatomists experiments'. The letter finally concludes with a sardonic piece of advice to the friend of Hastings, in which the Greek philosophers Heraclitus, Democritus and Pythagoras are evoked as the repositories of all wisdom:

> in reveiwing [sic] Mr. H –'s career, I perceive such picture as a Heraclitus might lament over, and a Democritus sneer at – to those who have benefited by the profusion of his government, and have persuaded themselves into his admirers, if they attempt a defence, I beg to recommend the observance of Pythagoras – to prevent enquiry, silence is the best antidote.

'Nothing new under the sun'

As far as the newspapers published in Britain are concerned, the trial of the Governor-General of Bengal and that of Verres appear to have been considered in juxtaposition right after Burke's 'Speech on Motion for Papers on Hastings' (20 February 1786). As I have noted in Chapter 4, in his address to the House of Commons, the Anglo-Irish orator compared Britain to Rome and suggested – though indirectly – that, as much as Warren Hastings could be regarded as a modern-day Verres, he himself could be thought of as a new Cicero. The following day, 21 February, all the major London papers, including the *General Advertiser, General Evening Post, London Chronicle, Morning Herald, Morning Chronicle and London Advertiser, Morning Post and Daily Advertiser, St. James's Chronicle: or, the British Evening Post*, and *Whitehall Evening Post*, summarized and commented on Burke's oration. According to the *General Advertiser*, Burke provokingly remarked that, in spite of Rome's rampant corruption and Verres's powerful connections, 'the Roman Senate allowed not only the time for digesting the matter of the accusation, but also opened, without reserve, all the cabinets which contained the documents the accuser called for'.[24] On the contrary – the Anglo-Irish orator continued – he himself was prevented from collecting documents against Hastings ('Can it now be said that the cause of justice is in liberal hands, if documents which the accuser demands are to be retained?').[25]

As a number of the London papers published between 1786 and 1788 suggest, the comparison between Burke and Cicero must have been a theme constantly debated outside the doors of Westminster Hall. Burke's own equation of himself with 'Tully' was discussed in at least two numbers of the *Public Advertiser*. In the 28 February 1786 issue, the newspaper commented ironically:

> In one of Mr. Burke's invective orations against Mr. Hastings, we were most obligeingly [sic] reminded, that Cicero, when accusing Verres, was supported by the whole power of the Roman Senate. This modest comparison of himself to Tully, must greatly endear Mr. Burke to those who have long admired him for that extreme diffidence, which is so opposite to the matchless intrepidity of face usually ascribed to other adventurers of his country.

The theme was resumed a week later (7 March 1786) in the same ironic vein:

> Mr. Burke very much resembles Cicero in the opinion of his friends, and he has ever emulated the character of the great orator; but it happens unfortunately, that neither Major Scott, nor Mr. Hastings, chuse [sic] to accept the part of Verres, which is absolutely necessary in order to fill up the *dramatis personae*.

What is interesting here is that, as much as Burke's supporters fostered an identification of the Anglo-Irish orator with Cicero, Hastings and, in this case, also John Scott-Waring ('Major Scott') were implicitly associated with Verres. Moreover, the reporter employs the expression *dramatis personae*, thus reinforcing the impression that the impeachment of Hastings was followed and commented on in the terms of a theatrical performance.

That the Governor-General of Bengal was cast in the role of Verres is further seen in numerous examples, such as the issue of *The Times* for 9 March 1787. Here, Jonathan Swift's 1710 translation of the *incipit* of the first Verrine oration was reproduced and prefaced by a short note:

> There is nothing new under the sun. Caius Verres was guilty of the same crimes above 18 hundred years ago, that are now laid to the charge of

Mr. H-s. The similarity is very striking, as will appear by the following extracts from an oration of Cicero translated by Dean Swift, and published in the Examiner, No. 17, November 30, 1710, and was intended by him to reflect the conduct of the Earl of Wharton, whilst he was Lord Lieutenant of Ireland. To apply it now, there needs only to substitute H-s for *Verres* – *Great Britain* for *Rome* – and *India* for *Sicily*.[26]

Had there been any doubt about the identity of 'Mr. H-s', the equation '*Great Britain* for *Rome*' and '*India* for *Sicily*' would have dispelled it. These observations, as well as Swift's translation, appeared verbatim a year later in a letter to the Editor of *The Times* (12 June 1788). On that occasion, however, the name of Hastings was printed in full.[27]

By 1788, the parallel between the Governor-General of Bengal and Verres, together with the equation of Edmund Burke with Cicero, was widely circulating among the reading nation and had long become the subject of public argument. This is also borne out by a series of articles published throughout the month of February 1788 in the columns of the *Public Advertiser* (5, 6, 7, 11, 13, and 15 February 1788).[28] In the preface to the six-part series, the author – a certain *Amicus Curiae* – suggests that the juxtaposition between the two pairs of men (Hastings and Verres; Burke and Cicero) originated 'from the *whisperings* of his [Hastings's] accusers [sic] friends' and, later, 'From conversation travelled to the public papers'.[29]

From the outset, the author of the letter proves to be biased towards Hastings and openly declares his intention to 'operate in favour of that Gentleman's exculpation'. According to *Amicus Curiae*, many readers were not conversant either with Roman history or with the British administration of India and, as such, they were unable to form 'a judgement upon the various volumes of *reports*, charges, paragraphs, inuendos [sic], &c. &c.' that before and since the commencement of the trial had gained currency around 'in prejudice' of the Governor-General.[30] As a remedy, the writer offers to draw a parallel that may lead the public 'to discriminate the *good* from the *bad*, the *frivolous* from the *wise* – the *patriot* from the *braggadocio*'.[31] The next five instalments are titled: 'A View of the Characters and Conduct of C. Verres, Praetor of Sicily, and Warren Hastings Esq; late Governor General of Bengal. With a Parallel between M. Tullius Cicero, and the Right Hon. Edmund Burke'. This title is significantly complemented by a sort of motto from Dr Johnson, which may somewhat be read as a defence of Hastings's (minor) faults: 'In all political regulations good cannot be complete, it can only be predominant'.

Both the second and third letters focus on the *propraetor* of Sicily. After highlighting how 'the administration of Rome was in every branch of it infamously corrupt', *Amicus Curiae* divides Verres's enormities into four heads: '1st corruption in judging of causes, 2d extortion in collecting the tythes and revennes [*sic*] of the Republic, 3d plundering the subjects of their statues and wrought plate, 4th illegal and tyrannical punishments'.[32] As Margaret M. Miles notes, 'The *Amicus Curiae* certainly read the *Verrines* closely and knew Cicero well'.[33] Each charge is, indeed, illustrated by an apt and detailed example that follows closely the Ciceronian text. Also, it looks likely that *Amicus Curiae* consulted *The History of the Life of Marcus Tullius Cicero* by Conyers Middleton, as the passages published in the 6 and 7 February editions of the *Public Advertiser* bear a striking resemblance to those included in Middleton's *Life*.

The accusation of corruption in the judging of cases is exemplified through the story of Dio of Halesa, a man of eminent fortune whose inheritance lawsuit was tried before Verres himself. The unlucky protagonist of the story was forced to pay 'about *nine thousand pounds*' and to hand over his celebrated breed of mares, as well as the valuable furniture of his house.[34] As for the charge of extortion, *Amicus Curiae* offers a distillation of the third *Verrine* of the *Actio Secunda*. In particular, he emphasizes that, by an edict of his own, Verres had ordered that 'the proprietor should pay *whatever the collector demanded*'.[35] Owing to the governor's greed, the Sicilian husbandmen were forced to leave their lands and houses, while 'Desolation spread itself around – most people thinking it safer to trust to chance, than to live under the fangs of such a tyrant'.[36]

In the edition for 7 February, the crime of plundering is delineated through the story of Antiochus, king of Syria.[37] After visiting Rome, Antiochus stopped at Syracuse, where Verres, who knew he was travelling with a great treasure, received him with particular civility. Pleased to have earned Verres's attention, Antiochus returned the invitation and incautiously displayed 'numberless vessels of solid gold, set round with the most precious stones'. Verres – *Amicus Curiae* comments – 'who had not only a *taste* for this kind of curiosities – but an *appetite* to make them his own', borrowed some of the vessels and 'took care never to return' them.[38] The *propraetor* also appropriated a candlestick of inestimable value that was intended as an offering to *Jupiter Capitolinus*. Subsequently, *Amicus Curiae* observes that when any vessel laden with valuable exotic goods arrived in the ports of Sicily, Verres seized its cargo and sent the whole crew ('those miserable captives in chains') to the *Laotomiae* [sic], quarries of stone converted into a prison by the tyrant Dionysius.[39]

Finally, in the two following instalments, *Amicus Curiae* explicitly compares Verres to Hastings (11 February 1788) and Cicero to Burke (13 February 1788). Both letters present a similar structure: after a preamble, they are divided into concise paragraphs concerned either with the Roman character or with its Anglo-Irish counterpart. Unsurprisingly, the parallel between Verres and Hastings is clearly biased in favour of the Governor-General. However, as in the preface to the series, the writer cunningly encourages his readers 'to draw their conclusions' from facts, thus giving the impression of leaving members of the public free to judge for themselves:

> I come now to state the character and conduct of Verres and Mr. Hastings, contrasting such *facts* as were *proved* against the former, with those generally in favour of the latter. Hence the public will be enabled to draw their conclusions without the false lights of partial and anticipated comparisons.[40]

In keeping with the introductory note, the governor of Sicily is depicted as a greedy, inhuman tyrant, with *Amicus Curiae* employing expressions such as 'pecuniary intoxication' and 'despotic manner'.[41] Conversely, Hastings is eulogized as a just and honourable ruler. In *Amicus Curiae*'s words, he 'not only left his Government in a state of established peace and security, but all the resources of its abundance unimpaired, and in many instances improved'.[42]

While the *propraetor* of Sicily and the Governor-General of Bengal appear to be the opposite of each other, the comparison between Cicero and Burke reveals surprising similarities. Indeed, *Amicus Curiae* suggests that 'it would be difficult to find, particularly at the distance of near two thousand years, such a striking resemblance of character as between the Roman and Modern Senator – Both the greatest orators of their time – both the wisest statesmen – both the champions of distressed provinces'.[43] This introduction is ironic and misleading, as in the course of the letter *Amicus Curiae* praises the ancient orator, but directs sarcastic barbs at Burke. For example, Cicero's appellations of *new man* and *foreigner* are presented as a matter of fact – Cicero was born at Arpinum, a province of Rome. The same remark is then extended to Burke, but not without a tinge of irony: 'Mr. Burke was born and educated in the kingdom of Ireland, *lately little better than a province to England* and it is said claims an *equal descent* with the Roman orator'.[44] In the following paragraphs, the accuser of Verres is portrayed as a talented orator and writer, as well as a skilful lawyer. On the contrary, Burke's description as philosopher and orator is full of mordant wit. For instance, whereas 'Cicero's writings touched all that was *useful and elegant in life*, Mr. Burke's pen has likewise treated on all that is *beautiful and sublime*; and as to the *utility* of his speeches, they will be as much the delight and admiration of posterity, as they are the *political land-marks* [sic] *of the present day*'.[45] Other parallels include Cicero's perilous voyage to Sicily, on the one hand, and ('at much less expence [sic]') Burke's 'travel' to the *India*-House, the London headquarters of the East India Company, on the other.[46]

Finally, in the last letter of the series, *Amicus Curiae* addresses the Lords ('that high Court of Judicature') and humbly suggests what 'they may perhaps consider' when formulating their final verdict on Hastings.[47] The text is interspersed with expressions that denote deference, respect and submission, such as 'That Right Honourable Court perhaps will consider' and 'they perhaps will keep in view'. Once again, *Amicus Curiae*'s reflections are aimed at defending Hastings. The writer also remarks how 'in the management of a great empire, [...] some unintentional errors must necessarily creep in'. In spite of some 'private' minor mistakes which Hastings may have made – *Amicus Curiae* continues – the Directors of the East India Company gave him a '*unanimous* vote of thanks for his good services'.[48] The writer concludes his letter by urging the Lords to take into account the repercussions of their verdict for 'all Governors, Commanders in Chief, &c. who may in future be employed under his Majesty's government in any part of the world'. Ironically, on the same day, in Westminster Hall, Edmund Burke came to the same conclusion, but sought the opposite outcome: 'my Lords [...]' – he thundered – 'You do not decide the Case only; you fix the rule. [...] It is according to the Judgment that you shall pronounce upon the past transactions of India, connected with those principles, that the whole rule, tenure, tendency and character of our future government in India is to be finally decided'.[49]

Two satirical prints

As *Amicus Curiae* acutely remarks in his first letter to the *Public Advertiser*, after slipping from whisperings to conversations and from conversations to newspapers, the parallel between Hastings and Verres, and between Burke and Cicero, travelled 'to the print-shops, where, under the character of the Roman Orator, the person and manner of Mr. Burke are too faithfully delineated to escape the observations of those who have ever once seen this very distinguished character'.[50] As is well known, satirical prints circulated widely in Britain at the time and such was their impact on moulding public opinion that, as Jim Davis has put it, 'the print shops themselves became an important cultural institution'.[51] Those who could not afford to buy prints, Davis continues, could, nonetheless, observe them in the windows of print shops, as shown in Gillray's renowned etching, *Very Slippy-Weather* (1808, BM 1851,0901.1248).[52] In particular, it is quite likely that *Amicus Curiae* had in mind two caricatures, namely James Sayers's *The Impeachment* (Figure 5.1) and John Boyne's *Cicero against Verres* (Figure 5.2). Even though these cartoons have already been discussed by a few critics, they deserve attention here, as – along with newspapers – they formed and forged the national imagination with regard to the trial of Hastings.[53]

As I mentioned above, in February 1786 the *Public Advertiser* drew attention to parallels between the Anglo-Irish orator and Cicero and between the *propraetor* of Sicily and Warren Hastings. Sayers picks up the analogy and represents Burke in the garb of a Roman (he is clothed in a tunic and long cloak), while wearing his own wig. The orator is portrayed in the act of brandishing the 'Articles of Impe[achme]nt', with his head turned menacingly towards a turbaned Hastings. On the extreme left of the etching, the latter is wearing an oriental dress, while his face, turned aside, is invisible. From his dramatic gesture – he stretches out his hands – we may assume that he is protesting his innocence. Above Hastings's head two papers fly in the air, as if lifted by the energetic movement of Burke's right arm: they are the 'Treaty of Peace with the Mahrattas' and the sketch of Chait Singh, the Raja of Benares, respectively. Both papers allude to the twenty-two 'Articles of Charge of High Crimes and Misdemeanors' that Burke produced against Hastings between 4 April and 5 May 1786.[54] Besides Hastings and Burke, the cartoon includes a third character hidden beneath the orator's cloak. The seated figure who holds

Fig. 5.1 James Sayers, *The Impeachment*, 17 March 1786. BM 1868,0808.5488. © Trustees of the British Museum.

his head with his hands in despair is John Powell (d. 1783), a 'defaulting cashier', in Nicholas K. Robinson's words, 'whom Burke, when in office, and amid much criticism, had reinstated to the Paymaster's staff'.[55] In front of Powell are visible an open account book and a noose – a clear reference to Powell's suicide in

Fig. 5.2 John Boyne, *Cicero against Verres*, 7 February 1787. BM 7138. © Trustees of the British Museum.

May 1783. Beneath the title, a few lines of verse spell out Sayers's unfavourable comparison between Cicero's rigorous morality and Burke's tainted reputation after his restoration of Powell:

> Had Hastings been accus'd in Verres' Time,
> And Asia's Preservation been his Crime,
> Tully, 'tis said, with all his Powers of Speech
> Had urg'd the Roman Senate – to impeach,
> But had that Tully lived in Powell's Day,
> And known the official 'Error of his Way'
> He wou'd have drop't [sic] the Impeachment and ye Halter
> And for his Merits screen'd the good Defaulter.

Burke is also dressed as a Roman in Boyne's cartoon. Despite wearing a voluminous toga, the Anglo-Irish orator is clearly recognizable by his characteristic spectacles. As the trial dragged on, these spectacles became a recurring trope in the satirical prints, and – as Daniel O'Quinn contends – 'were deployed in an increasingly complex fashion'.[56] Boyne represents Burke at the centre of the scene, in the act of declaiming a speech according to classical rhetorical prescriptions: his right arm is emphatically extended in the air, while his left hand rests on his hip.[57] This grave posture is somewhat spoilt by Burke's bald head and exaggeratedly big bare feet. Behind the orator, the heads and shoulders of Fox and North – who had forged an alliance in 1783 – are visible on the right-hand side, above a partition.[58] Fox looks on with melancholy and stares out to where Burke's audience is presumably sitting, while North, indifferent to the scene, reads a paper short-sightedly. On the left-hand side, two women are seated on the ground: they embody Britannia with a shield and, presumably, India. The former embraces and comforts the latter, who languishes exhausted, her head reclined on Britannia's shoulder. The image also reproduces Burke's speech:

> The time is come, Fathers, when that which has long been wished for, towards allaying the envy, your House has been subject to, & removing the imputations against trials, is (not by human contrivance, but superior direction) effectually put in our power. An opinion has long prevailed, not only here at home, but likewise in foreign countries, both dangerous to you, and pernicious to the state, viz. That, in prosecutions, men of wealth are always safe, however clearly convicted. There is now to be brought upon his trial

before you, to the confusion, I hope of the propagators of this slanderous imputation, one, whose life and actions condemn him in the opinion of all impartial persons; but who, according to his own reckoning, and declared dependence upon his riches, is already acquitted; I mean **W__H__**. I have undertaken this prosecution, Fathers, at the general desire, and with the great expectation of the **British People**, with the direct design of clearing your justice and impartiality before the world. For I have brought upon his trial, one, whose conduct has been such, that, in passing a just sentence upon him, you will have an opportunity of re-establishing the credit of such trials; of recovering whatever may be lost of the favour of the **British People**; and of satisfying foreign states and kingdoms in alliance with us, or tributary to us. I demand justice of you, Fathers, upon the robber of the public treasury, the oppressor of **Asia**, and the invader of the rights & privileges of **Britons**, the scourge and curse of **Indostan**. If that sentence is passed upon him which his crimes deserve, your authority, Fathers, will be venerable & sacred in the eyes of the public. But if his great riches should bias you in his favour, I shall still gain one point, viz. To make it apparent to all the world, that what was wanting in this case was not a criminal, nor a prosecutor; but justice, & adequate punishment.

In light of what we have seen so far, it comes as no surprise that this oration is an English translation of the beginning of Cicero's *Verrines*, namely *Verr*. I.1–3. Apart from a few ironic alterations, this is the same version published by the *Hicky's Bengal Gazette* (21 April–28 April 1781). As far as I have been able to ascertain, this anonymous translation was enormously successful in the last two decades of the eighteenth century. One finds it, for example, in British – and even American – schoolbooks of rhetoric, among instances of exemplary declamations.[59] Interestingly enough, Boyne's variations of the original text are emphasized by means of different types. Thus, Caius Verres turns into 'W_ H_'; 'Roman people' and 'Romans' are replaced by 'British people' and 'Britons'; while 'Asia Minor and Pamphylia' are substituted by 'Asia', and 'Sicily' by 'Indostan'.

It is clear that, from the earliest stages of Burke's campaign against Hastings, newspaper reporters, as well as caricaturists, explored and described the *cause célèbre* in terms of a re-enactment of the proceedings against Verres. Contemporary English-language papers published in India attest to the tendency to portray the former Governor-General of Bengal either as a latter-day Verres or, as with the speeches of MPs supportive of Hastings, as a celebrated statesman or general from Graeco-Roman antiquity. In parallel with the equation of Hastings–Verres, Burke was described as a British Cicero. In one example of this characterization, a certain Aristophanes referred to Burke with the pseudonym *Tullius Indianus*, combining classical antiquity with contemporary politics. An examination of the London press similarly shows that from 1786 Burke and Hastings were compared to Cicero and Verres. Beginning with a series of articles published in the *Public Advertiser* a few days before the opening of the trial, by early 1788 this parallel was widely explored amongst the reading nation and had become the subject of satirical cartoons. As we saw in Chapter 1, ancient Greek and Roman characters were not empty names from an alien and distant past, but rather, figures of real relevance who pervaded the discourse surrounding current political affairs.

Conclusion

Over the course of this book I have traced specific overlaps between classical culture and the trial of Warren Hastings. Through the analysis of Burke's and Sheridan's spectacular performances, as well as Burke's constant references to Cicero's *Verrines*, we have seen the extent to which British parliamentary oratory appropriated and inflected classical, particularly Roman, rhetorical strategies towards the close of the eighteenth century. At the time, Cicero's *Verrines* circulated widely among educated British gentlemen. Two possible explanations for this may lie in the promotion of a classical frame of mind by the British elite, on the one hand, and in the orations' relevance to an actively imperialist society on the other.

As I have pointed out, the education of the British elite was thoroughly modelled by and based on classical languages and cultures. It was thus not surprising that all parties in the British Parliament identified themselves with the Roman Senate and that eminent MPs trained their sons in classical models, particularly favouring Cicero. Burke himself had a wide-ranging knowledge of Greek and Latin antiquity, demonstrated by his writings and speeches, as well as the surviving catalogues of his library. Like many of his contemporaries, he followed classical models of rhetoric; hence his powerful grip on his hearers' emotions.

The Irish-born orator's particular empathy for and affinity with Cicero's writings and career encouraged him to adopt the *persona* of the great Roman lawyer, especially through the long years of the impeachment of Warren Hastings. As Burke modelled himself as Cicero, he found in Hastings a Verres, the notorious villain *propraetor* of Sicily, whom Cicero had brought to trial more than eighteen centuries beforehand.

In point of fact, this was not the first time that the character of Verres was evoked as the archetype of a powerful, corrupt man, as a close examination of the *Verrines*' circulation in eighteenth-century Britain and their manipulation in the political rhetoric of the age indicates. In the preceding pages I have described how Jonathan Swift's satirical attack on the first Earl of Wharton, for instance, was underpinned by the *incipit* of the first *Verrine*; similarly, the anonymous author of *Verres and his Scribblers* criticized Sir Robert Walpole's monetary policy through the medium of Cicero's speeches.

Alongside the contemporary context within which Burke's monumental prosecution of Hastings germinated, Lorna Hardwick reminds us that we should not lose sight of the 'two-way relationship' between the hypotext and the new work – specifically, in our case, Burke's 'Speech on the Opening of the Impeachment'. Indeed, it is by virtue of this 'two-way relationship' that sometimes we may 'frame new questions or retrieve aspects of the source which have been marginalized or forgotten'.[1] As a matter of fact, before the Governor-General of Bengal was arraigned by Burke, the *propraetor* of Sicily embodied two main vices in the British elite's collective imagination: rapacity and corruption. In the speeches delivered between 15 and 19 February 1788, the Irish-born orator also referred to such attributes as cruelty and monstrosity – characteristics of Verres that had, in fact, been brought into sharp relief by Cicero. In this sense, Burke's indictment of Hastings somehow affected the reception of the original text, for it illuminated some prominent aspects of the Latin text that British satirical writers had set aside.

If this book has proved the effectiveness of Burke's self-(re)presentation of a Cicero inveighing against the Governor's iniquities, then it has also shown that from the commencement of the impeachment, newspaper reporters followed and discussed the proceedings against Hastings in terms of a re-enactment of the arraignment of Verres, and satirists published cartoons representing Burke as a British Cicero and Hastings as a latter-day Verres. Tellingly, both Sayers and Boyne portrayed the Irish-born orator in the plastic pose of a Roman orator – his right arm emphatically lifted up in the air.

Welcoming the comparison with ancient *oratores*, Burke modelled his rhetoric on classical prescriptions, including Cicero's insistence on the superiority of *actio* or enactment (namely, air, gestures and enunciation, among others) over the contents of the oration. Indeed, his emphatic, theatrical histrionics which culminated in a (feigned) illness at the end of the account of the Rangpur atrocities may partly be ascribed to the Roman trend to transform legal debates into staged productions or spectacles of justice. Owing to its unusual emotional intensity and to Burke's sensational performance, the

18 February 1788 oration on the Rangpur horrors turned out to be immensely successful. Among the spectators, ladies swooned and gentlemen wept. No less importantly, many years later, Hastings himself would confess: 'I felt a villain under the magic of the orator'.[2]

Burke was not alone in acting out his speeches: with their histrionics, his fellow managers established parliamentary oratory as a theatrical show. Sheridan, in particular, showed that political debates could be turned into great public spectacles. In describing one of the impresario's spectacular performances, the lawyer Charles Butler (1750–1832) recalled: 'The rush to obtain places at the first commemoration of Handel, when all London seemed to pour into Westminster abbey, was not equal to the rush into Westminster-hall, on the day in which Mr. Sheridan brought his charges against Mr. Hastings'.[3] Certainly, contemporary cultural and social practices, such as the vogue for melodrama, influenced Hastings's prosecutors' exaggerated delivery. In my reading of Burke's and Sheridan's embodied language I have chosen to trace and emphasize classical rhetorical practices. As we have seen, in the Graeco-Roman tradition verbal eloquence went hand in hand with physical eloquence and particularly Cicero had stressed that oratory, 'like acting, is an embodied, public performance art'.[4]

The inextricable link between classical oratory and theatrical performances in the trial of Hastings can still be sensed in nineteenth-century declamations. Beginning around fifty years after the acquittal of the Governor-General, Burke's orations against Hastings were included in the programmes of the Speech Days of some of the most prestigious public schools, including Harrow and Eton: as Paul Elledge has noted, the structure where Speech Days were held became 'a theater packed with patrons expecting to be entertained by actors trained in the performance of roles'.[5] Interestingly, along with distinguished parliamentary speeches, as well as classical, Renaissance and, occasionally, contemporary dramas, the declamations delivered on Speech Days included excerpts from classical orations, such as 'Cicero in M. Antonium', 'Cicero in Catilinam' and 'Speech against Verres'.[6]

The fact that the *Verrines* were recited even in schools attests, once again, to their deep and far-reaching impact on the eighteenth- and nineteenth-century British elite. Their frequent resurfacing in a variety of different contexts – from education to parliamentary orations, from translations and satirical publications to cartoons – leads us to conclude that not only did they have a formative role in the perception of Roman rhetoric, but they also informed the British understanding of Roman rule. As such, Cicero's speeches against Verres had important ramifications for British rule overseas, with eighteenth-century Britons identifying themselves with the conquering classical Romans.

Britain might have replaced Rome in the creation of a vast empire but, in the minds of Burke and others at least, she was failing in the attempt to govern India according to the 'eternal laws of justice', and this was an area in which Verres's conviction could function as a relevant paradigm. By means of this authoritative Roman antecedent, Burke – though, in the end, unsuccessfully – endeavoured to prove that, after the rapacious years following the battle of Plassey, Britain had to secure a 'natural, immutable and substantial justice' for India's people before seeking any gain herself.[7]

This book has only begun the work of recovering the complex and multiple interfaces between classical culture and the impeachment of the first Governor-General of Bengal. In particular, what I have collected on Roman rhetoric and Burke's speeches against Hastings should be considered introductory. There is still much to be done, especially when considering that Burke regarded these orations as his greatest achievement, as he himself observed in a letter significantly penned on 28 July 1796, a year after the ending of the Hastings impeachment and a year before his own death. Addressed to his friend and close collaborator, French Laurence (1757–1809), the epistle gives us an image of Burke as a modern-day *pater patriae* who, in a titanic effort against 'this cruel, daring, unexampled act of publick [sic] corruption, guilt, and meanness' – namely, the acquittal of the Governor-General – constructs his orations as a monument-*monumentum* for posterity. It is presumably no coincidence that, as much as the *Verrines* constitute the only surviving Ciceronian prosecution oration, as well as the sole extant example of any Roman prosecution speech, so does Burke – on his 'departure from the public stage' – ask Laurence to let his speeches against Hastings be his 'monument; The only one I ever will have. Let' – the crusading prosecutor of Hastings concludes – 'everything I have done, said, or written be forgotten but this'.[8]

Notes

Introduction

1 William Eden, *The Journal and Correspondence of William, Lord Auckland*, 2 vols (London, 1861), i, p. 469. Mr. Storer to Mr. Eden (22 February 1788).
2 Gilbert Elliot, *Life and Letters of Sir Gilbert Elliot*, ed. The Countess of Minto, 3 vols (London, 1874), i, pp. 196–7. To Lady Elliot (3 March 1788).
3 Robin Theobald, 'Scandal in a scandalous age: the impeachment and trial of Warren Hastings, 1788–95', in J. Garrand and James L. Newell (eds), *Scandals in Past and Contemporary Politics* (Manchester and New York, 2006), p. 142.
4 I take the charges from P. J. Marshall, *The Impeachment of Warren Hastings* (Oxford, 1965), pp. xiv–xv. See also Nicholas B. Dirks, *The Scandal of Empire: India and the Creation of Imperial Britain* (Cambridge, MA, and London, 2006), pp. 19–20.
5 Theobald, 'Scandal in a scandalous age', p. 137.
6 Quoted in Conor Cruise O'Brien, *The Great Melody: A Thematic Biography and Commented Anthology of Edmund Burke* (London, 1992), p. 360.
7 Frances Burney, *Diary and Letters of Madame D'Arblay*, ed. C. Barrett, 7 vols (London, 1842–6), iv, p. 63. Other contemporaries also remarked on Hastings's sickly pallor. Sir Gilbert Elliot (the future Lord Minto and Governor-General of Bengal), for example, told his wife: 'I never saw Hastings till to-day, and had not formed anything like a just idea of him. I never saw a more miserable-looking creature, but indeed he has so much the appearance of bad health that I do not suppose he resembles even himself. He looks as if he could not live a week'. Elliot, *Life and Letters*, i, p. 194. To Lady Elliot (13 February 1788). Commenting on the third day of the trial, the politician Anthony Morris Storer similarly observed that 'the prisoner was but a mean-looking fellow, and did not appear at all as Alexander the Great ought to do at the Old Bailey'. Eden, *The Journal and Correspondence*, i, p. 468. Mr. Storer to Mr. Eden (15 February 1788).
8 The epistle is addressed to George Nesbitt Thompson (1753–1831), Hastings's former secretary in India. See S. Arthur Strong, 'Warren Hastings's own account of his impeachment', *Harper's Monthly Magazine*, 110 (1904–5), pp. 89–95 (p. 95).
9 F. P. Lock, *Edmund Burke, Volume One: 1730–84* and *Volume Two: 1784–1797* (Oxford, 1998–2006), ii, p. 159. P. J. Marshall has stressed that the managers

'constantly made allegations which bore no relation to the charges'. Marshall, *The Impeachment of Warren Hastings*, pp. 83–4.
10 Siraj Ahmed, 'The theater of the civilized self: Edmund Burke and the East India trials', *Representations*, lxxviii (2002), p. 44.
11 Daniel O'Quinn, *Staging Governance: Theatrical Imperialism in London 1700–1800* (Baltimore, MD, 2005), pp. 164–221.
12 Sara Suleri, *The Rhetoric of English India* (Chicago and London, 1992), pp. 49–74. Kate Teltscher has similarly argued that the trial of Hastings was a public spectacle in which British guilt over the colonization of India was given expression. See Kate Teltscher, *India Inscribed: European and British Writing on India 1600–1800* (Oxford, 1995), pp. 157–91.
13 Jennifer Pitts, *A Turn to Empire: The Rise of Imperial Liberalism in Britain and France* (Princeton, NJ, and Oxford, 2005), p. 69.
14 Marshall, *The Impeachment of Warren Hastings*. Richard Bourke, *Empire and Revolution: The Political Life of Edmund Burke* (Princeton, NJ, 2015), pp. 627–75; 820–50.
15 Tillman W. Nechtman, *Nabobs: Empire and Identity in Eighteenth-Century Britain* (Cambridge, 2010), p. 96. See also Marshall, *The Impeachment of Warren Hastings*, pp. 70–1.
16 Edmund Burke, *The Correspondence of Edmund Burke*, ed. T. W. Copeland et al., 10 vols (Cambridge, 1958–78), v, p. 357. To Henry Dundas (1 November 1787). The passage is quoted in Marshall, *The Impeachment of Warren Hastings*, p. 71.
17 Nechtman, *Nabobs*, p. 106.
18 David Francis Taylor, *Theatres of Opposition: Empire, Revolution, and Richard Brinsley Sheridan* (Oxford, 2012), p. 84.
19 Ibid.
20 Philip Dormer Stanhope, *Letters Written by the Late Right Honourable Philip Dormer Stanhope, Earl of Chesterfield, to His Son; with Some Account of His Life*, 4 vols (London, 1815), ii (24 November OS 1749), p. 297.
21 H. V. Canter, 'The impeachment of Verres and Hastings: Cicero and Burke', *The Classical Journal* ix (1914), pp. 199–211 and Geoffrey Carnall, 'Burke as modern Cicero', in G. Carnall and C. Nicholson (eds), *The Impeachment of Warren Hastings: Papers from a Bicentenary Commemoration* (Edinburgh, 1989), pp. 76–90.
22 See, for example, Paddy Bullard, *Edmund Burke and the Art of Rhetoric* (Cambridge, 2011), pp. 16–17.
23 Suleri, *The Rhetoric of English India*, p. 49.
24 Burney, *Diary and Letters*, iv, p. 96.

1 Cicero, Verres and the Classics in Eighteenth-Century Britain

1 M. L. Clarke, *Greek Studies in England 1700–1830* (Cambridge, 1945), p. 10. A good sense of the importance of the Classics in British education may also be derived from M. L. Clarke, *Classical Education in Britain 1500–1900* (Cambridge, 1959); J. A. K. Thomson, *The Classical Background of English Literature* (London, 1948); Robert Maxwell Ogilvie, *Latin and Greek: A History of the Influence of the Classics on English Life from 1600 to 1918* (Hamden, CT, 1964) and C. O. Brink, *English Classical Scholarship: Historical Reflections on Bentley, Porson, and Housman* (Cambridge, 1985).

2 See, for example, Joseph Addison, *A Discourse on Ancient and Modern Learning* (Dublin, 1739); John Gordon, *Occasional Thoughts on the Study and Character of Classical Authors, on the Course of Literature, and the Present Plan of a Learned Education. With Some Incidental Comparisons between Homer and Ossian* (London, 1762); James Beattie, *Essays: On Poetry and Music, as They Affect the Mind; on Laughter, and Ludicrous Composition: on the Utility of Classical Learning*, 2 vols (Edinburgh, 1776); Joseph Cornish, *An Attempt to Display the Importance of Classical Learning, Addressed to the Parents and Guardians of Youth: With Some Candid Remarks on Mr. Knox's Liberal Education* (London, 1783); William Stevenson, *Remarks on the Very Inferior Utility of Classical Learning* (London, 1796).

3 See John Locke, *Some Thoughts Concerning Education* (Oxford, 1989), p. 217 (§ 164).

4 Clarke, *Greek Studies*, p. 10.

5 John Stuart Mill served for three and a half decades at India House, while his father, James (1773–1836), was the author of the *History of British India* (1817).

6 John Stuart Mill, *Autobiography of John Stuart Mill Published from the Original Manuscript in the Columbia University Library* (New York and London, 1960), pp. 50–1.

7 Dunning's letter is included in *The Templar; or, Monthly Register of Legal and Constitutional Knowledge*, 2 vols (London, 1789), i, p. 11.

8 Carey McIntosh has calculated that in the first half the eighteenth century 'there were thirty-one editions of Aristotle, Quintilian, Longinus and Cicero's *De Oratore*, ten in translation and twenty-one in the original Latin or Greek'. See Carey McIntosh, 'Elementary rhetorical ideas and eighteenth-century English', *Language Sciences* xxii/3 (2000), pp. 231–49 (p. 233).

9 *The Letters of Sir William Jones*, ed. G. Cannon, 2 vols (Oxford, 1970), i, p. 125. To Viscount Althorp (23 April 1773). Other examples of renowned British politicians and orators who forged their rhetorical abilities on classical models, may be found

in Christopher Reid, *Imprison'd Wranglers: The Rhetorical Culture of the House of Commons 1760-1800* (Oxford, 2012), pp. 115-16; Philip Ayres, *Classical Culture and the Idea of Rome in Eighteenth-Century England* (Cambridge, 1997), p. 42; M. L. Clarke, 'Non hominis nomen, sed eloquentiae', in T. A. Dorey (ed.), *Cicero* (London, 1965), p. 100 and John L. Mahoney, 'The classical tradition in eighteenth century English rhetorical education', *History of Education Journal* ix/4 (1958), pp. 93-7.

10 Ayres, *Classical Culture*, p. 165.

11 C. A. Vince has collected a number of passages from Latin poets, which were quoted by British MPs in the eighteenth and nineteenth centuries. According to Vince's study, the most frequently cited Roman poets were Virgil, Horace, Juvenal and Ovid. See C. A. Vince, 'Latin poets in the British Parliament', *The Classical Review* xlvi (1932), pp. 97-104.

12 Robert Bisset, *The Life of Edmund Burke* (London, 1798), pp. 197-207.

13 Italics original. The author of the Preface to *Bellendenus* is the renowned classicist Samuel Parr. A list of newspapers and magazines commenting on Bisset's comparison of Burke and Cicero includes *True Briton* (24 August 1798); *The British Critic: A New Review for July, August, September, October, November, and December 1798* (London, 1798), pp. 296-300; *The Historical, Biographical, Literary, and Scientific Magazine. Miscellaneous Literature, for the Year 1799* (London, 1799), pp. 19-25; *The European Magazine, and London Review. From January to June 1799* (London, 1799), pp. 101-5.

14 David H. Solkin, 'The battle of the Ciceros: Richard Wilson and the politics of landscape in the age of John Wilkes', in S. Pugh (ed.), *Reading Landscape: Country – City – Capital* (Manchester, 1990), p. 49.

15 For a detailed description of Gillray's print, see the British Museum's website: http://www.britishmuseum.org/research/collection_online/collection_object_details.aspx?objectId=1628932&partId=1&searchText=design+for+the ew+gallery+of+busts+and+pictures&page=1 (accessed 20 September 2016).

16 Nollekens was commissioned to produce, among others, the busts of Charles James Fox (1791; 1801) and William Pitt the Younger (1807). Interestingly, John Kenworthy-Browne has described the 1801 bust of Fox as having 'the dignity of a Roman republican'. See Ayres, *Classical Culture*, p. 74.

17 Italics original.

18 Italics original.

19 *The New London Magazine*, vol. viii (1792), p. 36.

20 'Les membres du Parlement d'Angleterre aiment à se comparer aux anciens Romains autant qu'ils le peuvent'. See François Marie Arouet de Voltaire, *Lettres*

écrites de Londres sur les Anglois et autres sujets (Basle, 1734), p. 49. The English translation is mine. Even though Letter VIII – whence this quotation derives – is centred on the British Parliament, references to the Roman Senate, or Roman historical characters, such as Marius and Sulla, are abundant.

21 The authors most frequently cited were – in order of preference – Horace, Virgil, Ovid, Juvenal and Cicero. For a fuller discussion of the frequency with which Latin and Greek authors occurred in the *Spectator*, see 'Classicism' in *Brill's New Pauly: Encyclopaedia of the Ancient World*, eds H. Cancik, H. Schneider and M. Landfester, 22 vols (Leiden, 2002–), *Classical Tradition*, i, p. 881.

22 Solkin, 'The battle of the Ciceros', p. 50.

23 Other examples drawn from the *India Gazette* include: *Effects of War. Rome in the Reign of Romulus* (3 November 1788), concerning Rome's state of constant war 'to enslave the universe' and *Of the Supper Given to Cicero and Pompey, by Lucullus* (17 November 1788), about Lucullus's renowned sumptuous feasts, particularly that organized for Cicero and Pompey.

24 See, for example, the *India Gazette* (18 February 1788): *Horace, Book II. Ode III. Imitated* or the *India Gazette* (19 May 1788): *Horace. Ode XVI. Book II. Imitated*. Interestingly enough, on 15 February 1787, *The Calcutta Gazette; or, Oriental Advertiser* published *An Ode Written by Mr. Hastings, on Board the Berrington, in his Voyage from Bengal to England, in 1785. Addressed to John Shore, Esq. In Imitation of Horace, Book II. Ode 16*.

25 Edmund Burke, *The Correspondence of Edmund Burke*, ed. T. W. Copeland et al., 10 vols (Cambridge, 1958–78), vii, p. 501. To Arthur Murphy (8 December 1793).

26 Susanne Gippert, 'The poet and the statesman: Plutarchan biography in eighteenth century England' in L. De Blois, J. Bons, T. Kessels and D. M. Schenkeveld (eds), *The Statesman in Plutarch's Works: Proceedings of the International Conference of the International Plutarch Society, Nijmegen/Castle Hernen, May 1–5, 2002*, 2 vols (Leiden and Boston, 2004), i, p. 307.

27 *Plutarch's Lives. Translated from the Greek by Several Hands*, ed. J. Dryden, 5 vols (London, 1684–8).

28 Plutarch, *Plutarch's Lives Translated from the Original Greek; with Notes, Historical and Critical and a Life of Plutarch, by John and William Langhorne. A New Edition, Carefully Corrected, and the Index Much Amended, and Accurately Revised Throughout. In Four Volumes*, trans. J. Langhorne and W. Langhorne (Philadelphia, 1822), iv, pp. 10; 31–2.

29 Ibid., pp. 5; 7.

30 Ibid., p. 26.

31 Ibid., pp. 19; 35.
32 See George Lyttelton, *Observations on the Life of Cicero* (London, 1733), p. 3. An in-depth analysis of Lyttelton's text may be found in Matthew Fox, 'Cicero during the Enlightenment', in C. Steel (ed.), *The Cambridge Companion to Cicero* (Cambridge, 2013), pp. 329–31.
33 Lyttelton, *Observations*, p. 39.
34 Christine Gerrard, 'Lyttelton, George, first Baron Lyttelton (1709–1773)', in *Oxford Dictionary of National Biography*.
35 For an overview of the history of the composition and publication of Middleton's *Life of Cicero*, as well as the polemical quarrel from which it sprang, see, in particular, Robert G. Ingram, 'Conyers Middleton's *Cicero*: enlightenment, scholarship, and polemic', in William H. F. Altman (ed.), *Brill's Companion to the Reception of Cicero* (Leiden and Boston, 2015), pp. 95–123.
36 See Howard D. Weinbrot, 'History, Horace and Augustus Caesar: some implications for eighteenth-century satire', *Eighteenth-Century Studies*, vii/4 (1974), pp. 391–414 (p. 397, n. 18). In 1763, the *Critical Review* ironically observed that 'princes, nobles, and literati of all degrees had given their opinions, before they had read a single line of the work, that it was the finest performance that ever appeared'. See *Critical Review* xvi (1763), p. 401. I take this reference from Addison Ward, 'The Tory view of Roman history', *Studies in English Literature*, iv (1964), pp. 413–56 (p. 432).
37 See Howard D. Weinbrot, *Augustus Caesar in 'Augustan' England: The Decline of a Classical Norm* (Princeton, NJ, 1978), p. 74.
38 See Yasunari Takada, 'An Augustan representation of Cicero', in P. Robinson et al. (eds), *Enlightened Groves: Essays in Honour of Professor Zenzo Suzuki* (Tokyo, 1996), p. 245.
39 Conyers Middleton, *The Life of Marcus Tullius Cicero*, 3 vols (London, 1741), i, p. xxx. Cicero is further eulogized as a 'shining pattern of virtue' (iii, p. 301) and 'sublime specimen of perfection' (iii, p. 310).
40 Ibid., iii, p. 307.
41 See, for example, Ward, 'The Tory view of Roman history', pp. 435–56.
42 Anonymous, *The Death of M-L-N in the Life of Cicero: Being a Proper Criticism on That Marvellous Performance* (London, 1741), pp. 1–2.
43 Ibid., pp. 20; 22.
44 Ibid., pp. 46–7.
45 Colley Cibber, *The Character and Conduct of Cicero, Considered, From the History of his Life, by the Reverend Dr. Middleton. With Occasional Essays and Observations upon the Most Memorable Facts and Persons during That Period, By Colley Cibber, Esq; Servant to His Majesty* (London, 1747), p. 206.

46 Ibid., p. 209.
47 Joseph Warton, *An Essay on the Genius and Writings of Pope*, 2 vols (London, 1782), ii, pp. 260-1.
48 Anonymous, *A Free Translation of the Preface to Bellendenus; Containing Animated Strictures on the Great Political Characters of the Present Time* (London, 1788), p. 6.
49 Ibid., p. 8.
50 In 1983, M. L. Clarke reconsidered this pertinent question, reaching the conclusion that 'there is no justification for accusations of plagiarism'. See M. L. Clarke, 'Conyers Middleton's alleged plagiarism', *Notes and Queries*, xxx/1 (1983), pp. 44-6 (p. 45).
51 See P. J. Marshall, *The Impeachment of Warren Hastings* (Oxford, 1965), p. 14.
52 *Encyclopaedia Britannica; or, A Dictionary of Arts, Sciences, &c. Illustrated with above Two Hundred Copperplates*, 10 vols (Edinburgh, 1778-83), iii, p. 1976.
53 Ibid.
54 Ibid., p. 1975.
55 Ibid., p. 1979.
56 Ibid.
57 A note specifies that the 'modern writer' in question is Swinburne. See: *Encyclopaedia Britannica; or, A Dictionary of Arts, Sciences, and Miscellaneous Literature; ... Illustrated with Five Hundred and Forty-Two Copperplates*, 18 vols (Edinburgh, 1797), v, p. 5.
58 Ibid.
59 Ibid., p. 6.
60 Ibid.
61 See Conyers Middleton, *The Epistles of M.T. Cicero to M. Brutus and of Brutus to Cicero: with the Latin Text on the opposite page, and English notes to each epistle. Together with a prefatory dissertation, In which the Authority of the said Epistles is vindicated, and all the Objections of the Revd. Mr. Tunstall particularly considered and confuted* (London, 1743). In reply to Middleton, James Tunstall wrote *Observations on the present Collection of Epistles between Cicero and M. Brutus, representing several evident Marks of Forgery in those Epistles; and the true state of many important Particulars in the Life and Writings of Cicero, in answer to the late Pretences of the Reverend Dr. Conyers Middleton, by James Tunstall, B.D. Fellow etc.* (London, 1744). For an overview of the debate around the authenticity of Cicero's letters *Ad Marcum Brutum*, see, in particular, Ward, 'The Tory view', p. 435, n. 72.
62 Owing to the keen interest in English classical scholarship in Germany at the end of the century, Brüggemann also compiled a voluminous text listing all the English translations and editions of ancient orators published in Britain, as well as literary comments: *A view of the English Editions, Translations and Illustration of the ancient*

Greek and Latin authors with remarks by Lewis William Brüggemann, Counsellor of the consistory at Stettin in Pomerania, and Chaplain in Ordinary to his Prussian Majesty (Stettin, 1797).

63 Brüggemann, *A View of the English Editions, Translations and Commentaries of Marcus Tullius Cicero with Remarks* (Stettin, 1795), p. 27. This observation is taken from the *Critical Review* for February 1778, pp. 22–8.

64 Ibid., p. 22. This comment is derived from the *Monthly Review* for February 1755, pp. 96–8.

65 Ibid., p. 10. Here, Brüggemann is quoting from the *Critical Review* for June 1789, p. 427.

66 J. M. S. Tompkins, 'James White, Esq.: a forgotten humourist', *Review of English Studies*, iii/10 (1927), pp. 146–56 (p. 147). The following year, White published a pamphlet entitled *Hints for a Specific Plan for an Abolition of the Slave Trade, and for Relief of the Negroes in the British West Indies* and signed this work with the periphrasis 'By the translator of Cicero's Orations against Verres'.

67 Cicero, Marcus Tullius, *The Orations of Marcus Tullius Cicero against Caius Cornelius Verres, Translated from the Original, by James White, Esq. with Annotations*, trans. J. White (London, 1787), p. vii.

68 Ibid.

69 Ibid.

70 Margaret M. Miles, *Art as Plunder: The Ancient Origins of Debate about Cultural Property* (Cambridge, 2008), p. 302.

71 Ibid., p. 303.

72 Anonymous, *Verres and his Scribblers: A Satire in Three Cantos. To Which is Added an Examen of the Piece, and a Key to the Characters and Obscure Passages* (London, 1732), p. 60. Italics original.

73 Ibid., pp. 66–7.

74 Jonathan Swift, the *Examiner* (23–30 November 1710). Italics original.

75 Ibid. A detailed textual analysis of Swift's anonymous article and Cicero's *Verrines* may be found in Pat Rogers, 'Swift and Cicero: the character of Verres', *Quarterly Journal of Speech* lxi (1975), pp. 71–5. See also Fox, 'Cicero during the Enlightenment', pp. 322–3.

76 George Mackenzie, *An Idea of the Modern Eloquence of the Bar. Together with a Pleading out of Every Part of Law. Written by Sir George MacKenzie . . . Translated into English* (Edinburgh, 1711), p. 47. Italics original. For another example of the presence of Verres and the *Verrines* within legal contexts, see also John Taylor, *Elements of the Civil Law* (Cambridge, 1755), p. 215: in this case, Cicero's *Verrinae* are mentioned as a text offering 'many notable Instances' of a corrupt *praetor*.

77 Miles, *Art as Plunder*, p. 291.
78 John Breval, *Remarks on Several Parts of Europe, Relating Chiefly to Their Antiquities and History Collected Upon the Spot in Several Tours Since the Year 1723; And Illustrated by Upward of Forty Copper Plates, from Original Drawings; Among Which Are the Ruins of Several Temples, Theatres, Amphitheatres, Triumphal Arches, and Other Unpublish'd Monuments of the greek and Roman Times, in Sicily, and the South of France*, 2 vols (London, 1738), i, pp. 13, 26. Italics original.
79 Edward Chaney, *The Evolution of the Grand Tour: Anglo-Italian Cultural Relations since the Renaissance* (London and Portland, OR, 1998), p. 32.
80 Patrick Brydone, *A Tour through Sicily and Malta. In a Series of Letters to William Beckford, Esq. of Somerly in Suffolk; from P. Brydone, F. R. S.*, 2 vols (London, 1773), i, p. 353.
81 Richard Payne Knight, *Expedition into Sicily*, ed. C. Stumpf (London, 1986), p. 43.
82 John Campbell, *The Travels of Edward Brown, Esq; Formerly a Merchant in London. Containing His Observations on France and Italy, his Voyage to the Levant; his Account of the Island of Malta; his Remarks in his Journies through the Lower and Upper Egypt; Together with a Brief Description of the Abyssinian Empire ...*, 2 vols (London, 1739), i, p. 186.

2 A Clash of Characters

1 Clements R. Markham, George Bogle, Thomas Manning, *Narratives of the Mission of George Bogle to Tibet, and of the Journey of Thomas Manning to Lhasa* (London, 1876), p. 30.
2 Ibid., p. 6.
3 Among the most recent biographies of Burke, see, in particular, Conor Cruise O'Brien, *The Great Melody: A Thematic Biography and Commented Anthology of Edmund Burke* (London, 1992); Nicholas K. Robinson, *Edmund Burke: A Life in Caricature* (New Haven, CT, and London, 1996) and F. P. Lock's very detailed *Edmund Burke, Volume One: 1730–1784* and *Volume Two: 1784–1797* (Oxford, 1998–2006). The numerous studies on the life of Hastings include: George Robert Gleig, *Memoirs of the Right Hon. Warren Hastings, First Governor-General of Bengal ...*, 3 vols (London, 1841), which incorporates Macaulay's *Memoirs of the Life of Warren Hastings, First Governor-General of Bengal*; Alfred Comyn Lyall, *Warren Hastings* (London, 1889); Lionel J. Trotter, *Warren Hastings* (London and Toronto, 1925); A. Mervyn Davis, *A Biography of Warren Hastings* (New York, 1935); Penderel Moon, *Warren Hastings and British India* (London, 1947); Keith Feiling, *Warren*

Hastings (New York, 1954); Jeremy Bernstein, *Dawning of the Raj: The Life and Trials of Warren Hastings* (Chicago, 2000). Hastings himself wrote a book about his Indian years, *Memoirs relative to the State of India* (London, 1786), as well as an account of his impeachment, *The History of the Trial of Warren Hastings, Esq. Late Governor General of Bengal*, [...] (London, 1796).

4 James Boswell, *The Journal of a Tour to the Hebrides, with Samuel Johnson, LL.D.*, [...] (London, 1785), p. 257.

5 Paddy Bullard, *Edmund Burke and the Art of Rhetoric* (Cambridge, 2011), p. 16.

6 Sir Philip Francis, *A Letter Missive from Sir Philip Francis K. B. to Lord Holland* (London, 1816), p. 17. Italics original. Part of this passage is quoted by Robert Murray, *Edmund Burke: A Biography* (Oxford, 1931), p. 36, n. 4. In a letter penned to Burke in 1793, even the king of Poland, Stanislaw II Augustus (1732–98), called Cicero 'one of the most illustrious models of your eloquence'. Edmund Burke, *The Correspondence of Edmund Burke*, ed. T. W. Copeland et al., 10 vols (Cambridge, 1958–78), vii, p. 375. The King of Poland to Edmund Burke (12 June 1793).

7 The portrait of Burke is part of an article titled 'Memoirs of the celebrated Edmund Burke, Esq. Member for Wendover in Buckinghamshire'. *London Magazine*, xxxix (April 1770), pp. 174–5.

8 Ibid., p. 174. David H. Solkin mentions and comments on this plate in his article on Wilson's landscape, 'The battle of the Ciceros: Richard Wilson and the politics of landscape in the age of John Wilkes', in S. Pugh (ed.), *Reading Landscape: Country – City – Capital* (Manchester, 1990), pp. 56–7.

9 See Phiroze Vasunia, 'Barbarism and civilization: political writing, history and empire', in N. Vance and J. Wallace (eds), *The Oxford History of Classical Reception in English Literature*, 4 vols (Oxford, 2015), iv, p. 135. James Zetzel observes that, in the *Reflections*, Burke cites numerous Ciceronian texts, 'including the *Somnium Scipionis, pro Sestio, de Legibus* and *de Senectute*'. See James Zetzel, 'Plato with Pillows', in D. Braund and C. Gill (eds), *Myth, History and Culture in Republican Rome: Studies in Honour of T. P. Wiseman* (Exeter, 2003), p. 136, n. 35. Extending over a period of more than fifty years, Burke's *Correspondence* appears to be very significant in this sense. Indeed, references to Cicero's works are quite copious. In particular, Burke mentions or quotes from *Pro Archia Poeta* (To Richard Shackleton and Richard Burke, Sr, 25, 31 July 1746, i, p. 69); *Epistulae and Orationes* (To Richard Shackleton, 21 March 1746-7, i, pp. 89–90); *Orationes De Officiis* (To Richard Shackleton, 5 December 1746, i, p. 74); *Ad Atticum* (To William Baker, 1 October 1771, ii, p. 243); *De Amicitia* (To Dr William Markham, post 9 November 1771, ii, p. 257); *De Senectute* (To Richard Shackleton, 15 October 1744, i, p. 32; To Sir Charles Bingham, 30 October 1773, ii, p. 481 and To Earl Fitzwilliam, 5 June 1791,

vi, p. 275); *Pro Plancio* (To Charles O'Hara, 11 December 1773, ii, p. 496); and *In Vatinium* (To William Windham, 16 October 1794, viii, p. 41).

10 I have relied on the two surviving catalogues of Burke's library, a printed sale catalogue, *Catalogue of the Library of the Late Right Honourable Edmund Burke* (1833), included in *Sale Catalogues of Libraries of Eminent Persons*, ed. A. N. L. Munby et al., 12 vols (London, 1971–5), viii, pp. 183–240 and an earlier manuscript shelf-list held by the Bodleian Library, Oxford, *Catalogue of a Library of Books Late the Property of the Rt. Hon. Ed. Burke dcsd, August 17 1813* (Bod. MS 16978). For a comment on the books possessed by Burke, see Carl B. Cone, 'Edmund Burke's library', *Bibliographical Society of America, Papers* 44 (1950), pp. 153–72.

11 Some scholars believe, instead, that Burke was born in County Cork. See Daniel I. O'Neill, *Edmund Burke and the Conservative Logic of Empire* (Oakland, CA, 2016), p. 124.

12 Basing his rigorous research on parish registers and other evidence, Lock has come to the conclusion that Burke was probably born in 1730. For an in-depth exploration of the subject, see Lock, *Edmund Burke*, i, pp. 16–17.

13 Ibid., p. 49.

14 Bullard, *Edmund Burke*, p. 68. For an overview of the presence of classical studies at Trinity College Dublin, see, in particular, M. L. Clarke, *Classical Education in Britain 1500–1900* (Cambridge, 1959), pp. 160–6; Bullard, *Edmund Burke*, pp. 68–70 and Christopher Reid, *Imprison'd Wranglers: The Rhetorical Culture of the House of Commons 1760–1800* (Oxford, 2012), pp. 128–9. For an in-depth analysis of the practice of rhetoric at Trinity College, see Jean Dietz Moss, '"Discordant Consensus": Old and new rhetoric at Trinity College, Dublin', *Rhetorica* xiv/4 (1996), pp. 383–441.

15 Burke, *Correspondence*, iv, p. 48. To William Jones (12 March 1779). Elsewhere the orator confessed: 'My knowledge of Greek was never perfect and critical'. See ibid., vii, p. 582. Appendix I, *Edmund Burke's Character of His Son and Brother*.

16 Ibid., iv, p. 48. To William Jones (12 March 1779).

17 Michael J. Franklin, 'Accessing India: orientalism, anti-"Indianism" and the rhetoric of Jones and Burke', in T. Fulford and P. J. Kitson (eds), *Romanticism and Colonialism: Writing and Empire, 1780–1830* (Cambridge, 1998), p. 48. For a survey of the relationships between Burke and Jones, see Garland Cannon, 'Sir William Jones and Edmund Burke', *Modern Philology* liv/3 (1957), pp. 165–86.

18 Edmund Burke, *The Writings and Speeches of Edmund Burke*, ed. P. Langford et al., 9 vols to date (Oxford, 1981–), i, pp. 187–8.

19 I derive this quotation from Carl B. Cone, *Burke and the Nature of Politics: The Age of the American Revolution*, 2 vols (Lexington, 1957–64), i, p. 162.

20 Donald Cross Bryant, 'The contemporary reception of Edmund Burke's speaking', in R. F. Howes (ed.), *Historical Studies of Rhetoric and Rhetoricians* (Ithaca, NY, 1961), p. 292. For an insightful overview of Burke's rhetoric, see Christopher Reid 'Burke as a rhetorician and orator', in D. Dwan and C. J. Insole (eds), *The Cambridge Companion to Edmund Burke* (Cambridge, 2012), pp. 41–52.

21 Cone, 'Edmund Burke's library', p. 154. For a general survey of the influence of British theatre on Burke, see, among others, Paul Hindson and Tim Gray, *Burke's Dramatic Theory of Politics* (Aldershot, 1988), in particular pp. 6–8 and Lia Guerra, '"The great theatre of the world": Edmund Burke's dramatic perspective', in L. M. Crisafulli and C. Pietropoli (eds), *The Language of Performance in British Romanticism* (Bern, 2008), pp. 195–9. Notably, Burke's *Reflections on the Revolution in France* (1790) is pervaded by references to the theatre. Among the rich critical literature that explores the relationship between the orator's theatrical style and his counterrevolutionary argument, see, for example, Christopher Reid, 'Burke's tragic muse: Sarah Siddons and the "feminization" of the *Reflections*', in S. Blakemore (ed.), *Burke and the French Revolution: Bicentennial Essays* (Athens, GA, and London, 1992), pp. 1–27; Frans De Bruyn, 'Theater and counter-theater in Burke's *Reflections on the Revolution in France*', in R. DeMaria (ed.), *British Literature 1640–1789: A Critical Reader* (Oxford, 1999), pp. 271–86 and Anne Mallory, 'Burke, boredom, and the theater of counterrevolution', *PMLA* cxviii/2 (2003), pp. 224–38.

22 See Bullard, *Edmund Burke*, p. 20.

23 For a discussion of this famous scene and how it was represented by contemporaries, see, among others, Gillian Russell, 'Burke's dagger: theatricality, politics and print culture in the 1790s', *British Journal for Eighteenth-Century Studies* xx (1997), pp. 1–16; Bullard, *Edmund Burke*, pp. 20–1 and Reid, *Imprison'd Wranglers*, p. 227.

24 Ian Haywood, *Bloody Romanticism: Spectacular Violence and the Politics of Representation, 1776–1832* (Basingstoke, 2006), pp. 141–2.

25 I borrow this expression from Robert W. Jones, *Literature, Gender and Politics in Britain during the War for America 1770–1785* (Cambridge, 2011), p. 72.

26 Burke, *Writing and Speeches*, iii, p. 356.

27 Haywood, *Bloody Romanticism*, p. 157.

28 Burke, *Writing and Speeches*, iii, p. 356.

29 Ibid., p. 358.

30 Ibid., p. 361.

31 Ibid., p. 358.

32 Burke, *Writing and Speeches*, iii, pp. 363–4.

33 See Luke Gibbons, *Edmund Burke and Ireland: Aesthetics, Politics and the Colonial Sublime* (Cambridge, 2003), p. 183. Gibbons offers a detailed analysis of the McCrea episode; see pp. 183–93.

34 Burke, *Writing and Speeches*, vi, p. 421.
35 I take this comment from Paul Langford, 'Burke, Edmund (1729/30–1797)', in *Oxford Dictionary of National Biography*.
36 Langford, 'Burke, Edmund (1729/30–1797)'.
37 Cone, 'Edmund Burke's library', p. 165.
38 Other texts on the Indian subcontinent and the relationship between Britain and India included in the catalogue of sale of Burke's library are: Maurice's *Indian Antiquities* (no date is provided); *On Indian Stock* (1764–6) by Lord Clive and Johnstone; Ives's *Voyage from England to India* (1773); Macpherson's *History of the East India Company* (1779); *Reports Relative to the Affairs in India* (1781); *Debates on the East India Bill* (1784); *Debates on Pitt's East India Bill* (1784); *Papers Relating to the Nabob of Arcot and Rajah of Tanjore* (1785); *Transactions in India* (1786); *Correspondence in India between the Country Powers and East India Company* (1787); Raynal's *History of the East and West Indies, by Justamond* (1788); and *Manuscript Papers Relating to India. Proceedings of the Governor-General and Council in Consequence of the Insurrection at Rungpore* (no date is provided). See *Sale Catalogues of Libraries of Eminent Persons*, viii, pp. 183–240 and *Catalogue of a Library of Books Late the Property of the Rt. Hon. Ed. Burke*.
39 Burke, *Writings and Speeches*, vi, p. 20. Burke's detailed speech on the wide diversities among Indian cultures and religions performed on the first day of his 'Speech on the Opening of the Impeachment' attests to the Anglo-Irish orator's avid interest in India. See ibid., pp. 300–12.
40 For a discussion of Burke's devotion to the interests of Indians, see, in particular, P. J. Marshall, *The Impeachment of Warren Hastings* (Oxford, 1965), pp. 186–7.
41 Frederick G. Whelan, *Edmund Burke and India: Political Morality and Empire* (Pittsburgh, PA, 1996), p. 303. Among the vast number of studies exploring the deep affinities between Burke's and Cicero's political thought, see, in particular, Leo Strauss, *Natural Right and History* (Chicago and London, 1953), pp. 295; 321; Reed Browning, 'The origin of Burke's ideas revisited', *Eighteenth-Century Studies* xviii/1 (1984), pp. 57–71 and Iain Hampsher-Monk, 'Rhetoric and opinion in the politics of Edmund Burke', *History of Political Thought* ix (1988), pp. 455–84 (p. 459). More recently, Gary Remer has studied Cicero's anticipation of modern representation in the writings of theorists of political representation, including Burke. See Gary Remer, 'The classical orator as political representative: Cicero and the modern concept of representation', *The Journal of Politics* lxxii/4 (2010), pp. 1063–82 (in particular, pp. 1073–6).
42 Peter J. Stanlis, *Edmund Burke and the Natural Law* (Ann Arbor, MI, 1958), p. 36.
43 Burke, *Writings and Speeches*, vi, p. 350.
44 Ibid., p. 268.

45 Ibid.
46 Ibid., pp. 346; 350; 28.
47 This resemblance has been noted by H. V. Canter: see H. V. Canter, 'The impeachment of Verres and Hastings: Cicero and Burke', *The Classical Journal* ix (1914), pp. 199–211 (p. 209). For a definition of 'geographical morality', see Jennifer Pitts, *A Turn to Empire: The Rise of Imperial Liberalism in Britain and France* (Princeton, NJ, and Oxford, 2005), p. 77.
48 Burke, *Writings and Speeches*, vi, p. 346.
49 Cicero is referring here to Verres's unjust promulgation of edicts governing inheritances. Marcus Tullius Cicero, *The Verrine Orations*, trans. L. H. G. Greenwood, 2 vols (London and Cambridge, MA, 1966).
50 Marshall, *The Impeachment of Warren Hastings*, p. 13.
51 Bullard, *Edmund Burke*, p. 141.
52 Burke, *Correspondence*, vi, p. 46. To Charles-Jean-François Depont (November 1789).
53 *Remarks on the Policy of the Allies with Respect to France* (1793), in Burke, *Writings and Speeches*, viii, p. 461.
54 Quoted in O'Brien, *The Great Melody*, p. 431.
55 F. P. Lock, 'Burke's life' in D. Dwan and C. J. Insole (eds), *The Cambridge Companion to Edmund Burke* (Cambridge, 2012), p. 24.
56 For an overview of the caricatures of Burke and his *Reflections*, see Nicholas K. Robinson, *Edmund Burke*, pp. 136–70.
57 Burke, *Correspondence*, vi, p. 183. Pierre Gaëton Dupont to Edmund Burke (30 November 1790). For a fuller discussion of the contemporary reception of Burke's *Reflections*, see, in particular, F. P. Lock, *Burke's Reflections on the Revolution in France* (London, 1985), pp. 132–65.
58 See Walter Sichel, *Sheridan* (Boston and New York, 1909), p. 404.
59 Andrew Rudd, *Sympathy and India in British Literature, 1770–1830* (Basingstoke, 2011), p. 26.
60 For a comment on the expensive garments worn by Hastings in his 1766–8 portrait, see Aileen Ribeiro, *The Gallery of Fashion* (Princeton, NJ, 2000), p. 124.
61 Hermione De Almeida and George H. Gilpin, *Indian Renaissance: British Romantic Art and the Prospect of India* (Aldershot and Burlington, VT, 2005), p. 110.
62 P. J. Marshall, 'Hastings, Warren (1732–1818)', in *Oxford Dictionary of National Biography*.
63 According to the sale catalogue of Hastings's, library, his collection of Latin authors included: Cicero's *Orationes* (1684); Horace's *Art of Poetry* (1783); *Horace Translated by Boscawen* (1795); *Works of Horace, translated into Prose* (1787); *Lucani Pharsalia* (1760); *Terentius, accesserunt variae Lectiones* (1751); *Terence's Comedies* (1768);

Virgil Translated into Blank Verse (1794); *Virgilius, a Heyne* (1793); *Virgil's Works, Translated by Warton* (1778); *Virgile, par Delille* (1804). See *Sale Catalogues of Libraries of Eminent Persons*, viii, pp. 243–76.

64 See Bernstein, *Dawning of the Raj*, p. 56.
65 As P. J. Marshall explains, the fortune amassed by the Governor-General of Bengal was not large, but still a sizable one. Hastings lost most of his fortune 'by his generosity, carelessness and extravagance'. P. J. Marshall, 'The personal fortune of Warren Hastings', *The Economic History Review* xvii/2 (1964), pp. 284–300 (p. 299). At the end of the trial, in 1795, Hastings pleaded poverty. In spite of the annuity granted to him by the East India Company, he left at his death several debts unpaid.
66 Bernard S. Cohn, *Colonialism and its Forms of Knowledge: The British in India* (Princeton, NJ, 1996), p. 24.
67 The sketch is mentioned in P. J. Marshall, 'Hastings, Warren (1732–1818)', in *Oxford Dictionary of National Biography*.
68 De Almeida and Gilpin, *Indian Renaissance*, p. 109.
69 See P. J. Marshall, 'The making of an imperial icon: the case of Warren Hastings', *Journal of Imperial and Commonwealth History* xxvii/3 (1999), pp. 1–16 (pp. 7–8); Sudipta Sen, 'Imperial subjects on trial: on the legal identity of Britons in late eighteenth-century India', *Journal of British Studies* xlv/3 (2006), pp. 532–55 (p. 544); and Michael S. Dodson, *Orientalism, Empire, and National Culture: India 1770–1880* (Basingstoke, 2007), p. 20.
70 P. J. Marshall, 'Warren Hastings as scholar and patron', in A. Whiteman, J. S. Bromley and P. G. M. Dickson (eds), *Statesmen, Scholars and Merchants: Essays in Eighteenth-Century Literature presented to Dame Lucy Sutherland* (Oxford, 1973), p. 246.
71 Feiling, *Warren Hastings*, p. 236. See also S. N. Mukherjee, *Sir William Jones: A Study in Eighteenth-Century British Attitudes to India* (London, 1987), p. 73.
72 Nathaniel Brassey Halhed, *A Code of Gentoo Laws, or, Ordinations of the Pundits, from a Persian Translation, Made from the Original, Written in the Shanscrit* [sic] *Language* (London, 1776), pp. ix–x.
73 Quoted in Cohn, *Colonialism and Its Forms of Knowledge*, p. 70.
74 Quoted in Phiroze Vasunia, *The Classics and Colonial India* (Oxford, 2013), p. 3.
75 Ibid.
76 Mukherjee, *Sir William Jones*, p. 73.
77 Charles Wilkins, *The Bhagvat-Geeta, or Dialogues of Kreeshna and Arjoon; in Eighteen Lectures; with Notes* (London, 1785), p. 10. The quotation is taken from a letter that Hastings wrote to Nathaniel Smith, Chairman of the East India Company, dated 4 October 1784. For an in-depth analysis of Hastings's letter, see, among others, De Almeida and Gilpin, *Indian Renaissance*, pp. 112–14 and Vasunia, *Classics and Colonial India*, p. 243.

78 Jones's study of Sanskrit and his formulation of the Indo-European family of languages is well documented. See, for example, Garland Cannon, *The Life and Mind of Oriental Jones: Sir William Jones, the Father of Modern Linguistics* (Cambridge, 1990), pp. 241–70; Javed Majeed, *Ungoverned Imaginings: James Mill's The History of British India and Orientalism* (Oxford, 1992), pp. 12–16; Michael J. Franklin, *Orientalist Jones: Sir William Jones, Poet, Lawyer, and Linguist, 1746–1794* (Oxford, 2011), pp. 1–42.

79 Jones asserted the linguistic ascendancy of Sanskrit, as well as its affinity with Greek and Latin, in his 'Third Anniversary Discourse' to the Asiatick Society (2 February 1786). See Majeed, *Ungoverned Imaginings*, p. 13.

80 Vasunia, *Classics and Colonial India*, p. 17. The citation is from Thomas R. Trautmann, quoted in ibid.

81 See Burke, *Writings and Speeches*, vi, pp. 79–91.

82 Ibid., p. 106.

83 For a discussion of the tensions between Hastings and Francis, see, in particular, Nicholas B. Dirks, *The Scandal of Empire: India and the Creation of Imperial Britain* (Cambridge, MA, and London, 2006), pp. 94–100.

3 Classical Oratory and Theatricality in the Trial against Warren Hastings

1 *The Times* (13 February 1788).
2 Ibid.
3 Daniel O'Quinn, *Staging Governance: Theatrical Imperialism in London 1700–1800* (Baltimore, MD, 2005), p. 168.
4 For an overview of Lady Charlotte Schreiber's fans and fan-leaves collection, see, in particular, Lionel Cust, *Catalogue of the Collection of Fans and Fan-leaves Presented to the British Museum by Lady Charlotte Schreiber* (London, 1893) and Charlotte Schreiber, *Fans and Fan-leaves – English, Collected and Described by Lady Charlotte Schreiber*, 2 vols (London, 1888).
5 MacIver Percival, *The Fan Book* (New York, 1921), p. 110.
6 Nicholas B. Dirks, *The Scandal of Empire: India and the Creation of Imperial Britain* (Cambridge, MA, and London, 2006), p. 87.
7 Glynis Ridley, 'Sheridan's courtroom dramas: the impeachment of Warren Hastings and the trial of the *Bounty* mutineers', in J. E. Derochi and D. J. Ennis (eds), *Richard Brinsley Sheridan: The Impresario in Political and Cultural Context* (Lewisburg, PA, 2013), p. 178.

8 See, for instance, Siraj Ahmed, 'The theater of the civilized self: Edmund Burke and the East India trials', *Representations*, lxxviii (2002), pp. 28–55; Anna Clark, *Scandal: The Sexual Politics of the British Constitution* (Princeton, NJ, 2004), pp. 84–112; Dirks, *The Scandal of Empire*, pp. 87–131; O'Quinn, *Staging Governance*, pp. 164–257; Jennifer Pitts, *A Turn to Empire: The Rise of Imperial Liberalism in Britain and France* (Princeton, NJ, 2005), pp. 74–5; Ridley, 'Sheridan's courtroom dramas', pp. 177–90; Julie Stone Peters, 'Theatricality, legalism, and the scenography of suffering: the trial of Warren Hastings and Richard Brinsley Sheridan's *Pizarro*', *Law and Literature*, xviii (2006), pp. 15–45.

9 Lock has calculated that temporary stands could hold around 2,000 people. See F. P. Lock, *Edmund Burke, Volume One: 1730–1784* and *Volume Two: 1784–1797* (Oxford, 1998–2006), ii, pp. 149; 189, n. 136. This was not the first time that temporary stands had been constructed. The Office of Works, which built the wooden structure inside Westminster Hall, followed plans used on previous occasions.

10 Gilbert Elliot, *Life and Letters of Sir Gilbert Elliot*, ed. The Countess of Minto, 3 vols (London, 1874), i, p. 193. To Lady Elliot (13 February 1788).

11 Gerald Campbell, *Edward and Pamela Fitzgerald; Being Some Account of their Lives, Compiled from the Letters of Those Who Knew Them* (London, 1904), p. 41. The diary of Lady Sophia Fitzgerald is quoted by Lock, *Edmund Burke*, ii, p. 190.

12 Eddy Kent, *Corporate Character: Representing Imperial Power in British India, 1786–1901* (Toronto, 2014), p. 44. Similar solemn processions into Westminster Hall had been held on the occasion of previous trials, such as that of Lawrence Earl Ferrers (1720–60) in 1760, and that of William Lord Byron, Baron Byron of Rochdale (1722–98) in 1765. For a detailed description of these processions, see Thomas Bayly Howell et al., *A Complete Collection of State Trial and Proceedings for High Treason and Other Crimes and Misdemeanors from the Earliest Period to the Present Time*, 21 vols (London, 1816), xix, pp. 885–7 and 1177–8 respectively.

13 *London Chronicle* (13 February 1788). Quoted in Kent, *Corporate Character*, pp. 44–5. The *London Chronicle*'s account appears almost verbatim in Warren Hastings's *The History of the Trial of Warren Hastings, Esq. Late Governor General of Bengal* (London, 1796), Part I, pp. 1–2.

14 *The Gentleman's Magazine: and Historical Chronicle. For the Year MDCCXCIX. Volume LXIX. Part the First* (London, 1799), p. 76.

15 *The Times* (14 February 1788).

16 *Morning Post and Daily Advertiser* (14 February 1788). Emphasis original.

17 Elizabeth D. Samet, 'A prosecutor and a gentleman: Edmund Burke's idiom of impeachment', *ELH* lxviii/2 (2001), pp. 397–418. For extensive comments on the importance of Burney's diary to understand the theatrical atmosphere of the impeachment, see also Betsy Bolton, 'Imperial sensibilities, colonial ambivalence:

Edmund Burke and Frances Burney', *ELH* lxxii/4 (2005), pp. 871–99 and O'Quinn, *Staging Governance*, pp. 222–57.
18 Frances Burney, *Diary and Letters of Madame D'Arblay*, ed. C. Barrett, 7 vols (London, 1842–6), iv, p. 63.
19 Jean Marsden, 'Shakespeare and sympathy', in P. Sabor and P. Yachnin (eds), *Shakespeare and the Eighteenth Century* (Aldershot, 2008), p. 33.
20 James Boaden, *Memoirs of the Life of John Philip Kemble*, 2 vols (Philadelphia, 1825), i, p. 80.
21 Jeffrey N. Cox, 'Spots of time: the structure of the dramatic evening in the theater of Romanticism', *Texas Studies in Literature and Language* xvi (1999), pp. 403–25 (p. 405).
22 Burney, *Diary and Letters*, iv, p. 84.
23 See Lock, *Edmund Burke*, ii, pp. 149–50.
24 Catherine Eagleton, *The Collections of Sarah Sophia Banks* (Annual Lecture 2013, Sir Joseph Banks Society). Available at http://www.joseph-banks.org.uk/members/research-papers/annual-lecture-2013/ (accessed 13 January 2017). Besides a substantial collection of printed ephemera, Miss Banks assembled a significant numismatic collection. For an overview of the latter, see Catherine Eagleton, 'Collecting African money in Georgian London: Sarah Sophia Banks and her collection of coins', *Museum History Journal* vi/1 (2013), pp. 23–38. For a survey of Miss Banks's collecting practices, see Arlene Leis, 'Cutting, arranging, and pasting: Sarah Sophia Banks as collector', *Early Modern Women: An Interdisciplinary Journal* ix/1 (2014), pp. 127–40.
25 Anthony Pincott, 'The book tickets of Miss Sarah Sophia Banks (1744–1818)', *The Bookplate Journal*, II/1 (March 2004), pp. 3–30 (p. 13). Although it focuses on Miss Banks's collection of book tickets, Pincott's article also offers an excellent overview of Sarah Sophia's life and her collecting interests.
26 *St. James's Chronicle: or, British Evening Post* (16–19 February 1788).
27 *London Chronicle* (12–14 February 1788).
28 In the tickets collected by Sarah Sophia we read, for example, the names of Hampden (BM J,9.36), Cardiff (BM J,9.39), Jersey (BM J,9.71) and Stanhope (BM J,9.79).
29 The practice of changing tickets 'in colour as well as in the form of the engraving, so that forgery is rendered impracticable' is confirmed by a report in the *Gazetteer and New Daily Advertiser* (20 February 1788).
30 See Tillman W. Nechtman, *Nabobs: Empire and Identity in Eighteenth-Century Britain* (Cambridge, 2010), p. 105, n. 38.
31 Edmund Burke, *The Correspondence of Edmund Burke*, ed. T. W. Copeland et al., 10 vols (Cambridge, 1958–78), v, p. 380. To Sir Peter Burrell (February 1788).
32 *Gazetteer and New Daily Advertiser* (20 February 1788).

33 For a detailed description of James Sayers's *For the Trial of Warren Ha[stings]/ Seventh Day* and James Gillray's *Impeachment ticket. For the trial of W-RR-NH-ST-NGS Esqr*, see Lock, *Edmund Burke*, ii, p. 150 and Nicholas K. Robinson, *Edmund Burke: A Life in Caricature* (New Haven, CT, and London, 1996), p. 101. See also the British Museum online description and curator's comments. Available at http://www.britishmuseum.org/research/collection_online/collection_object_details.aspx?objectId=1627140&partId=1&searchText=impeachment%20ticket (accessed 16 January 2016) and http://www.britishmuseum.org/research/collection_online/collection_object_details.aspx?objectId=1461440&partId=1&searchText=james+sayers+ticket&page=1 (accessed 16 January 2016), for Gillray's print and Sayer's parody respectively.
34 *The World* (19 February 1788). Italics original.
35 Lock, *Edmund Burke*, ii, p. 150.
36 Burke, *Correspondence*, v, p. 380. To Sir Peter Burrell (February 1788). Burke's letter to Burrell is mentioned by Locke, *Edmund Burke*, ii, p. 150, n. 27.
37 Ibid.
38 Jeffrey N. Cox, 'Spots of time', p. 411.
39 Sophie von La Roche, *Sophie in London, 1786; Being the Diary of Sophie v. la Roche. Translated from the German, with an Introductory Essay, by Clare Williams. With a Foreword by G.M. Trevelyan* (London, 1933), p. 133.
40 BM J,9.1; BM J,9.2; BM J,9.3; BM J,9.4; BM J,9.5. The hand that wrote the annotations added on BM J,9.3 is definitely neither that of Sir William, nor that of Sarah Sophia. The other tickets bear no inscription. As with official passes, also the tickets to enter the box of Sir William Chambers were printed in different colours: green (BM J,9.1), blue (BM J,9.2; BM J,9.3; BM J,9.4) and brown (BM J,9.5).
41 In 1770, Sir William Chambers was appointed *riddare* (knight) of the order of the Polar Star by Gustav III of Sweden. Consequently, George III permitted Sir William to adopt the address of English knighthood.
42 Or so it seems, for on the back of a ticket bearing the inscription 'Great Chamberlains Box' (BM J,9.20), Sarah Sophia added the date 'Feb. 12. 1788'. Peeresses and their daughters only were entitled to seats in Westminster Hall (later this prerogative was extended also to the wives of the eldest sons of peers). Miss Banks did not enjoy this privilege, nor did Lady Banks, as Sir Joseph was not a member of the Lords.
43 On the back of this ticket Sarah Sophia wrote: 'Feb. 12. 1788'. Presumably, the ticket was given to Sir Joseph on that day.
44 Burney, *Diary and Letters*, iv, p. 110.
45 William Eden, *The Journal and Correspondence of William, Lord Auckland*, 2 vols (London, 1861), i, p. 469. Mr. Storer to Mr. Eden (22 February 1788).
46 Elliot, *Life and Letters*, i, p. 205. To Lady Elliot (3 June 1788).

47 Ibid.
48 Ibid., p. 197. To Lady Elliot (3 March 1788).
49 Nicoll Allardyce, *The Garrick Stage* (Manchester, 1980), p. 82.
50 'The worst crush of the century' – White continues – 'was at the Little Theatre in February 1794. Fifteen died when someone tripped descending a staircase to the pit'. Jerry White, *London in the Eighteenth Century: A Great and Monstrous Thing* (London, 2012), pp. 308–9.
51 *London Chronicle* (3–5 June 1788).
52 Elliot, *Life and Letters*, i, p. 206. To Lady Elliot (3 June 1788).
53 *Letters Written by the Late Right Honourable Philip Dormer Stanhope, Earl of Chesterfield, to His Son; with Some Account of His Life*, 4 vols (London, 1815), i (8 February 1746), p. 284.
54 Paddy Bullard, 'Rhetoric and eloquence: the language of persuasion', in J. A. Harris (ed.), *The Oxford Handbook of British Philosophy in the Eighteenth Century* (Oxford, 2013), p. 92.
55 This translation is provided in a footnote.
56 Joseph Addison, *The Spectator*, ed. D. F. Bond, 5 vols (Oxford, 1965), iii, p. 522.
57 David Hume, *Essays, Moral, Political, and Literary* (Edinburgh, 1742), I.XIII.19.
58 Ibid., I.XIII.2; I.XIII.6. For a thorough discussion of this essay, see, in particular, Adam Potkay, *The Fate of Eloquence in the Age of Hume* (Ithaca, NY, 1994), pp. 24–30.
59 Paul Goring, *The Rhetoric of Sensibility in Eighteenth-Century Culture* (Cambridge, 2005), p. 38. Italics original. For a recent survey of the rhetorical treatises and cultural practices that constituted the elocutionary movement see also Paul Goring, 'The elocutionary movement in Britain', in M. J. MacDonald (ed.), *The Oxford Handbook of Rhetorical Studies* (Oxford, 2017).
60 James Burgh, *The Art of Speaking* (London, 1761), p. 2. Italics original. Burgh's detailed manual had eight English and ten American editions. For a comment on this text, see Peter De Bolla, *The Discourse of the Sublime: Readings in History, Aesthetics and the Subject* (Oxford, 1989), p. 159.
61 John Ward, *A System of Oratory, Delivered in a Course of Lectures Publicly Read at Gresham College, London*, 2 vols (London, 1759), ii, 334.
62 Classical rhetoric has been the subject of innumerable publications. As far as Roman eloquence is concerned, an overview may be found in *Roman Eloquence: Rhetoric in Society and Literature*, ed. W. J. Dominik (London and New York, 1997); Joy Connolly, *The State of Speech: Rhetoric and Political Thought in Ancient Rome* (Princeton, NJ, and Oxford, 2007); *Form and Function in Roman Oratory*, ed. D. H. Berry and A. Erskine (Cambridge, 2010); Catherine Steel, *Roman Oratory* (Cambridge, 2006); M. L. Clarke, *Rhetoric at Rome: A Historical Survey* (London, 1953), George Alexander

Kennedy, *The Art of Rhetoric in the Roman World* (Princeton, NJ, 1972); *A Companion to Roman Rhetoric*, ed. W. Dominik and J. Hall (Oxford, 2007).

63 The best commentary on Cicero's *De Oratore* is still Anron D. Leeman, Harm Pinkster (and others), *M. T. Cicero. De Oratore libri III. Kommentar*, 5 vols (Heidelberg, 1981-2008). A selection of the rich bibliography on *De Oratore* includes: James M. May, *Trials of Character: The Eloquence of Ciceronian Ethos* (Chapel Hill, NC, and London, 1988); Elaine Fantham, *The Roman World of Cicero's De Oratore* (Oxford, 2004); Marcus Tullius Cicero, *Cicero. On the Ideal Orator (De Oratore)*, ed. and trans. J. M. May and J. Wisse (New York and Oxford, 2001); Jon Hall, 'Persuasive design in Cicero's *De Oratore*', *Phoenix* xlviii/3 (1994), pp. 210-25.

64 For a detailed discussion of this acclaimed speech, see, in particular, Lock, *Edmund Burke*, ii, pp. 114-18 and P. J. Marshall, *The Impeachment of Warren Hastings* (Oxford, 1965), pp. 52-3.

65 *Additional Supplement to the Calcutta Gazette* (21 June 1787).

66 George Gordon Byron, *Lord Byron's Letters and Journals*, ed. L. A. Marchand, 13 vols (London, 1973-94), iii, p. 239 (17, 18 December 1813).

67 Sara Suleri, *The Rhetoric of English India* (Chicago and London, 1992), pp. 53-4. According to Lock, this inordinate price is not believable. See Lock, *Edmund Burke*, ii, p. 190, n. 137. Sir Gilbert Elliot gives the more credible sum of twenty-five guineas. See Elliot, *Life and Letters*, i, p. 204. To Lady Elliot (28 May 1788).

68 Ibid., pp. 204-5. To Lady Elliot (2 June 1788).

69 The letter is dated 25 April 1788 but was published in *The World* issue for 14 May 1788. Emphasis in the original. Burke himself wrote to Sir Peter Burrell to request 'two or three Tickets for Sheridans [sic] day, in addition to my personal Stock'. See Burke, *Correspondence*, v, p. 401. To Sir Peter Burrell (ante 3 June 1788).

70 Christopher Reid, *Edmund Burke and the Practice of Political Writing* (Dublin, 1985), p. 98.

71 Ibid.

72 Thomas Moore, *Memoirs of the Life of the Right Honourable Richard Brinsley Sheridan*, 2 vols (London, 1825), i, p. 452. For Sheridan's resistance to the commercial circulation of his speeches and writings, see Frank Donoghue, 'Avoiding the "cooler tribunal of the study": Richard Brinsley Sheridan's writer's block and late eighteenth-century print culture', *ELH* lxviii/4 (2001), pp. 831-56.

73 See, for example, James M. May, 'Ciceronian oratory in context', in J. M. May (ed.), *Brill's Companion to Cicero: Oratory and Rhetoric* (Leiden, 2002), p. 59. For the close similarities existent between orators and actors, see in particular *De Orat*. I.18; I.118; I.125; I.128-9; I.156; I.251; II.242; II.244; II.251-2; III. 83. Marcus Tullius Cicero, *De Oratore*, trans. E. W. Sutton, 2 vols (London and Cambridge, MA, 1959). *Brut*. 290. Marcus Tullius Cicero, *Brutus*, trans. G. L. Hendrickson, *Orator*,

trans. H. M. Hubbell (London and Cambridge, MA, 1962). *Inst.* I.11.1–3. Marcus Fabius Quintilian, *The Orator's Education*, ed. and trans. D. A. Russell, (Cambridge, MA, and London, 2001). Unless otherwise stated, further references to Cicero's and Quintilian's texts, as well as their translation into English, are to these editions.

74 *Orat.* I.156. The translation is mine. In his account of Cicero's life, Plutarch stresses how both the great Roman orator as well as his Greek counterpart, Demosthenes, had frequently turned to theatre. See Plutarch's *Life of Cicero*, 4–6. Similarities between orators and actors in ancient Rome have been discussed by numerous scholars. Cicero's familiarity with drama is amply demonstrated by numerous references with which his corpus abounds. For references to theatre and drama, see Frederick Warren Wright, *Cicero and the Theater* (Northampton, MA, 1931); Emanuele Narducci, *Cicerone e l'eloquenza romana: Retorica e progetto culturale* (Rome and Bari, 1997), pp. 82–7 and Alberto Cavarzere, *Gli arcani dell'oratore: alcuni appunti sull'actio dei Romani* (Rome and Padua, 2011), pp. 126–41. For comedy, in particular, see Jerzy Axer, *The Style and the Composition of Cicero's Speech 'Pro Q. Roscio Comoedo': Origin and Function* (Warsaw, 1979); Katherine A. Geffcken, *Comedy in the Pro Caelio, with an Appendix on the In Clodium et Curionem* (Leiden, 1973); Ann Vasaly, 'The masks of rhetoric: Cicero's *Pro Roscio Amerino*', *Rhetorica* iii (1985), pp. 1–20; Joseph J. Hughes, *Comedic Borrowing in Selected Orations of Cicero* (Ph.D. Diss. University of Iowa, 1987) and Joseph J. Hughes, '*Inter tribunal and scaenam*: comedy and rhetoric in Rome', in W. J. Dominik (ed.), *Roman Eloquence*, pp. 182–97.

75 See William Batstone, 'The drama of rhetoric at Rome', in E. Gunderson (ed.), *The Cambridge Companion to Ancient Rhetoric* (Cambridge, 2009), p. 212.

76 Ibid.

77 *Inst.* VI.2.35: *Vidi ego saepe histriones atque comoedos, cum ex aliquo graviore actu personam deposuissent, flentes adhuc egredi. Quod si in alienis scriptis sola pronuntiatio ita falsis accendit adfectibus, quid nos faciemus, qui illa cogitare debemus ut moveri periclitantium vice possimus?* Emphasis in the original translation.

78 *De Orat.* III.56.214.

79 '...when the speaker rises the whole throng will give a sign for silence, then expressions of assent, frequent applause; laughter when he wills it, or if he wills, tears; so that a mere passer-by observing from a distance, though quite ignorant of the case in question, will recognize that he is succeeding and that a Roscius is on the stage' (*Brut.* 290: ... *cum surgat is qui dicturus sit, significetur a corona silentium, deinde crebrae assensiones, multae admirationes; risus cum velit, cum velit fletus, ut qui haec procul videat, etiam si quid agat nesciat, at placere tamen et in scaena esse Roscium intellegat*).

80 Stone Peters, 'Theatricality, legalism, and the scenography of suffering', p. 27. Commenting on the *Letters from Simpkin*, Stone Peters notes that 'Rather than

causing the audience to mistake theater for reality (as the truly artful actor does), the managers have caused the audience disturbingly to mistake reality for theater'. Ibid., p. 27.
81 Ralph Broome, *Letters from Simpkin the Second to his Dear Brother in Wales, Containing an Humble Description of the Trial of Warren Hastings, Esq. From the Commencement to the Close of the Sessions in 1789* (London, 1789), p. 19. Emphasis original.
82 Ibid., p. 7. Emphasis original.
83 Jay Fliegelman, *Declaring Independence: Jefferson, Natural Language, and the Culture of Performance* (Stanford, CA, 1993), p. 81.
84 John Hill, *The Actor: A Treatise on the Art of Playing* (London, 1750), p. 106. Emphasis in the original. Horace's prescription is in the *Ars Poetica* 102–3: 'If you would have me weep, you must first feel grief yourself' (*si vis me flere, dolendum est | primum ipsi tibi*). Horace, *Satires, Epistles and Ars Poetica*, trans. H. Rushton Fairclough (London and Cambridge, MA, 1966), pp. 458–9. An admirably detailed commentary on the *Ars Poetica* is still C. O. Brink, *Horace on Poetry: The 'Ars Poetica'* (Cambridge, 1971). For an overview of the vast bibliography on the *Ars Poetica*, see Andrew Laird, 'The *Ars Poetica*', in S. Harrison (ed.), *The Cambridge Companion to Horace* (Cambridge, 2007), p. 143. For a discussion of the reception of the *Ars Poetica*, see Leon Golden, 'Reception of Horace's *Ars Poetica*', in G. Davis (ed.), *A Companion to Horace* (Oxford, 2010), pp. 391–413.
85 Hugh Blair, *Lectures on Rhetoric and Belles Lettres*, ed. L. Ferreira-Buckley and S. M. Halloran (Carbondale, IL, 2005), p. 361.
86 Ibid., p. 363.
87 Marshall, *The Impeachment of Warren Hastings*, p. 141. For an overview of the prosecution of Sir Elijah Impey, see ibid., pp. 60–2; 132–42.
88 Burke, *Correspondence*, v, pp. 368–9. To Lady Elliot (13 December 1787). For a recent comment on this passage, see Richard Bourke, *Empire and Revolution: The Political Life of Edmund Burke* (Princeton, NJ, 2015), p. 673.
89 Elliot, *Life and Letters*, i, p. 177. To Lady Elliot (13 December 1787). Italics original.
90 *De Orat.* II.188. See also Quintilian, *Inst.* VI.2.26: 'The heart of the matter as regards arousing emotions, so far as I can see, lies in being moved by them oneself' (*Summa, enim, quantum ego quidem sentio, circa movendos adfectus in hoc posita est, ut moveamur ipsi*).
91 *De Orat.* II.190: *Ut enim nulla materies tam facilis ad exardescendum est, quae nisi admoto igni ignem conciper possit, sic nulla mens est tam ad comprehendendam vim oratoris parata, quae possit incendi, nisi ipse inflammatus ad eam et ardens accesserit.* See also, for example, *Orat.* 132: 'and I am sure that the audience would never be set on fire unless the words that reached him were fiery' (*nec unquam is qui audiret incenderetur, nisi ardens ad eum perveniret oratio*).

92   A fuller discussion of Sir Gilbert reading Sheridan may be found in David Francis Taylor, *Theatres of Opposition: Empire, Revolution, and Richard Brinsley Sheridan* (Oxford, 2012), pp. 82–8.
93   Elliot, *Life and Letters*, i, pp. 208; 210. To Lady Elliot (5 June 1788).
94   Ibid., pp. 208–9. Italics original.
95   *Speeches of the Managers and Counsel in the Trial of Warren Hastings*, ed. E. Bond, 4 vols (London, 1859–61), i, pp. 493–4. Emphasis added.
96   For an in-depth analysis of this passage, see, in particular, Taylor, *Theatres of Opposition*, pp. 100–1.
97   Elliot, *Life and Letters*, i, p. 209. To Lady Elliot (5 June 1788).
98   Ibid., p. 214. To Lady Elliot (7 June 1788).
99   Ibid., p. 213.
100 *Speeches of the Managers and Counsel in the Trial of Warren Hastings*, i, p. 562. Emphasis added.
101 Elliot does not mention Sheridan's third oration. After speaking for almost two and a half hours, Sheridan was taken ill. As a result, the proceedings were abruptly suspended. Lock wonders whether Sheridan's illness may be seen as a (perhaps unconscious) imitation of Burke's similar indisposition after the Rangpur speech, also on his third day of speaking. See Lock, *Edmund Burke*, ii, p. 188.
102 Elliot, *Life and Letters*, i, p. 218. To Lady Elliot (14 June 1788).
103 *The Times* (14 June 1788).
104 Ibid.
105 Julie A. Carlson, 'Trying Sheridan's *Pizarro*', *Texas Studies in Literature and Language*, xxxviii/3–4 (1996), pp. 359–73 (p. 366).
106 *Speeches of the Managers and Counsel in the Trial of Warren Hastings*, i, p. 689.
107 O'Quinn, *Staging Governance*, p. 210.
108 *Speeches of the Managers and Counsel in the Trial of Warren Hastings*, i, p. 690.
109 Thomas Sheridan, *A Course of Lectures on Elocution: Together with Two Dissertations on Language; and Some Other Tracts Relative to Those Subjects* (London, 1762), p. 132.
110 Ibid., pp. 132–3.
111 Elliot, *Life and Letters*, i, p. 218. To Lady Elliot (14 June 1788).
112 Edward Gibbon, *The Letters of Edward Gibbon*, ed. J. E. Norton, 3 vols (New York, 1956), iii, p. 109.
113 To George Nesbitt Thompson (17 July 1788), in S. Arthur Strong, 'Warren Hastings's own account of his impeachment', *Harper's Monthly Magazine*, 110 (1904–5), pp. 89–95 (p. 93).
114 Ridley, 'Sheridan's courtroom dramas', p. 181.

115 For a discussion of Garrick's acting style, see, for example, Shearer West, *The Image of the Actor: Verbal and Visual Representation in the Age of Garrick and Kemble* (London, 1991), pp. 58–68.
116 Thomas Davies, *Memoirs of the Life of David Garrick*, 2 vols (London, 1780), ii, p. 339. This passage is quoted in Reid, *Edmund Burke*, p. 100. For another example of Burke's high esteem for Garrick, see Paul Hindson and Tim Gray, *Burke's Dramatic Theory of Politics* (Aldershot, 1988), p. 58.
117 Jim Davis, 'Spectatorship', in J. Moody and D. O'Quinn (eds), *The Cambridge Companion to British Theatre, 1730–1830* (Cambridge, 2007), p. 59.
118 Elliot, *Life and Letters*, i, pp. 201–2. To Lady Elliot (10 May 1788).
119 Ibid., p. 202.
120 The demand for an immediate engagement of the audience's sympathy in eighteenth-century British theatre needs to be placed within the context of the contemporary culture of sensibility. A good survey of sensibility in the Romantic period may be found in Julie Ellison, 'Sensibility', in J. Faflak and J. M. Wright (eds), *A Handbook of Romanticism Studies* (Oxford, 2012), pp. 37–53. For a discussion of the vocabulary of the sentimental (sympathy, sentimentality, sensibility) and how it underwent significant alterations throughout the eighteenth century, see Lynn Festa, *Sentimental Figures of Empire in Eighteenth-Century Britain and France* (Baltimore, MD, 2006), pp. 14–36. John Mullan offers an analysis of the 'signs' of sentiment, especially in the fiction of novelists such as Richardson, Sterne, Henry Brooke and Henry Mackenzie in *Sentiment and Sociability: The Language of Feeling in the Eighteenth Century* (Oxford, 1988). For a discussion of the importance of sympathy in the acting of the period, see Leigh Woods, *Garrick Claims the Stage: Acting as Social Emblem in Eighteenth-Century England* (Westport, CT, 1984); for an overview of sentimental drama, see Janet Todd, *Sensibility: An Introduction* (New York, 1986), in particular pp. 32–48.
121 May, 'Ciceronian oratory in context', p. 61. In his *Orator* (*Orat*. 130), describing his own ability to arouse pity (*miseratio*), Cicero proudly observes how 'even though there were several speakers on our side, they always let me make the closing speech. I owe my reputation for excellence on such occasions, not to any natural gift, but to a genuine sympathy' (*etiam si plures dicebamus, perorationem mihi tamen omnes relinquebant; in quo ut viderer excellere non ingenio sed dolore assequebar*). Among the several instances of highly pathetic Ciceronian perorations, see, for instance, *Pro Milone* (*On Behalf of Milo*) 105: 'But no more. Indeed I can no longer speak for tears, and my client forbids that tears should plead his cause' (*Sed finis sit; neque enim prae lacrimis iam loqui possum, et hic se lacrimis defendi vetat*). Marcus Tullius Cicero, *The Speeches: Pro T. Annio Milone*

– In L. Calpurnium Pisonem – Pro M. Aemilio Scauro – Pro M. Fonteio – Pro C. Rabirio Postumo – Pro M. Marcello – Pro Ligario – Pro Rege Deiotaro, trans. N. H. Watts (London and Cambridge, MA, 1964), pp. 122–3. For other examples of passages of high emotion, see May, 'Ciceronian oratory in context', p. 61, n. 31.

122 *De Orat.* II.45.189: *Neque fieri potest, ut doleat is, qui audit, ut oderit, ut invideat, ut pertimescat aliquid, ut ad fletum misericordiamque deducatur, nisi omnes illi motus, quos orator adhibere volet iudici, in ipso oratore impressi esse atque inusti videbuntur.* Quintilian, as well, observed and recommended: 'Nothing but fire can burn, nothing but water can make us wet, and "nothing gives colour but what colour has". The first thing, then, is that those feelings should be strong in us which we want to be strong in the judge, and that we should ourselves be moved before we try to move others' (*Inst.* VI.2.28: *nec incendit nisi ignis nec madescimus nisi umore 'nec res ulla dat alteri colorem| quem non ipsa habet'. Primum est igitur ut apud nos valeant ea quae valere apud iudicem volumus, adficiamurque antequam adficere conemur*).

123 In the late Republic, persuasive appeals to the audience were based both on emotions and on character. The latter was indeed extremely important in the social and political milieu of Cicero's Rome, as we are explicitly told in *De Orat.* II.182: 'A potent factor in success, then, is for the characters, principles, conduct and course of life [...] of those who are to plead cases' (*Valet igitur multum ad vincendum probari mores et instituta et facta et vitam eorum, qui agent causas*). The best account of pathos and ethos (emotion and character) as crucial means of persuasion is still Jakob Wisse, *Ethos and Pathos from Aristotle to Cicero* (Amsterdam, 1989). See, also, Alberto Cavarzere, 'La voce delle emozioni: "Sincerità" e "simulazione" nella teoria retorica dei Romani', in G. Petrone (ed.), *Le passioni della retorica* (Palermo, 2004), pp. 11–28.

124 *Brut.* 89: *cum duae sint in oratore laudes, una subtiliter disputandi ad docendum, altera graviter agendi ad animos audientium permovendos, multoque plus proficiat is qui inflammet iudicem quam ille qui doceat.*

125 A thorough account of the Rangpur episode can be found in Lock, *Edmund Burke*, ii, pp. 158–61.

126 Edmund Burke, *The Writings and Speeches of Edmund Burke*, ed. P. Langford et al., 9 vols to date (Oxford, 1981–), vi, p. 268.

127 Burke, *Correspondence*, v, p. 372. To Philip Francis (*circa* 3 January 1788).

128 Bourke, *Empire and Revolution*, p. 672.

129 Lock, *Edmund Burke*, ii, p. 160.

130 Burke, *Writings and Speeches*, vi, pp. 410–27.

131 Ibid., p. 269.

132 Ibid., p. 421. Sara Suleri pays close attention to this episode. See Suleri, *The Rhetoric of English India*, pp. 60–1. Among others, see, also, Michael J. Franklin, 'Accessing

India: orientalism, anti-"Indianism" and the rhetoric of Jones and Burke', in T. Fulford and P. J. Kitson (eds), *Romanticism and Colonialism: Writing and Empire, 1780-1830* (Cambridge, 1998), pp. 53-6.
133 Burke, *Writings and Speeches*, vi, p. 420.
134 *London Chronicle* (16-19 February 1788).
135 Eden, *The Journal and Correspondence*, i, p. 469. Mr. Storer to Mr. Eden (22 February 1788). The daughter of Tantalus and Dione or Euryanassa, and wife of the Theban king Amphion, Niobe had seven sons and seven daughters, who were all exterminated by Apollo and Artemis. Overcome by pain, Niobe turned into a rock, with tears incessantly flowing from it. The best-known source of Niobe's myth is Ovid's *Metamorphoses* (6.146-316).
136 Edmund Burke, *Revolutionary Writings*, ed. I. Hampsher-Monk (Cambridge, 2014), p. 83.
137 *Gazetteer and New Daily Advertiser* (19 February 1788). The same consideration appears verbatim in the *London Chronicle* (16-19 February 1788).
138 *Morning Chronicle and London Advertiser* (19 February 1788).
139 Elliot, *Life and Letters*, i, p. 178. To Lady Elliot (13 December 1787).
140 *The Times* (5 March 1788).
141 Burney, *Diary and Letters*, iv, p. 114.
142 Burke, *Writings and Speeches*, vi, p. 426.
143 *The World* (19 February 1788).
144 Ahmed, 'The theater of the civilized self', p. 44.
145 Stone Peters, 'Theatricality, legalism, and the scenography of suffering', p. 20.
146 Horace Walpole, *Journal of the Reign of King George the Third, from the Year 1771 to 1783*, 2 vols (London, 1859), i, p. 338.

4 Spectacles of Passion: Cicero's *In Verrem* and Burke's 'Speech on the Opening of the Impeachment'

1 H. V. Canter, 'The impeachment of Verres and Hastings: Cicero and Burke', *The Classical Journal* ix (1914), pp. 199-211.
2 Geoffrey Carnall, 'Burke as modern Cicero', in G. Carnall and C. Nicholson (eds), *The Impeachment of Warren Hastings: Papers from a Bicentenary Commemoration* (Edinburgh, 1989), pp. 76-90.
3 See such studies as Edmund Burke, *The Writings and Speeches of Edmund Burke*, ed. P. Langford et al., 9 vols to date (Oxford, 1981-), vi, pp. 28-30; Frederick G. Whelan's *Edmund Burke and India: Political Morality and Empire* (Pittsburgh, PA, 1996),

pp. 302–3; Philip Ayres's *Classical Culture and the Idea of Rome in Eighteenth-Century England* (Cambridge, 1997), pp. 42–7; Margaret M. Miles's *Art as Plunder: The Ancient Origins of Debate about Cultural Property* (Cambridge, 2008), pp. 302–7; Paddy Bullard's *Edmund Burke and the Art of Rhetoric* (Cambridge, 2011), pp. 16–7; Andrew Rudd's *Sympathy and India in British Literature 1770–1830* (Basingstoke, 2011), p. 27; Eddy Kent, *Corporate Character: Representing Imperial Power in British India, 1786–1901* (Toronto, 2014), pp. 47–50; and Richard Bourke, *Empire and Revolution: The Political Life of Edmund Burke* (Princeton, NJ, 2015), pp. 631–2.

4 The collection of Burke's speeches pronounced against Hastings throughout the eight years of the trial is a massive work. It comprises, in fact, two volumes (VI and VII) and over one thousand pages of the Oxford edition.

5 I take this phrase from Burke, *Writings and Speeches*, vi, p. 264.

6 F. P. Lock, *Edmund Burke, Volume One: 1730–84* and *Volume Two: 1784–97* (Oxford, 1998–2006), ii, p. 154.

7 See ibid., p. 153. See also Burke, *Writings and Speeches*, vi, pp. 266–7.

8 Burke, *Writings and Speeches*, vii, p. 1.

9 'I was over-persuaded by Lord and Lady Amherst to go to the trial, and heard Burke's famous oration of three hours and a quarter without intermission' – Hannah More confessed to one of her sisters – 'Such a splendid and powerful oration I never heard [...]'. William Roberts, *Memoirs of the Life and Correspondence of Mrs. Hannah More*, 2 vols (New York, 1834), i, p. 287. The account refers to the speech pronounced by Burke on 18 February 1788. Similarly, Frances Burney recorded in her *Diary* how 'His [Burke's] opening had struck me with the highest admiration of his powers, from the eloquence, the imagination, the fire, the diversity of expression, and the ready flow of language, with which he seemed gifted, in a most superior manner, for any and every purpose to which rhetoric could lead. And [...] when he related the particulars of those dreadful murders, he interested, he engaged, he at last overpowered me; I felt my cause lost. I could hardly keep on my seat. My eyes dreaded a single glance towards a man so accused as Mr. Hastings; I wanted to sink on the floor, that they might be saved so painful a sight. I had no hope he could clear himself; not another wish in his favour remained'. Frances Burney, *Diary and Letters of Madame D'Arblay*, ed. C. Barrett, 7 vols (London, 1842–6), iv, pp. 119–20. For an overview of contemporary opinions about Burke's four-day speech, see Burke, *Writings and Speeches*, vi, pp. 459–60.

10 I follow the version provided in the Oxford edition.

11 Bullard, *Edmund Burke*, p. 19.

12 A full discussion of the transcription of Burke's 'Speech on the Opening of the Impeachment' may be found in Burke, *Writings and Speeches*, vi, pp. 264–6. In this

chapter, further references to Burke's *Writings and Speeches*, vi, will be provided parenthetically in the text.
13 Christopher Reid, *Edmund Burke and the Practice of Political Writing* (Dublin, 1985), p. 129. See, also, Lock, *Edmund Burke*, ii, p. 152.
14 I take this quotation from Ayres, *Classical Culture*, p. 45. In fact, this sentence does not appear in the volumes of *The Writings and Speeches of Edmund Burke* edited by P. J. Marshall. Ayres derives it from *The Works of the Right Honourable Edmund Burke* (London, 1887).
15 Burke, *Writings and Speeches*, vii, pp. 662–3. According to M. L. Clarke, it is not credible that all Burke's audience had read the *Verrines*. However, 'that he himself had read them cannot be doubted'. Presumably, Burke read them in the original, while a student at Trinity College Dublin. See M. L. Clarke, 'Non hominis nomen, sed eloquentiae', in T. A. Dorey (ed.), *Cicero* (London, 1965), p. 101. Margaret M. Miles contends that Burke may also have read Cicero's orations against Verres in his school days (as the expression 'in our early education' seems to suggest). See Miles, *Art as Plunder*, p. 305, n. 40.
16 Here, I utilize the terms 'appropriation' and 'adaptation' according to Lorna Hardwick's definitions. See Lorna Hardwick, *Reception Studies* (Oxford, 2003), p. 9.
17 Ann Vasaly, 'Cicero's early speeches', in J. M. May (ed.), *Brill's Companion to Cicero: Oratory and Rhetoric* (Leiden, 2002), p. 89. A perceptive analysis of how Cicero publicly positioned himself on the question of judicial corruption and the senatorial monopoly of the juries can be found in Ann Vasaly, 'Cicero, domestic politics, and the first action of the Verrines', *Classical Antiquity* xxviii/1 (2009), pp. 101–37.
18 As soon as the trial of Verres came to an end, the *lex Cornelia iudiciaria* was abolished and replaced by the *lex Aurelia iudicia* (70 BC). This latter decreed that the juries of tribunals were to be equally drawn from *senatores*, *equites* and *tribuni aerarii*. For a survey of Roman tribunals, see, for example, Emanuele Narducci, *Processi ai politici nella Roma antica* (Rome and Bari, 1995), pp. 13–23.
19 Throughout the *Actio Prima* Cicero constantly alludes to the close relationship between money (*pecunia*) and Verres's hope to be acquitted by bribing the judges. See, for example, *Verr.* I.2: 'Gaius Verres appears, to stand his trial before you [...] already acquitted, according to his own confident assertions, by his vast fortune' (*reus in iudicium adductus est C. Verres* [...] *pecuniae magnitudine sua spe et praedicatione absolutus*); I.10: 'he looked upon his money as his only possible means of escape' (*omnem rationem salutis in pecunia constitueret*). See also *Verr.* I.3–4; I.16–17 and I.19. Marcus Tullius Cicero, *The Verrine Orations*, trans. L. H. G. Greenwood, 2 vols (London and Cambridge, MA, 1966). Further references to Cicero's *Verrines* are to this edition.

20 The adjective *divinitus* – and, therefore, the idea that the trial against Verres is a heaven-sent opportunity – appears repeatedly throughout the *Verrines*. See, for example, I.43 and II.3.178.

21 Cicero often refers to the people present at the trial. See, for instance, *Verr.* I.4; I.15; I.48 and I.54. Among the several passages in which Cicero refers to foreign peoples, see, for example, II.4.64 and II.4.68.

22 Whelan, *Edmund Burke and India*, p. 303.

23 See also the following expressions: 'crimes not against forms, but against those eternal laws of *justice*' (p. 275); 'you are not bound by any rules whatever except those of natural, immutable and substantial *justice*' (p. 276); 'God forbid that [...] it should be supposed that that narrow partiality, so destructive of *justice*, should guide us' (p. 278); 'enlarge the circle of *justice* to the necessities of the Empire' (p. 279); 'Your Lordships will exercise the great plenary powers with which you are invested in a manner that will do honour to your *justice*, to the protecting *justice* of this Kingdom' (p. 279); 'those reports [...] have only got abroad to be defeated and entirely overturned by the humanity, simplicity, dignity and nobleness of your Lordships' *justice*' (p. 279). Emphasis added.

24 Ann Vasaly, *Representations: Images of the World in Ciceronian Oratory* (Berkeley, CA, 1993), p. 164. For an analysis of the Roman point that, the East conquered, Rome is herself conquered by oriental licentiousness, see, among others, Erich S. Gruen, *The Hellenistic World and the Coming of Rome*, 2 vols (Berkeley, CA, 1984), i, pp. 260–6.

25 See, for example, *Verr.* I.5: 'as he has been quite open in amassing his stolen wealth, so he has revealed quite clearly to everybody the plans and schemes by which he aims at corrupting his judges' (*ut apertus in corripiendis pecuniis fuit, sic in spe corrumpendi iudicii perspicua sua consilia conatusque omnibus fecit*) and I.38–9. Cicero repeatedly warns the Senate against the perils of bribery, as in I.36, where he passionately thunders against 'all those who are in the habit of depositing or receiving deposits for bribery, of undertaking to offer or offering bribes, or of acting as agents or go-betweens for the corruption of judges in our courts' (*qui aut deponere aut accipere aut recipere aut polliceri aut sequestres aut interpretes corrumpendi iudicii solent esse*).

26 Burke's preoccupation that the Lords may be corrupted is evident from a number of expressions. See, for example: 'My Lords, I must confess that [...] the Commons do not approach your Lordships' Bar without some considerable degree of anxiety. I hope and trust that the magnitude and interests which we have in hand will reconcile some degree of solicitude for the event with the undoubting confidence with which we impose ourselves upon your Lordships' *justice*' (p. 270).

27 Emphasis original.

28 Emphasis original.

29 David Hume, *Essays and Treatises on Several Subjects*, 4 vols (Basil, 1793), ii, p. 28. For a general discussion of maladministration in the provinces and the close political affinity between British and Roman imperial practice, see Peter N. Miller, *Defining the Common Good: Empire, Religion and Philosophy in Eighteenth-Century Britain* (Cambridge, 1994), pp. 190–4.

30 Tillman W. Nechtman, *Nabobs: Empire and Identity in Eighteenth-Century Britain* (Cambridge, 2010), p. 13.

31 A critical analysis of *The Nabob* may be found in Daniel O'Quinn's *Staging Governance: Theatrical Imperialism in London, 1770–1800* (Baltimore, MD, 2005), pp. 43–73 and Rudd, *Sympathy and India*, pp. 37–9.

32 Rudd, *Sympathy and India*, p. 35.

33 Quoted in Philip Lawson and Jim Phillips, '"Our Execrable Banditti": perceptions of nabobs in mid-eighteenth-century Britain', *Albion* xvi/3 (1984), pp. 225–41 (p. 238).

34 Burke, *Writings and Speeches*, v, p. 402.

35 Ibid., p. 403.

36 Iain Hampsher-Monk, 'Edmund Burke and empire', in D. Kelly (ed.), *Lineages of Empire: The Historical Roots of British Imperial Thought* (Oxford, 2009), p. 133. For more on Burke's concern that Indian wealth and luxury may debilitate Britain, see Kate Teltscher, *India Inscribed: European and British Writing on India 1600–1800* (Oxford, 1995), pp. 169–72.

37 Phiroze Vasunia, *The Classics and Colonial India* (Oxford, 2013), p. 255.

38 See Pierre Boyancé, 'Cicéron et l'empire romain en Sicile', *Latomus* cxxi/1970, pp. 140–59.

39 Cicero reasserts the same concept over and over again. See, in particular, *Verr.* II.3.219–22.

40 William Godwin, *Political and Philosophical Writings of William Godwin*, ed. Martin Fitzpatrick et al., 7 vols (London, 1993), i, p. 253.

41 Jonathan Sachs, *Romantic Antiquity: Rome in the British Imagination, 1789–1832* (Oxford, 2010), p. 67.

42 Godwin, *Political and Philosophical Writings*, i, p. 283.

43 Ibid.

44 Ibid., p. 287.

45 Ibid.

46 By means of ancient Rome Godwin is, in fact, referring to contemporary Britain. The comparison between Rome and Britain is indeed constant throughout the letter, General Burgoyne being, for example, compared to Caesar and Lord Clive to Dolabella. See Ibid., pp. 284–5.

47 Ibid., p. 284. For a discussion of this point, see Sachs, *Romantic Antiquity*, p. 68.

48 See, for example, I.36: 'To all those who are in the habit of depositing or receiving deposits for bribery, of undertaking to offer or offering bribes, or of acting as agents or go-betweens for the corruption of judges in our courts, [...] in this present trial, take care that your hands and your minds are kept clear of this vile crime' (*qui aut deponere aut accipere aut recipere aut polliceri aut sequestres aut interpretes corrumpendi iudicii solent esse,* [...] <u>abstineant</u> *in hoc iudicio manus animosque ab hoc scelere nefario*). Emphasis added.

49 See, for instance, I.43: 'Now I entreat you, gentlemen, in God's name to take thought, and to devise measures, to meet this state of affairs' (*Cui loco, per deos immortales, iudices,* <u>consulite</u> *ac* <u>providete</u>*!*); II.1.22: 'You, gentlemen, you must take thought and make provision for what concerns the credit, the good name, the safe existence of you all' (*Vos, quod ad vestram famam existimationem salutemque communem pertinet, iudices,* <u>prospicite</u> *atque* <u>consulite</u>). Emphasis added.

50 See the expressions: 'your Lordship have great and plenary power' (p. 272); your Lordships [...] are not bound by any rules whatever except those natural, immutable and substantial justice' (p. 276); 'Your Lordships always had a boundless power; I mean, always within the limits of justice. Your Lordships always had a boundless power and unlimited jurisdiction' (p. 277).

51 See, for example, 'God forbid [...] that your Lordships should ever reject evidence on any pretended nicety, which I am sure you will not (p. 277); 'God forbid it should be said that no nation under heaven equals the British in substantial violence and informal justice' (p. 278).

52 A few illustrative examples of the major contrasts between the trial of Hastings and that of Verres may be found in Canter, 'The impeachment of Verres and Hastings', pp. 202–3.

53 Throughout the *Actio Prima* Cicero repeatedly argues that Verres brought about the devastation of Asia, Pamphylia and Sicily. See, for example, *Verr.* I.11 and I.40.

54 Anna Clark, *Scandal: The Sexual Politics of the British Constitution* (Princeton, NJ, 2004), p. 102.

55 Emphasis added.

56 See, for example, II.1.1: *tam audacem, tam amentem, tam impudentem*; II.1.6: *eius audacia atque amentia*; II.3.64: *in tanta audacia, in tanta impudentia*; II.3.166: *crimen tantae audaciae tantaeque impudentiae*; II.5.34: *vi et audacia*; II.5.39: *tuam cupiditatem et audaciam*; II.5.62: *Huncine hominem, hancine impudentiam, iudices, hanc audaciam!*

57 *Verr.* II.3.22: *Eorum omnium qui decumani vocabantur princeps erat Q. ille Apronius* [...]. *Hic est Apronius quem* [...] *Verres* [...] *nequitia, luxuria, audacia sui simillimum iudicavit*.

58 *Verr.* II.3.30: *homine nequissimo ac turpissimo*; *Verr.* II.3.140: *homo improbus atque impurus*; *Verr.* II.3.134: *contaminatum, perditum, flagitiosum, qui non modo animum integrum sed ne animam quidem puram conservare potuisset.*
59 C. E. W. Steel, *Cicero, Rhetoric, and the Empire* (Oxford, 2001), pp. 37–43.
60 Ibid., p. 43.
61 P. J. Marshall, *The New Cambridge History of India. Bengal: The British Bridgehead. Eastern India 1740–1828* (Cambridge, 1987), p. 119. For an account of Ganga Govind Singh, see P. J. Marshall, 'Indian officials under the East India Company in eighteenth-century Bengal', *Bengal Past and Present* lxxxiv (1965), pp. 95–120 (pp. 111–20).
62 'Arcadians both, ready to sing and to reply'. I take this translation from Burke, *Writings and Speeches*, vi, p. 408, n. 1. Burke did not provide the Lords with an English version of Virgil's verses, thus reinforcing the idea of an audience with a strong classical background. Virgil was quoted repeatedly by Burke during the trial. For an overview of Burke's citations of Virgil, see Vasunia, *The Classics and Colonial India*, pp. 258–60.
63 Cicero's indignation reaches its climax in the rhetorical question phrased in II.1.93: 'Could you not keep your hands from outraging your guardian's duty, your ward, your friend's son?' (*manus a tutela, manus a pupillo, manus a sodalis filio abstinere non potuisti?*). In 80 Verres was legate (*legatus*) on the staff of Gnaeus Cornelius Dolabella, governor of Cilicia. When Gaius Malleolus, Dolabella's *quaestor*, died, Verres replaced him, and together with the governor plundered the provinces until Dolabella's trial in 78. The governor of Cilicia was ironically convicted mainly on Verres's evidence.
64 *Verr.* II.2.93: *Malleolus a me productus est et mater eius atque avia, quae miserae flentes eversum a te puerum patriis bonis esse dixerunt.*
65 Nechtman, *Nabobs*, p. 13.
66 Lock, *Edmund Burke*, ii, p. 157.
67 Cicero suggests that avarice is often accompanied by either wickedness (*nequitia*) or crime (*scelus*). See, for example, *Verr.* II.3.152: 'Well then, gentlemen, this man's avaricious greed, his unblushing and criminal wickedness, are already proved, and proved unmistakably' (*Tenetur igitur iam, iudices, et manifesto tenetur avaritia, cupiditas hominis, scelus, improbitas, audacia*); II.5.24: 'this scoundrel's cupidity' (*avaritiae scelerique*); II.5.59: 'your greed and wickedness' (*avaritia ac nequitia tua*); II.5.91: 'the iniquitous cupidity of Verres' (*istius avaritia nequitiaque*).
68 See II.3.48: 'After such dishonesty, after such cruelty, after the infliction of so many grievous wrongs' (*tu in tanta improbitate, in tanta acerbitate, in tot ac tantis iniuriis*). As this example shows, the repetition of the adjective *tanta, tanta, tantis*, with polyptoton and *variatio* in the third *colon*, gives special emphasis to the cruelties repeatedly inflicted on the Sicilians. See, also, II.3.153: 'Verres' criminal wickedness'

(*istius scelere atque improbitate*); II.5.141: 'Verres' rascality and wickedness' (*istius improbitate atque nequitia*); II.5.92: 'what a matchless piece of foul wickedness on the part of Verres!' (*o istius nequitiam ac turpitudinem singularem!*).

69 For a discussion of Hastings's criminality in terms of corruption, see, in particular, Kent, *Corporate Character*, pp. 26–58. While focusing on Burke's accusation of corruption, Kent also refers to the trial of Verres. See ibid., p. 50.

70 See, for example, *Verr.* II.1.42: 'What shall be done with a man like this? For what possible use should you keep so treacherous and savage a creature?' (*Quid hoc homine faciatis? aut ad quam spem tam perfidiosum, tam importunum animal reservetis?*); II.5.109: 'But why do I speak of the bond of hospitality in connexion with this beast and monster? [...] Nay, is it the cruelty of a human being that we have here – is it not the monstrous savagery of a wild beast?' (*Sed quid ego hospitii iura in hac immani belua commemoro? [...] Cum homine crudeli nobis res est an cum fera atque immani belua?*).

71 Vasaly, *Representations*, p. 117.

72 I take this quotation from Vasunia, *The Classics and Colonial India*, p. 259.

73 Ayres, *Classical Culture and the Idea of Rome*, p. 44.

74 Warren Hastings, *The History of the Trial of Warren Hastings, Esq. Late Governor General of Bengal*, ... (London, 1796), Part VII, p. 151. Emphasis original. This section is referred to as *Curious Collection of Mr. BURKE's Abuse of Mr. HASTINGS* in the table of contents (under Part VII).

75 Ibid., p. 152. Italics original.

76 Ibid., p. 153. Italics original.

77 Ibid., p. 155.

78 Ibid., p. 152. Italics original.

79 See, for example, the speech pronounced on 19 February 1788: 'these were the very lands of the Rajah of Dinagepore, from whom or from whose Country he had taken a bribe of £40,000. My Lords, this appears to be a monstrous thing' (p. 444). Burke also utilizes phrases such as 'monstrous head of corruption'; 'monstrous consequences' (p. 379); 'monstrous raised revenues' (p. 382); and 'monstrous failure' (p. 383).

80 A fuller discussion of this caricature may be found in Daniel O'Quinn's *Staging Governance: Theatrical Imperialism in London, 1770–1800* (Baltimore, MD, 2005), pp. 172–80; Nicholas K. Robinson's *Edmund Burke: A Life in Caricature* (New Haven, CT, and London, 1996), pp. 99–101; and the British Museum's website, available at http://www.britishmuseum.org/research/collection_online/collection_object_details.aspx?objectId=1634523&partId=1&searchText=the+raree+show&page=1 (accessed 28 April 2016).

81 See Mark Neocleous, 'The monstrous multitude: Edmund Burke's political teratology', *Contemporary Political Theory* iii (2004), pp. 70–88.

82 Mary Fairclough, *The Romantic Crowd: Sympathy, Controversy and Print Culture* (Cambridge, 2013), p. 69. Lia Guerra has shown how the term monstrosity 'as a disquieting presence' connected to the French Revolution had, in fact, already appeared in a 1789 letter penned to Burke's son: 'the Elements that compose Human Society seem all to be dissolved, and a world of Monsters to be produced in the place of it'. Guerra further notes how even in successive works, such as *Further Reflections of the Revolution in France* and *Letters on a Regicide Peace*, 'the imagery of monstrosity continued to interfere with Burke's writings'. See Lia Guerra, '"The great theatre of the world": Edmund Burke's dramatic perspective', in L. M. Crisafulli and C. Pietropoli (eds), *The Languages of Performance in British Romanticism* (Oxford, 2008), p. 197.
83 Paul Youngquist, *Monstrosities: Bodies and British Romanticism* (Minneapolis, MN, 2003), p. 24. In his article on Burke's use of the metaphor of the monstrous, Mark Neocleous has also observed that 'the monster is in essence a threat to order'. See Neocleous, 'The monstrous multitude', p. 79.
84 J. G. A. Pocock, *The Machiavellian Moment: Florentine Political Thought and the Atlantic Republican Tradition* (Princeton, NJ, 1975), p. 477.
85 Isaac Kramnick has contended that 'the bitterest example' probably occurred on 22 July 1727, when the paper pictured Walpole as a famous monster in exhibition in Westminster: 'The Body of this Creature covered at least an Acre of Ground, was party-colour'd, and seemed to be swelled and bloated as if full of *Corruption*. He had Claws like an [sic] *Harpy*; his Wings resembled *Parchment*, and he had above *five hundred Mouths* and as many *Tongues*; from whence he took the name of POLYGLOTT' [sic]. Emphasis original. For a detailed analysis of the *Craftsman*'s characterization of Walpole as a giant and a monster, see Isaac Kramnick, *Bolingbroke and His Circle: The Politics of Nostalgia in the Age of Walpole* (Cambridge, MA, 1968), p. 21. Commenting on the image of the Prime Minister in English prose fiction, Jerry B. Beasley has further observed that the anti-Walpole narrative portrays him 'as a grotesque, even bestial figure, a creature of enormous excesses'. See Jerry C. Beasley, 'Portraits of a monster: Robert Walpole and early English prose fiction', *Eighteenth-Century Studies* xiv/4 (1981), pp. 406–31 (p. 419).
86 James M. May, 'Cicero and the beasts', *Syllecta Classica* vii (1995), pp. 143–53 (p. 144, n. 3).
87 Ibid.
88 See, for example, *Verr.* II.3.171: 'I felt that it was something too monstrously unnatural to be called a mere robbery' (*Non mihi iam furtum sed monstrum ac prodigium videbatur*); II.4.47: 'Think what this means. What monstrous abortion is this that we sent to rule our province?' (*Quid hoc est? quod hoc monstrum, quod prodigium in provinciam misimus?*); II.5.145: 'After long years Sicily was once more

the prey [...] of a new and monstrous creature' (*Versabatur in Sicilia longo intervallo* [...] *quoddam novum monstrum*).

89 According to Graeco-Roman mythology, Scylla was a six-headed sea monster with a triple row of teeth and twelve feet. This creature lived in a cave opposite Charybdis, a cliff with a dangerous whirlpool. Three times a day Charybdis sucked in everything, then spat it all out. The Cyclopes were one-eyed giant man-eaters. The most famous of them was Polyphemus, whom Odysseus cunningly blinded.

90 *Verr.* II.5.146: *Non enim Charybdim tam infestam neque Scyllam nautis quam istum in eodem freto fuisse arbitror: hoc etiam iste infestior quod multo se pluribus et immanioribus canibus succinxerat: Cyclops alter multo importunior, hic enim totam insulam obsidebat, ille Aetnam solam et eam Siciliae partem tenuisse dicitur.*

91 E.g. *hic tyrannus* (II.4.123); *tyrannicis interdictis tuis* (II.5.21); *importunus atque amens tyrannus* (II.5.103); *nefario tyranno* (II.5.117).

92 In his 'Cicéron et les tyrans de Sicile', *Ciceroniana* 4 (1980), pp. 63–74 (p. 63), Pierre Grimal has pointed out that, since an early age, ancient Romans were familiar with Sicilian tyrants. Romans residing in Syracuse, for example, envisaged themselves as the heirs of the greatest Sicilian tyrant, 'le "roi" Hiéron'. For an overview of the Sicilian tyrants mentioned in Cicero's works, see ibid., pp. 63–74.

93 Vasaly, *Representations*, p. 117. For other characteristics of Verres as a tyrant, see also pp. 122–4.

94 Steel, *Cicero, Rhetoric, and Empire*, p. 30. Italics original.

95 Kathryn Tempest, 'Saints and sinners: some thoughts on the presentation of character in Attic oratory and Cicero's *Verrines*', in J. R. W. Prag (ed.), *Sicilia Nutrix Plebis Romanae: Rhetoric, Law, and Taxation in Cicero's Verrines* (London, 2007), p. 35.

96 See, for instance, the expressions: *singulari crudelitate* (*Verr.* II.3.52); *tuo scelere, importunitate, avaritia, crudelitate* (II.3.126); *dissolutissimus crudelissimusque semper fuisti* (II.3.129); *tua crudelitate* (II.5.21); *culpas istius maximas avaritiae, maiestatis, dementiae, libidinis, crudelitatis* (II.5.42); *tantam crudelitatem inhumanitatemque* (II.5.115). An analysis of Verres's cruelty in the second section of *In Verrem* II.5 may be found in Thomas D. Frazel, *The Rhetoric of Cicero's 'In Verrem'* (Göttingen, 2009), pp. 158–60.

97 Among the numerous references to Hastings's cruelty, see, for example: 'We bring him [Hastings] before you for having cruelly injured persons in India; [...] he has cruelly injured them' (p. 370); 'there is undoubtedly oppression, breach of faith, cruelty, perfidy charged upon him [Hastings]' (p. 377); 'the last act of Mr. Hastings's life was to be an accomplice in the most cruel and perfidious breach of faith' (p. 439). Burke also uses expressions, such as 'cruel exaction' (p. 383); 'cruel scourge of oppression' (p. 417); 'cruel and savage war made upon the country' (p. 418);

'scenes of horrors and cruelty' (p. 421); and 'horrid and nefarious cruelties' (p. 424).

98 Verr.II.3.6: 'Shall one who deplores our allies' wrongs and our provinces' misfortunes feel no resentment towards you for stripping Asia, and making havoc of Pamphylia, and plunging Sicily into tears and mourning?' (*Qui sociorum iniuriis provinciarumque incommodis doleat, is in te non expilatione Asiae, vexatione Pamphyliae, squalore et lacrimis Siciliae concitetur?*). In order to induce his audience to sympathize with Verres's victims, Cicero utilizes a highly pathetic language. To offer but a few examples, we can think of the Sicilians' *dolorem et iniurias, incommoda, agros vexatos* (II.3.103); Cicero also refers to *aratorum fugae, calamitates, exilia, suspendia* (II.3.144).

99 See, for instance, the expressions: *magnum et acerbum dolorem* (II.4.47); *maximo dolore* (II.4.52); *Hic dolor erat tantus* (II.4.111) *Mediocrine tandem dolore eos affectos esse arbitramini?* (II.4.132); *mirum quaendam dolorem* (II.4.135); *eorum dolorem* (II.4.140).

100 In II.3.24, for example, the Sicilians are described as 'loyal allies and worthy fellow-citizens' (*fidelissimos socios optimosque cives*). See also II.2.2: 'No other nation has equalled her in loyal goodwill towards us: once the various states in the island had embraced our friendship, they never thereafter seceded from it; and most of them, and those the most notable, remained, without a break, our firm friends' (*Sola fuit ea fide benevolentiaque erga populum Romanum ut civitates eius insulae, quae semel in amicitiam nostram venissent, numquam postea deficerent, pleraeque autem et maxime illustres in amicitia perpetuo manerent*).

101 See, for example, II.2.2: 'She was the first of all to receive the title of province, the first such jewel in our imperial crown' (*Prima omnium, id quod ornamentum imperii est, provincia est appellata*); II.2.5: 'Cato Sapiens called her [...] "the nation's storehouse, the nurse at whose breast the Roman people is fed"' (*ille M. Cato Sapiens cellam penariam rei publicae nostrae, nutricem plebis Romanae Siciliam nominabat*). For Sicily as a source of profit (*fructosamque provinciam*), see, in particular, II.2.6.

102 The emphasis is mine.

103 It is worth remembering that the *Actio Secunda* was never delivered. As Ann Vasaly has suggested, it 'would not have been written until after the suspension of the trial'. See Vasaly, 'Cicero's early speeches', p. 90.

104 Beth Innocenti, 'Towards a theory of vivid description as practiced in Cicero's *Verrine* orations', *Rhetorica* xii (1994), pp. 355–81 (pp. 356–7).

105 Ibid.

106 See *inst.* VIII.3.64: 'Cicero is outstanding in this area, as in all others' (*Plurimum in hoc genere sicut ceteris eminet Cicero*). Marcus Fabius Quintilian, *The Orator's*

Education, ed. and trans. D. A. Russell, (Cambridge, MA, and London, 2001). Further references to Quintilian's *Institutio Oratoria* are to this edition.

107 On Verres's thefts of art, see, in particular, Thomas D. Frazel, '*Furtum* and the description of stolen objects in Cicero *In Verrem* 2.4', *American Journal of Philology* cxxvi/3 (2005), pp. 363–76; Renaud Robert, 'Ambiguïté du collectionnisme de Verrès', in J. Dubouloz and S. Pittia (eds), *La Sicile de Cicéron: Lectures des Verrines. Actes du colloque de Paris, 19–20 mai 2006* (Besançon, 2007), pp. 15–34 and Miles, *Art as Plunder*, pp. 152–217.

108 *Verr*. II.4.52: *Quem concursum in oppido factum putatis, quem clamorem, quem porro fletum mulierum? qui videret equum Troianum introductum, urbem captam diceret. Efferri sine thecis vasa, extorqueri alia e manibus mulierum, ecfringi multorum fores, revelli claustra.*

109 Vasaly, *Representations*, p. 127. For a comment on the Ceres of Henna episode, see, among others, Domenico Romano, 'Cicerone e il ratto di Proserpina', *Ciceroniana* iv (1980), pp. 191–201.

110 The semantic field of mourning appears repeatedly in Cicero's 'miniature dramas'. See, for instance, the case of Sagesta, where Verres removed the statue of Diana. Cicero suggests that the image (*simulacrum*) of the goddess was taken away amidst tears and laments: 'Amid the grief and lamentation of the whole community, with tears and cries of grief from every man and every woman in it' (*Verr*. II.4.76: *Magno cum luctu et gemitu totius civitatis, multis cum lacrimis et lamentationibus virorum mulierumque omnium*).

111 II.4.110: 'I think of that sanctuary, that sacred spot, that solemn worship: before my eyes rises the picture of the day when I visited Henna, my reception by the priests of Ceres wearing their fillets and carrying their sacred boughs, my address to the assembled townsfolk, in which my words were heard amid such groans and weeping as showed the whole town to be a prey to the bitterest distress' (*Venit enim mihi fani, loci, religionis illius in mentem; versantur ante oculos omnia, dies ille quo, cum ego Hennam venissem, praesto mihi sacerdotes Cereris cum infulis ac verbenis fuerunt, contio conventusque civium, in quo ego cum loquerer tanti gemitus fletusque fiebant ut acerbissimus tota urbe luctus versari videretur*).

112 John Granger Cook, *Crucifixion in the Mediterranean World* (Tübingen, 2014), p. 62. For a critical comment on the crucifixion of Gavius within its historical context, see ibid., pp. 62–9.

113 *Verr*. II.5.159: 'I will put the bare facts before you. They speak so forcibly for themselves that there is no need of eloquence, from my own feeble lips or from the lips of anyone else, to kindle your indignation' (*rem in medio ponam; quae tantum habet ipsa gravitatis ut neque mea, quae nulla est, neque ciuiusquam ad inflammandos vestros animos eloquentia requiratur*).

114 Cook, *Crucifixion in the Mediterranean World*, p. 65.
115 *Verr.* II.5.170: 'To bind a Roman citizen is a crime, to flog him is an abomination, to slay him is almost an act of murder: to crucify him is – what? There is no fitting word that can possibly describe so horrible a deed' (*Facinus est vincire civem Romanum, scelus verberare, prope parricidium necare: quid dicam in crucem tollere? Verbo satis digno tam nefaria res appellari nullo modo potest*).
116 See, also, II.5.163; II.5.166 and II.5.169.
117 See, for example, *Inst.* IV.2.113: 'Does not Cicero, when he describes the flogging of a Roman citizen, move every emotion in a few words, not only by emphasizing the victim's standing, the scene of the outrage, and the sort of flogging, but also by praising the man's courage? He shows us a hero who, when beaten with rods, neither groaned nor begged for mercy, but only cried out that he was a Roman citizen' (*An non M. Tullius circa verbera civis Romani omnis brevissime movit adfectus, non solum condicione ipsius, loco iniuriae, genere verberum, sed animi quoque commendatione? Summum enim virum ostendit, qui cum virgis caederetur non ingemuerit, non rogaverit, sed tantum civem se Romanum esse.*
118 Vasaly, 'Cicero's early speeches', p. 93.
119 *Verr.* II.5.161: 'Then he made for the market-place, on fire with mad and wicked rage, his eyes blazing, and cruelty showing clearly in every feature of his face' (*Ipse inflammatus scelere et furore in forum venit; ardebant oculi, toto ex ore crudelitas eminebat*). The image of flames and fire associated with Verres (*Ipse inflammatus*) and in his eyes (*ardebant oculi*) encourages the readers to visualize and to construct their own picture of the governor.
120 See *De orat.* III.53.202: 'For a great impression is made by dwelling on a single point, and also by clear explanation and almost visual presentation of events as if practically going on – which are very effective both in stating a case and in explaining and amplifying the statement, with the object of making the fact we amplify appear to the audience as important as eloquence is able to make it' (*Nam et commoratio una in re permultum movet et illustris explanatio rerumque quasi gerantur sub aspectum paene subiectio, quae et in exponenda re plurimum valet et ad illustrandum id quod exponitur et ad amplificandum, ut eis qui audient illud quod augebimus quantum efficere oratio poterit tantum esse videatur*). Marcus Tullius Cicero, *De Oratore*, trans. E. W. Sutton, 2 vols (London and Cambridge, MA, 1959).
121 Italics original. *Inst.* IX.2.40: *Illa vero, ut ait Cicero, sub oculos subiectio tum fieri solet cum res non gesta indicatur sed ut sit gesta ostenditur, nec universa sed per partis*. Throughout his *Institutio Oratoria*, Quintilian repeatedly refers to the technique of vivid descriptions. In *Inst.* VI.2.29, for example, Quintilian notes that 'The person who will show the greatest power in the expression of emotions will be the person who has properly formed what the Greeks call *phantasiai* (let us call

them "visions"), by which the images of absent things are presented to the mind in such a way that we seem actually to see them with our eyes and have them physically present to us' (*Quas φαντασίας Graeci vocant (nos sane visiones appellemus), per quas imagines rerum absentium ita repraesentantur animo ut cernere oculis ac praesentes habere videamur, has quisquis bene ceperit is erit in adfectibus potentissimus*).

122 *Gell.* X.3.10: 'the mere words "he ordered that he be stripped and bound, and rods brought" arouse such emotion and horror that you do not seem to hear the act described, but to see it acted before your face' (*Iam haec medius fidius sola verba: 'nudari ac deligari et virgas expediri iubet' tanti motus horrorisque sunt, ut non narrari quae gesta sunt, sed rem geri prosus videas*). Aulus Gellius, *Attic Nights*, trans. J. C. Rolfe, 2 vols (London and Cambridge, MA, 1927).

123 Ian Haywood, *Bloody Romanticism: Spectacular Violence and the Politics of Representation, 1776-1832* (Basingstoke, 2006), p. 3.

124 Ibid., p. 4.

125 Among the many publications looking at violence in representations of slavery, see ibid., pp. 11–59; Lynn Festa, *Sentimental Figures of Empire in Eighteenth-Century Britain and France* (Baltimore, MD, 2006), pp. 190–7; and Karen Halttunen, 'Humanitarianism and the pornography of pain in Anglo-American culture', *The American Historical Review* c/2 (1995), pp. 303–34 (pp. 321–5).

126 Teltscher, *India Inscribed*, p. 167.

127 Although movement is a central feature in the episode of Gavius, as Donovan J. Ochs notes, 'many stories of Verres' atrocities display character in action rather than character as reported'. Donovan J. Ochs, 'Rhetorical detailing in Cicero's Verrine Orations', *Central State Speech Journal* xxxiii (1982), pp. 310–18 (p. 315).

128 Innocenti, 'Towards a theory', p. 370.

129 *Verr.* II.5.162: 'and all the while, amid the crack of the falling blows, no groan was heard from the unhappy man, no words came from his lips in his agony except "I am a Roman citizen"' (*Cum interea nullus gemitus, nulla vox alia illius miseri inter dolorem crepitumque plagarum audiebatur nisi haec: 'Civis Romanus sum'*).

130 Frans De Bruyn has notably associated 'this harrowing and at times extraordinarily explicit account' with the celebrated passage in the *Reflections on the Revolution in France* in which Burke describes Marie Antoinette's narrow escape from a gang of French revolutionaries. See Frans De Bruyn, 'Edmund Burke's Gothic romance: the portrayal of Warren Hastings in Burke's writings and speeches on India', in *Criticism* xxix/4 (1987), pp. 415–38 (p. 432).

131 Indian virgins were violated 'in the presence of the day, in the public Court'; the wives, instead, 'lost their honour in the bottom of the most cruel dungeons', but

'were dragged out, naked and exposed to the public view, and scourged before all the people'. Burke, *Writings and Speeches*, vi, pp. 420–1.

132 Innocenti, 'Towards a theory', pp. 378–9.

133 'They bound the father and son face to face, arm to arm, body to body; and in that situation they scourged and whipped them, in order with a refinement of cruelty that every blow that escaped the father should fall upon the son, that every stroke that escaped the son should strike upon the parent; so that where they did not lacerate and tear the sense, they should wound the sensibilities and sympathies of nature'. Burke, *Writings and Speeches*, vi, p. 420.

134 *Verr.* II.1.76: *Constituitur in foro Laodiceae spectaculum acerbum et miserum et grave toti Asiae provinciae, grandis natu parens adductus ad supplicium, ex altera parte filius: ille quod pudicitiam liberorum, hic quod vitam patris famamque sororis defenderat. Flebat uterque non de suo supplicio, sed pater de filii morte, de patris filius.* For an analysis of the Philodamus episode, see Manfred Fuhrmann, 'Tecniche narrative nella seconda orazione contro Verre', *Ciceroniana* iv (1980), pp. 27–42.

135 *Inst.* IV.2.114: 'Take the misfortunes of Philodamus. Does not Cicero both fan the flame of indignation throughout his account, and fill our eyes with tears at the moment of punishment, when he describes, or rather sets before our eyes, the father weeping for his son's death and the son for his father's? What more pitiful effect could any Epilogue produce? (*Philodami casum nonne cum per totam expositionem incendit invidia tum in supplicio ipso lacrimis implevit, cum flentis non tam narraret quam ostenderet patrem de morte filii, filium de patris? Quid ulli epilogi possunt magis habere miserabile?*).

136 Ibid.

137 Richard Bourke, *Empire and Revolution*, p. 629. For Burke's use of 'the moral psychology of "sympathy"', see, in particular, Daniel I. O'Neill, *Edmund Burke and the Conservative Logic of Empire* (Oakland, CA, 2016), pp. 94–5.

138 The court had allowed Cicero one hundred and ten days to collect the evidence against Verres, but the Roman lawyer used but fifty: *Verr.* I.6: 'I covered the whole of Sicily in fifty days, so effectively, that I took cognisance of the wrongs, and the documents recording the wrongs, of all the communities and individuals concerned' (*ego Siciliam totam quinquaginta diebus sic obii ut omnium populorum privatorumque litteras iniuriasque cognoscerem*). On Cicero's rapid tour of Sicily, see, among others, Vasaly, 'Cicero's early speeches', p. 88 and Andrew Lintott, 'The citadel of the allies', in J. R. W. Prag (ed.), *Sicilia Nutrix Plebis Romanae: Rhetoric, Law, and Taxation in Cicero's Verrines* (London, 2007), pp. 7–8.

139 See, for example, *Verr.* I.6: *Itaque cum <u>ego</u> diem inquirendi in Siciliam perexiguam postulavissem, [...] <u>ego meo</u> labore et vigiliis consecutus sum [...] <u>ego</u> Siciliam*

totam quinquaginta diebus sic obii ('That is why, when I had applied for a very short space of time in which to go and collect my evidence in Sicily [...] I have achieved with my own hard work and watchfulness [...] I covered the whole of Sicily in fifty days'). Emphasis added.

140 Verr. I.33: *hominem tabulis, testibus, privatis publicisque litteris auctoritatibusque accusemus.* The evidence that Cicero intends to bring before the tribunal is mentioned again in I.56: 'we will use witnesses, and private records, and official written statements' (*Hoc testibus, hoc tabulis privatis publicisque auctoritatibus*). In Shane Butler's reconstruction of the opening day of the trial of Verres (5 August 70 BC), at around three in the afternoon, Cicero – waiting for the jurors – was not alone: besides his assistants and witnesses, there was a vast number of document boxes (*capsae*), which certainly were guarded. See Shane Butler, *The Hand of Cicero* (London and New York, 2002), p. 63. A perceptive analysis of Cicero's strategic use of witnesses may be found in Luca Fezzi, *Il corrotto. Un'inchiesta di Marco Tullio Cicerone* (Rome and Bari, 2016), pp. 62–5 and Lintott, 'The citadel of the allies', pp. 11–14. For a list of the staggering number of witnesses and documentary evidence against Verres in the *Actio Secunda*, see, in particular, Fezzi, *Il corrotto*, pp. 208–15; Michael C. Alexander, *The Case for the Prosecution in the Ciceronian Era* (Ann Arbor, MI, 2002), pp. 255–62; and Ettore Ciccotti, *Il processo di Verre: Un capitolo di storia romana* (Milan, 1895), pp. 183–92.

141 For a survey of the Indian testimonials, see Teltscher, *India Inscribed*, pp. 177–86.

5 The Reception of the Hastings Trial in the Newspapers and Satirical Prints

1 Christopher Reid, *Imprison'd Wranglers: The Rhetorical Culture of the House of Commons 1760–1800* (Oxford, 2012), p. 10.
2 David Musselwhite, 'The trial of Warren Hastings', in F. Barker, P. Hulme, M. Iversen and D. Loxley (eds), *Literature, Politics and Theory: Papers from the Essex Conference 1976–84* (London and New York, 1986), p. 92.
3 Paul Langford, 'Burke, Edmund (1729/30–1797)', in *Oxford Dictionary of National Biography*. For an account of Burke's editorship of the *Register*, see F. P. Lock, *Edmund Burke, Volume One: 1730–84* and *Volume Two: 1784–97* (Oxford, 1998–2006), i, pp. 165–79.
4 'When Cicero came forward as the accuser of Verres, what were the arguments he advanced why the prosecution should be committed to him? "Because," said he, "I am acquainted with the evasions and sophistry of his advocate Hortensius. I am accustomed to combat and to overthrow them"'. *Annual Register* (1788), p. 143.

5   As with Chapter 1, I have based my research on eighteenth-century British newspapers issued in India on the collection held by the British Library.
6   *Hicky's Bengal Gazette; or the Original Calcutta General Advertiser*, no. xi (31 March–7 April 1781) and no. xiv (21 April–28 April 1781). Emphasis original. Even though the second article is described as the 'continuance' of the first, the version appearing in no. xi is a translation of the opening of the *Divinatio in Caecilium*, while that published in no. xiv is the *incipit* of the *Actio Prima*. It is worth noting here that, besides comprising the *Actio Prima* and *Actio Secunda*, the Verrine orations also include the *Divinatio in Caecilium*, 'the only example', as Ann Vasaly explains, 'of an oration delivered at a preliminary hearing before a court empowered to decide who would be allowed to prosecute a given defendant'. See Ann Vasaly, 'Cicero's early speeches', in J. M. May (ed.), *Brill's Companion to Cicero: Oratory and Rhetoric* (Leiden, 2002), p. 87.
7   *Hicky's Bengal Gazette; or the Original Calcutta General Advertiser* (21 April–28 April 1781). Emphasis original. I have reproduced the name 'Pillage' with a slightly bigger type, as in the original.
8   P. J. Marshall, *The Impeachment of Warren Hastings* (Oxford, 1965), p. 14.
9   Ibid., p. 12. Marshall goes on to suggest that, even though Thomas Rumbold was 'the immediate victim' and scapegoat for the British defeat in Madras, 'accusations were also made against Hastings'. In a letter to Sir Thomas Rumbold (23 March 1781), Burke described Hastings as the author of 'the present ruinous Maratta War'. See Edmund Burke, *The Correspondence of Edmund Burke*, ed. T. W. Copeland et al., 10 vols (Cambridge, 1958–78), iv, pp. 344–5. To Sir Thomas Rumbold (23 March 1781).
10 Other phrases emphasized in the two issues include: 'daring impiety', 'Wanton Cruelty', 'miserable helpless people', 'Exemplary Justice', 'Vindication', 'Delinquents', 'distressed', 'clearly convicted', 'scourge', 'Mankind at defiance', 'tryal' [*sic*], 'exemplary justice', 'abusers of power', 'mal administration' [*sic*], 'great riches', 'money', 'presents', and 'ruin'.
11 A brief introduction to the article explains that 'the following debate, which we have extracted from the MADRAS COURIER, upon the Subject of Mr. HASTING'S [*sic*] IMPEACHMENT, exhibits very different Opinions and Views of his Conduct, from what we have observed in former Speeches upon it'. Emphasis original. In spite of this reference to the *Madras Courier*, it should be noted that the same story appears verbatim in the *Morning Chronicle and London Advertiser* (10 May 1787).
12 *India Gazette: or, Calcutta Public Advertiser* (7 January 1788). Emphasis original.
13 Unlike the *India Gazette*, this article is only partially derived from the *Morning Chronicle and London Advertiser* (10 May 1787).
14 *Calcutta Gazette; or, Oriental Advertiser* (9 May 1787). Emphasis original.

15 According to *The Times* (10 May 1787), 'He [Mr. Courtenay] observed, that Mr. Hastings had been compared to Verres and the two Scipios. He might be like the first, but he could not conceive how he resembled the two Scipios'.
16 Warren Hastings, *The History of the Trial of Warren Hastings, Esq. Late Governor General of Bengal*, ... (London, 1796), Part I, p. 16.
17 Ibid., p. 19.
18 According to the *Calcutta Gazette*, while focusing on Cortés, Courtenay remarked how the Archbishops 'contrived to get several affidavits sworn, that the deponents heard a chorus of angels sing in the Mexican language, *Gloria in Excelsis*, and the blessings of heaven upon the head of Ferdinando Cortez, for his humanity and benevolence to the Mexicans and Peruvians. The Archbishop of Toledo transmitted these to bench of his reverend brother Chief of Justice; they persuaded the people to believe the facts deposed; a general credulity prevailed, and at the same time, Cortez sent Charles the fifth some jewels [...] and all Spain rang with the praises of Ferdinando Cortez'. The *Calcutta Gazette* does not specify whether Courtenay explicitly suggested (or left it, instead, implicit) that also the Governor-General of Bengal was seeking out testimonies from Indian elites asserting his virtue and benevolence, or, that Hastings had bribed the king. This section of the *Gazette* concludes rather abruptly that: 'Mr. Courtenay dwelt for some time on the analogy between the conduct of Cortez, and the conduct of Mr. Hastings, and at length concluded a very long speech'. The *Calcutta Gazette; or, Oriental Advertiser* (17 January 1788).
19 Sara Suleri, *The Rhetoric of English India* (Chicago and London, 1992), p. 69. For criticism concerning *Pizarro* and the trial of Hastings, see also Julie A. Carlson, 'Trying Sheridan's *Pizarro*', *Texas Studies in Literature and Language*, xxxviii/3–4 (1996), pp. 359–78; Julie Stone Peters, 'Theatricality, legalism, and the scenography of suffering: the trial of Warren Hastings and Richard Brinsley Sheridan's *Pizarro*', *Law and Literature*, xviii (2006), pp. 15–45 (pp. 29–40); and David Francis Taylor, *Theatres of Opposition: Empire, Revolution, and Richard Brinsley Sheridan* (Oxford, 2012), pp. 121–41.
20 I am referring here to the early English-language Indian newspaper. It should not be confused with *The World* published in London.
21 *The World* (4 January 1794). I was not able to trace the epistle Aristophanes here refers to, as the British Library collection of *The World* includes only the 4 January 1794 issue.
22 Edmund Burke, *The Writings and Speeches of Edmund Burke*, ed. P. Langford et al., 9 vols to date (Oxford, 1981–), vi, p. 346.
23 Jennifer Pitts, *A Turn to Empire: The Rise of Imperial Liberalism in Britain and France* (Princeton, NJ, and Oxford, 2005), p. 78. Insightful discussions of the term

'geographical morality' may be found, among others, in ibid., pp. 77–85 and Frederick G. Whelan, *Edmund Burke and India: Political Morality and Empire* (Pittsburgh, PA, 1996), pp. 281–91.

24 Burke, *Writings and Speeches*, vi, p. 63.

25 Ibid. The theme of corruption – both in Britain and ancient Rome – was not new in Burke's writings. An epistle penned on 22 June 1784 proves that at least four years before the commencement of the trial of Hastings Burke had complained about Britain's moral decline: 'At present the picture of the English Nation does not appear to me in a very favourable light', he confided to his friend William Baker (1743–1824). Indeed, so depraved did the Court and Ministry appear to the Anglo-Irish orator that he dishearteningly observed: 'I do not think any thing was correspondent, even in the worst times of the Roman Republick' [*sic*]. See Burke, *Correspondence*, v, p. 155. To William Baker (22 June 1784).

26 Emphasis original. Swift is called 'Dean', as he was Dean of Saint Patrick Cathedral in Dublin from 1713 until his death in 1745. The issue of the *Examiner* in which Swift published his translation was not 'No. 17', but No 18. Probably owing to space restrictions, the translation printed in *The Times* is slightly abridged.

27 The article published on 9 March 1787 and the letter printed in the issue for 12 June 1788 are identical but for the introduction to Swift's translation. As for the letter to the Editor, it begins as follows: 'Sir, among the many proofs that the world has been the same in all ages, it may not be unworthy of observation, that Caius Verres was guilty of the same crimes above eighteen hundred years ago, that are now laid to the charge of Mr. Hastings'.

28 The series is mentioned by P. J. Marshall in Burke, *Writings and Speeches*, vi, p. 29, n. 2; Lock, *Edmund Burke*, ii, p. 91, n. 151; and Margaret M. Miles, *Art as Plunder: The Ancient Origins of Debate about Cultural Property* (Cambridge, 2008), pp. 306–7.

29 *Public Advertiser* (5 February 1788). Italics original.

30 Ibid. Italics original.

31 In particular, *Amicus Curiae*'s programme asserts: 'First to state the characters and conduct of Verres and Hastings from *facts*: Next to draw a parallel between *Marcus Tuilius* [*sic*] *Cicero*, the accuser of *Verres*, and *The Right Hon. Edmund Burke*, the accuser of *Warren Hastings*, Esq; And lastly, to suggest such reasons drawn from the conduct of Mr. Hastings, as, in my opinion, should operate in favour of that Gentleman's exculpation'. Ibid. Emphasis original.

32 *Public Advertiser* (6 February 1788).

33 Miles, *Art as Plunder*, p. 307.

34 *Public Advertiser* (6 February 1788). Italics original. See *Verr.* II.2.19–22. Marcus Tullius Cicero, *The Verrine Orations*, trans. L. H. G. Greenwood, 2 vols (London and Cambridge, MA, 1966).

35 *Public Advertiser* (6 February 1788). Italics original.
36 Ibid.
37 The story of Antiochus is reported in *Verr.* II.4.61–68.
38 Italics original.
39 Italics original. See *Verr.* II.5.146. A description of the *Lautumiae* may be found in *Verr.* II.5.68 and II.5.143
40 *Public Advertiser* (11 February 1788). Italics original.
41 Ibid. Among the many examples he cites of Verres's cruelty, *Amicus Curiae* notes that 'so wantonly and inhumanly did he [Verres] oppress the natives, the tributaries and allies, and so scandalously degrade the character of the Roman arms, as not only to produce a famine, but eat up all resources of public revenues'; 'Verres, during his short government, pushed his avarice to such barbarous and unheard of lengths'; 'he immediately overturned [Sicily's police and finance] in the most direct and despotic manner – making his will the laws of the province, and his avarice and extortions the panders of his will'. Ibid.
42 Ibid. The writer further highlights that 'so far from having a *single petition against him*, [Hastings] parted from his government with the expressed regret of his fellow-servants and countrymen; on his return to his own country, so far was he from being thought guilty of high crimes and misdemeanors, that he received the *unanimous thanks* of his own immediate masters, the Court of Directors'. Ibid. Italics original.
43 *Public Advertiser* (13 February 1788).
44 Ibid. Italics original.
45 Ibid. Italics original.
46 Ibid. Italics original.
47 *Public Advertiser* (15 February 1788).
48 Ibid. Emphasis original.
49 Burke, *Writings and Speeches*, vi, pp. 270–1.
50 *Public Advertiser* (5 February 1788).
51 Jim Davis, 'Spectatorship', in J. Moody and D. O'Quinn (eds), *The Cambridge Companion to British Theatre, 1730–1830* (Cambridge, 2007), p. 63.
52 Ibid.
53 Among the scholars who have touched on Sayers's and/or Boyne's satirical print, see, in particular, Nicholas K. Robinson, *Edmund Burke: A Life in Caricature* (New Haven, CT, and London, 1996), p. 82 and Lock, *Edmund Burke*, ii, p. 91.
54 See Marshall, *The Impeachment of Warren Hastings*, pp. xiv–xv. For the Benares charge, see, in particular, ibid., pp. 88–108.
55 Robinson, *Edmund Burke*, p. 82. A fuller discussion of this episode may be derived from Lock, *Edmund Burke*, ii, p. 5.

56 Daniel O'Quinn, *Staging Governance: Theatrical Imperialism in London, 1770–1800* (Baltimore, MD, 2005), p. 190.
57 The only extant Roman text which provides detailed information about oratorical gestures is the eleventh chapter of Quintilian's *Institutio Oratoria*. A discussion of the orator's movements and gestures may be found in *Inst.* XI.3.66–137. Quintilian, Marcus Fabius, *The Orator's Education*, ed. and trans. D. A. Russell, (Cambridge, MA, and London, 2001).
58 After the Shelburne administration fell in February 1783, Fox and Lord North formed a coalition, which was ousted in December the same year. A study that is especially useful for getting a sense of the Fox–North coalition within the years of acute crisis of the constitution (1782–4) is John Cannon's *The Fox–North Coalition: Crisis of the Constitution 1782–1784* (Cambridge, 1969).
59 See, for example, Noah Webster, *An American Selection of Lessons in Reading and Speaking* (Philadelphia, 1787), pp. 298–302; John Walker, *The Academic Speaker* (Dublin, 1796), pp. 146–52; and Lindley Murray, *The English Reader* (London, 1799), pp. 153–7.

Conclusion

1 Lorna Hardwick, *Reception Studies* (Oxford, 2003), p. 4.
2 Quoted in Robert Murray, *Edmund Burke: A Biography* (Oxford, 1931), p. 336.
3 Charles Butler, *Reminiscences* (London, 1822), 3rd edition, p. 207. The passage is quoted in Christopher Reid, *Imprison'd Wranglers: The Rhetorical Culture of the House of Commons 1760–1800* (Oxford, 2012), p. 16.
4 Michael J. MacDonald, 'Introduction', in M. J. MacDonald (ed.), *The Oxford Handbook of Rhetorical Studies* (Oxford, 2017), p. 17.
5 Paul Elledge, *Lord Byron at Harrow School: Speaking Out, Talking Back, Acting Up, Bowing Out* (Baltimore, MD, and London, 2000), p. 9. For a list of the speeches declaimed at Harrow which included Burke's orations against Hastings, see, for example, *The Times* (6 July 1846; 1 July 1870). As for Eton, see, for instance, *The Times* (5 June 1875).
6 See *The Times* (25 July 1853; 6 July 1854) and *The Morning Post* (6 July 1877), among others.
7 Edmund Burke, *The Writings and Speeches of Edmund Burke*, ed. P. Langford et al., 9 vols to date (Oxford, 1981–), vi, p. 276.
8 Edmund Burke, *The Correspondence of Edmund Burke*, ed. T. W. Copeland et al., 10 vols (Cambridge, 1958–78), ix, p. 62. To French Laurence (28 July 1796).

Bibliography

Primary sources

Addison, Joseph, *A Discourse on Ancient and Modern Learning* (Dublin, 1739).
——, *The Spectator*, ed. D. F. Bond, 5 vols (Oxford, 1965).
Additional Supplement to the Calcutta Gazette.
Anonymous, *Verres and his Scribblers: A Satire in Three Cantos. To Which is Added an Examen of the Piece, and a Key to the Characters and Obscure Passages* (London, 1732).
——, *The Death of M-L-N in the Life of Cicero: Being a Proper Criticism on That Marvellous Performance* (London, 1741).
——, *A Free Translation of the Preface to Bellendenus; Containing Animated Strictures on the Great Political Characters of the Present Time* (London, 1788).
Annual Register.
Beattie, James, *Essays: On Poetry and Music, as They Affect the Mind; on Laughter, and Ludicrous Composition: on the Utility of Classical Learning*, 2 vols (Edinburgh, 1776).
Bisset, Robert, *The Life of Edmund Burke* (London, 1798).
Blair, Hugh, *Lectures on Rhetoric and Belles Lettres*, ed. L. Ferreira-Buckley and S. M. Halloran (Carbondale, IL, 2005).
Boaden, James, *Memoirs of the Life of John Philip Kemble*, 2 vols (Philadelphia, 1825).
Boswell, James, *The Journal of a Tour to the Hebrides, with Samuel Johnson, LL.D.*, ... (London, 1785).
Breval, John, *Remarks on Several Parts of Europe, Relating Chiefly to Their Antiquities and History Collected Upon the Spot in Several Tours Since the Year 1723; And Illustrated by Upward of Forty Copper Plates, from Original Drawings; Among Which Are the Ruins of Several Temples, Theatres, Amphitheatresm Triumphal Arches, and Other Unpublish'd Monuments of the Greek and Roman Times, in Sicily, and the South of France*, 2 vols (London, 1738).
The British Critic.
Broome, Ralph, *Letters from Simpkin the Second to his Dear Brother in Wales, Containing an Humble Description of the Trial of Warren Hastings, Esq. From the Commencement to the Close of the Sessions in 1789* (London, 1789).

Brüggemann, Ludwig Wilhelm, *A view of the English Editions, Translations and Commentaries of Marcus Tullius Cicero, with Remarks* (Stettin, 1795).

———, *A view of the English Editions, Translations and Illustration of the ancient Greek and Latin authors with remarks by Lewis William Brüggemann, Counsellor of the consistory at Stettin in Pomerania, and Chaplain in Ordinary to his Prussian Majesty* (Stettin, 1797).

Brydone, Patrick, *A Tour through Sicily and Malta. In a Series of Letters to William Beckford, Esq. of Somerly in Suffolk; from P. Brydone, F. R. S.*, 2 vols (London, 1773).

Burgh, James, *The Art of Speaking* (London, 1761).

Burke, Edmund, *The Works of the Right Honourable Edmund Burke* (London, 1887).

———, *The Correspondence of Edmund Burke*, ed. T. W. Copeland et al., 10 vols (Cambridge, 1958–78).

———, *The Writings and Speeches of Edmund Burke*, ed. P. Langford et al., 9 vols to date (Oxford, 1981–).

———, *Revolutionary Writings*, ed. I. Hampsher-Monk (Cambridge, 2014).

Burney, Frances, *Diary and Letters of Madame D'Arblay*, ed. C. Barrett, 7 vols (London, 1842–6).

Butler, Charles, *Reminiscences* (London, 1822), 3rd edition.

Byron, George Gordon, *Lord Byron's Letters and Journals*, ed. L. A. Marchand, 13 vols (London, 1973–94).

Calcutta Chronicle: And General Advertiser.

The Calcutta Gazette; or, Oriental Advertiser.

Campbell, John, *The Travels of Edward Brown, Esq; Formerly a Merchant in London. Containing His Observations on France and Italy, his Voyage to the Levant; his Account of the Island of Malta; his Remarks in his Journies through the Lower and Upper Egypt; Together with a Brief Description of the Abyssinian Empire . . .*, 2 vols (London, 1739).

Catalogue of a Library of Books Late the Property of the Rt. Hon. Ed. Burke dcsd, August 17 1813 (Bod. MS 16978).

Cibber, Colley, *The Character and Conduct of Cicero, Considered, From the History of his Life, by the Reverend Dr. Middleton. With Occasional Essays and Observations upon the Most Memorable Facts and Persons during That Period, By Colley Cibber, Esq; Servant to His Majesty* (London, 1747).

Cicero, Marcus Tullius, *The Orations of Marcus Tullius Cicero against Caius Cornelius Verres, Translated from the Original, by James White, Esq. with Annotations*, trans. J. White (London, 1787).

———, *De Oratore*, trans. E. W. Sutton, 2 vols (London and Cambridge, MA, 1959).

———, *Brutus*, trans. G. L. Hendrickson, *Orator*, trans. H. M. Hubbell (London and Cambridge, MA, 1962).

——, *The Speeches: Pro T. Annio Milone – In L. Calpurnium Pisonem – Pro M. Aemilio Scauro – Pro M. Fonteio – Pro C. Rabirio Postumo – Pro M. Marcello – Pro Ligario – Pro Rege Deiotaro*, trans. N. H. Watts (London and Cambridge, MA, 1964).

——, *The Verrine Orations*, trans. L. H. G. Greenwood, 2 vols (London and Cambridge, MA, 1966).

——, *Cicero. On the Ideal Orator (De Oratore)*, ed. and trans. J. M. May and J. Wisse (New York and Oxford, 2001).

Cornish, Joseph, *An Attempt to Display the Importance of Classical Learning, Addressed to the Parents and Guardians of Youth: with Some Candid Remarks on Mr. Knox's Liberal Education* (London, 1783).

The Craftsman.

Critical Review.

Cust, Lionel, *Catalogue of the Collection of Fans and Fan-leaves Presented to the British Museum by Lady Charlotte Schreiber* (London, 1893).

Davies, Thomas, *Memoirs of the Life of David Garrick*, 2 vols (London, 1780).

Eden, William, *The Journal and Correspondence of William, Lord Auckland*, 2 vols (London, 1861).

Elliot, Gilbert, *Life and Letters of Sir Gilbert Elliot*, ed. The Countess of Minto, 3 vols (London 1874).

Encyclopaedia Britannica; or, A Dictionary of Arts, Sciences, &c. Illustrated with above Two Hundred Copperplates, 10 vols (Edinburgh, 1778–83).

Encyclopaedia Britannica; or, A Dictionary of Arts, Sciences, and Miscellaneous Literature; ... Illustrated with Five Hundred and Forty-Two Copperplates, 18 vols (Edinburgh, 1797).

The European Magazine, and London Review.

Examiner.

Francis, Sir Philip, *A Letter Missive from Sir Philip Francis K. B. to Lord Holland* (London, 1816).

Gazetteer and New Daily Advertiser.

Gellius, Aulus, *Attic Nights*, trans. J. C. Rolfe, 2 vols (London and Cambridge, MA, 1927).

The Gentleman's Magazine: and Historical Chronicle.

Gibbon, Edward, *The Letters of Edward Gibbon*, ed. J. E. Norton, 3 vols (New York, 1956).

Gleig, George Robert, *Memoirs of the Right Hon. Warren Hastings, First Governor-General of Bengal...*, 3 vols (London, 1841).

Godwin, William, *Political and Philosophical Writings of William Godwin*, ed. Martin Fitzpatrick et al., 7 vols (London, 1993).

Gordon, John, *Occasional Thoughts on the Study and Character of Classical Authors, on the Course of Literature, and the Present Plan of a Learned Education. With Some Incidental Comparisons between Homer and Ossian* (London, 1762).

Grub Street Journal.

Halhed, Nathaniel Brassey, *A Code of Gentoo Laws, or, Ordinations of the Pundits, from a Persian Translation, Made from the Original, Written in the Shanscrit* [sic] *Language* (London, 1776).

Hastings, Warren, *Memoirs relative to the State of India* (London, 1786).

——, *The History of the Trial of Warren Hastings, Esq. Late Governor General of Bengal,* . . . (London, 1796).

Hicky's Bengal Gazette; or the Original Calcutta General Advertiser.

Hill, John, *The Actor: A Treatise on the Art of Playing* (London, 1750).

Hircarrah.

The Historical, Biographical, Literary, and Scientific Magazine.

Horace, *Satires, Epistles and Ars Poetica*, trans. H. Rushton Fairclough (London and Cambridge, MA, 1966).

Howell, Thomas Bayly et al., *A Complete Collection of State Trial and Proceedings for High Treason and Other Crimes and Misdemeanors from the Earliest Period to the Present Time . . .*, 21 vols (London, 1816).

Hull Packet and Humber Mercury.

Hume, David, *Essays, Moral, Political, and Literary* (Edinburgh, 1742).

——, *Essays and Treatises on Several Subjects*, 4 vols (Basil, 1793).

India Gazette: Or, Calcutta Public Advertiser.

Jones, Sir William, *The Letters of Sir William Jones*, ed. G. Cannon, 2 vols (Oxford, 1970).

Knight, Richard Payne, *Expedition into Sicily*, ed. C. Stumpf (London, 1986).

London Chronicle.

London Magazine.

Locke, John, *Some Thoughts Concerning Education* (Oxford, 1989).

Lyall, Alfred Comyn, *Warren Hastings* (London, 1889).

Lyttelton, George, *Observations on the Life of Cicero* (London, 1733).

Mackenzie, George, *An Idea of the Modern Eloquence of the Bar. Together with a Pleading out of Every Part of Law. Written by Sir George MacKenzie . . . Translated into English* (Edinburgh, 1711).

Madras Courier.

Markham, Clements R., Bogle, George, Manning, Thomas, *Narratives of the Mission of George Bogle to Tibet, and of the Journey of Thomas Manning to Lhasa* (London, 1876).

Middleton, Conyers, *The Life of Marcus Tullius Cicero*, 3 vols (London, 1741).

——, *The Epistles of M.T. Cicero to M. Brutus and of Brutus to Cicero: with the Latin Text on the opposite page, and English notes to each epistle. Together with a prefatory dissertation, In which the Authority of the said Epistles is vindicated, and all the*

Objections of the Revd. Mr. Tunstall particularly considered and confuted (London, 1743).

Mill, John Stuart, *Autobiography of John Stuart Mill Published from the Original Manuscript in the Columbia University Library* (New York and London, 1960).

Monthly Review.

Moore, Thomas, *Memoirs of the Life of the Right Honourable Richard Brinsley Sheridan*, 2 vols (London, 1825).

Morning Chronicle and London Advertiser.

The Morning Post.

Morning Post and Daily Advertiser.

Murray, Lindley, *The English Reader* (London, 1799).

The New London Magazine.

North, Thomas, *The Lives of the noble Grecians and Romanes, compared together by that grave, learned philosopher and historiographer Plutarke of Chaeronea: translated out of Greeke into French by I. Amyot and into Englishe by T. North* (London, 1579).

Oracle Bell's New World.

Plutarch, *Plutarch's Lives. Translated from the Greek by Several Hands*, ed. J. Dryden, 5 vols (London, 1684–8).

——, *Plutarch's Lives Translated from the Original Greek; with Notes, Historical and Critical and a Life of Plutarch, by John and William Langhorne. A New Edition, Carefully Corrected, and the Index Much Amended, and Accurately Revised Throughout. In Four Volumes*, trans. J. Langhorne and W. Langhorne (Philadelphia, 1822).

Public Advertiser.

Quintilian, Marcus Fabius, *The Orator's Education*, ed. and trans. D. A. Russell, (Cambridge, MA, and London, 2001).

Roberts, William, *Memoirs of the Life and Correspondence of Mrs. Hannah More*, 2 vols (New York, 1834).

Schreiber, Charlotte, *Fans and Fan-leaves – English, Collected and Described by Lady Charlotte Schreiber*, 2 vols (London, 1888).

Sheridan, Thomas, *A Course of Lectures on Elocution: Together with Two Dissertations on Language; and Some Other Tracts Relative to Those Subjects* (London, 1762).

Spectator.

Speeches of the Managers and Counsel in the Trial of Warren Hastings, ed. E. Bond, 4 vols (London, 1859–61).

St. James's Chronicle: or, British Evening Post.

Stanhope, Philip Dormer, *Letters Written by the Late Right Honourable Philip Dormer Stanhope, Earl of Chesterfield, to His Son; with Some Account of His Life*, 4 vols (London, 1815).

Stevenson, William, *Remarks on the Very Inferior Utility of Classical Learning* (London, 1796).

Strong, S. Arthur, 'Warren Hastings's own account of his impeachment', *Harper's Monthly Magazine*, 110 (1904–5), pp. 89–95.

Taylor, John, *Elements of the Civil Law* (Cambridge, 1755).

The Templar; or, Monthly Register of Legal and Constitutional Knowledge, 2 vols (London, 1789).

The Times.

True Briton.

Tunstall, James, *Observations on the present Collection of Epistles between Cicero and M. Brutus, representing several evident Marks of Forgery in those Epistles; and the true state of many important Particulars in the Life and Writings of Cicero, in answer to the late Pretences of the Reverend Dr. Conyers Middleton, by James Tunstall, B.D. Fellow etc.* (London, 1744).

Voltaire, François Marie Arouet de, *Lettres écrites de Londres sur les Anglois et autres sujets* (Basle, 1734).

von La Roche, Sophie, *Sophie in London, 1786; Being the Diary of Sophie v. la Roche. Translated from the German, with an Introductory Essay, by Clare Williams. With a Foreword by G.M. Travelyan* (London, 1933).

Walker, John, *The Academic Speaker* (Dublin, 1796).

Walpole, Horace, *Journal of the Reign of King George the Third, from the Year 1771 to 1783*, 2 vols (London, 1859).

Ward, John, *A System of Oratory, Delivered in a Course of Lectures Publicly Read at Gresham College, London*, 2 vols (London, 1759).

Warton, Joseph, *An Essay on the Genius and Writings of Pope*, 2 vols (London, 1782).

Webster, Noah, *An American Selection of Lessons in Reading and Speaking* (Philadelphia, 1787).

White, James, *Hints for a Specific Plan for an Abolition of the Slave Trade, and for Relief of the Negroes in the British West Indies* (London, 1788).

Wilkins, Charles, *The Bhagvat-Geeta or Dialogues of Kreeshna and Arjoon; in Eighteen Lectures; with Notes* (London, 1785).

The World (London).

The World (Calcutta).

Secondary sources

Ahmed, Siraj, 'The theater of the civilized self: Edmund Burke and the East India trials', *Representations*, lxxviii (2002), pp. 28–55.

Alexander, Michael C., *The Case for the Prosecution in the Ciceronian Era* (Ann Arbor, MI, 2002).
Allardyce, Nicoll, *The Garrick Stage* (Manchester, 1980).
Axer, Jerzy, *The Style and the Composition of Cicero's Speech 'Pro Q. Roscio Comoedo': Origin and Function* (Warsaw, 1979).
Ayres, Philip, *Classical Culture and the Idea of Rome in Eighteenth-Century England* (Cambridge, 1997).
Batstone, William, 'The drama of rhetoric at Rome', in E. Gunderson (ed.), *The Cambridge Companion to Ancient Rhetoric* (Cambridge, 2009).
Beasley, Jerry C., 'Portraits of a monster: Robert Walpole and early English prose fiction', *Eighteenth-Century Studies* xiv/4 (1981), pp. 406–31.
Bernstein, Jeremy, *Dawning of the Raj: The Life and Trials of Warren Hastings* (Chicago, 2000).
Bolton, Betsy, 'Imperial sensibilities, colonial ambivalence: Edmund Burke and Frances Burney', *ELH* lxxii/4 (2005), pp. 871–99.
Bourke, Richard, *Empire and Revolution: The Political Life of Edmund Burke* (Princeton, NJ, 2015).
Boyancé, Pierre, 'Cicéron et l'empire romain en Sicile', *Latomus* 121 (1970), pp. 140–59.
Brill's New Pauly: Encyclopaedia of the Ancient World, eds H. Cancik, H. Schneider and M. Landfester, 22 vols (Leiden, 2002–).
Brink, C. O., *Horace on Poetry: The 'Ars Poetica'* (Cambridge, 1971).
——, *English Classical Scholarship. Historical Reflections on Bentley, Porson, and Housman* (Cambridge, 1985).
Browning, Reed, 'The origin of Burke's ideas revisited', *Eighteenth-Century Studies* xviii/1 (1984), pp. 57–71.
Bryant, Donald Cross, 'The contemporary reception of Edmund Burke's speaking', in R. F. Howes (ed.), *Historical Studies of Rhetoric and Rhetoricians* (Ithaca, NY, 1961).
Bullard, Paddy, *Edmund Burke and the Art of Rhetoric* (Cambridge, 2011).
——, 'Rhetoric and eloquence: the language of persuasion', in J. A. Harris (ed.), *The Oxford Handbook of British Philosophy in the Eighteenth Century* (Oxford, 2013).
Butler, Shane, *The Hand of Cicero* (London and New York, 2002).
Campbell, Gerald, *Edward and Pamela Fitzgerald; Being Some Account of their Lives, Compiled from the Letters of Those Who Knew Them* (London, 1904).
Cannon, Garland, 'Sir William Jones and Edmund Burke', *Modern Philology* liv/3 (1957), pp. 165–86.
——, *The Life and Mind of Oriental Jones: Sir William Jones, the Father of Modern Linguistics* (Cambridge, 1990).
Cannon, John, *The Fox-North Coalition: Crisis of the Constitution 1782–1784* (Cambridge, 1969).

Canter, H. V., 'The impeachment of Verres and Hastings: Cicero and Burke', *The Classical Journal* ix (1914), pp. 199-211.

Carlson, Julie, 'Trying Sheridan's *Pizarro*', *Texas Studies in Literature and Language*, xxxviii/3-4 (1996), pp. 359-78.

Carnall, Geoffrey, 'Burke as modern Cicero', in G. Carnall and C. Nicholson (eds), *The Impeachment of Warren Hastings: Papers from a Bicentenary Commemoration* (Edinburgh, 1989).

Catalogue of the Library of the Late Right Honourable Edmund Burke (1833), in *Sale Catalogues of Libraries of Eminent Persons*, ed. A. N. L. Munby et al., 12 vols (London, 1971-5).

Cavarzere, Alberto, 'La voce delle emozioni. "Sincerità" e "simulazione" nella teoria retorica dei Romani', in G. Petrone (ed.), *Le passioni della retorica* (Palermo, 2004).

———, *Gli arcani dell'oratore: alcuni appunti sull'actio dei Romani* (Roma-Padova, 2011).

Chaney, Edward, *The Evolution of the Grand Tour: Anglo-Italian Cultural Relations since the Renaissance* (London and Portland, OR, 1998).

Ciccotti, Ettore, *Il processo di Verre. Un capitolo di storia romana* (Milano, 1895).

Clark, Anna, *Scandal: The Sexual Politics of the British Constitution* (Princeton, NJ, 2004).

Clarke, M. L., *Greek Studies in England 1700-1830* (Cambridge, 1945).

———, *Rhetoric at Rome: A Historical Survey* (London, 1953).

———, *Classical Education in Britain 1500-1900* (Cambridge, 1959).

———, 'Non hominis nomen, sed eloquentiae', in T. A. Dorey (ed.), *Cicero* (London, 1965).

———, 'Conyers Middleton's alleged plagiarism', *Notes and Queries*, xxx/1 (1983), pp. 44-6.

Cohn, Bernard S., *Colonialism and its Forms of Knowledge: The British in India* (Princeton, NJ, 1996).

A Companion to Roman Rhetoric, ed. W. Dominik and J. Hall (Oxford, 2007).

Cone, Carl B., 'Edmund Burke's library', *Bibliographical Society of America, Papers* 44 (1950), pp. 153-72.

———, *Burke and the Nature of Politics: The Age of the American Revolution*, 2 vols (Lexington, 1957-64).

Connolly, Joy, *The State of Speech: Rhetoric and Political Thought in Ancient Rome* (Princeton, NJ, and Oxford, 2007).

Cook, John Granger, *Crucifixion in the Mediterranean World* (Tübingen, 2014).

Cox, Jeffrey N., 'Spots of time: the structure of the dramatic evening in the theater of Romanticism', *Texas Studies in Literature and Language* xvi (1999), pp. 403-25.

Davis, A. Mervyn, *A Biography of Warren Hastings* (New York, 1935).

Davis, Jim, 'Spectatorship', in J. Moody and D. O'Quinn (eds), *The Cambridge Companion to British Theatre, 1730–1830* (Cambridge, 2007).
De Almeida, Hermione and Gilpin, George H., *Indian Renaissance: British Romantic Art and the Prospect of India* (Aldershot and Burligton, VT, 2005).
De Bolla, Peter, *The Discourse of the Sublime: Readings in History, Aesthetics and the Subject* (Oxford, 1989).
De Bruyn, Frans, 'Edmund Burke's Gothic romance: the portrayal of Warren Hastings in Burke's writings and speeches on India', in *Criticism* xxix/4 (1987), pp. 415–38.
——, 'Theater and counter-theater in Burke's *Reflections on the Revolution in France*', in R. DeMaria (ed.), *British Literature 1640–1789: A Critical Reader* (Oxford, 1999).
Dirks, Nicholas B., *The Scandal of Empire: India and the Creation of Imperial Britain* (Cambridge, MA, and London, 2006).
Dodson, Michael S., *Orientalism, Empire, and National Culture: India 1770–1880* (Basingstoke, 2007).
Donoghue, Frank, 'Avoiding the "cooler tribunal of the study": Richard Brinsley Sheridan's writer's block and late eighteenth-century print culture', *ELH* lxviii/4 (2001), pp. 831–56.
Eagleton, Catherine, 'Collecting African money in Georgian London: Sarah Sophia Banks and her collection of coins', *Museum History Journal* vi/1 (2013), pp. 23–38.
Elledge, Paul, *Lord Byron at Harrow School: Speaking Out, Talking Back, Acting Up, Bowing Out* (Baltimore, MD, and London, 2000).
Ellison, Julie, 'Sensibility', in J. Faflak and J. M. Wright (eds), *A Handbook of Romanticism Studies* (Oxford, 2012).
Fairclough, Mary, *The Romantic Crowd: Sympathy, Controversy and Print Culture* (Cambridge, 2013).
Fantham, Elaine, *The Roman World of Cicero's De Oratore* (Oxford, 2004).
Feiling, Keith, *Warren Hastings* (London, 1954).
Festa, Lynn, *Sentimental Figures of Empire in Eighteenth-Century Britain and France* (Baltimore, MD, 2006).
Fezzi, Luca, *Il corrotto. Un'inchiesta di Marco Tullio Cicerone* (Roma–Bari, 2016).
Fliegelman, Jay, *Declaring Independence: Jefferson, Natural Language, and the Culture of Performance* (Stanford, CA, 1993).
Form and Function in Roman Oratory, ed. D. H. Berry and A. Erskine, (Cambridge, 2010).
Fox, Matthew, 'Cicero during the Enlightenment', in C. Steel (ed.), *The Cambridge Companion to Cicero* (Cambridge, 2013).
Franklin, Michael J., 'Accessing India: orientalism, anti-"Indianism" and the rhetoric of Jones and Burke', in T. Fulford and P. J. Kitson (eds), *Romanticism and Colonialism: Writing and Empire, 1780–1830* (Cambridge, 1998).

——, *Orientalist Jones: Sir William Jones, Poet, Lawyer, and Linguist, 1746-1794* (Oxford, 2011).

Frazel, Thomas D., '*Furtum* and the description of stolen objects in Cicero *In Verrem* 2.4', *American Journal of Philology* cxxvi/3 (2005), pp. 363-76.

——, *The Rhetoric of Cicero's »In Verrem«* (Göttingen, 2009).

Fuhrmann, Manfred, 'Tecniche narrative nella seconda orazione contro Verre', *Ciceroniana* iv (1980), pp. 27-42.

Geffcken, Katherine A., *Comedy in the Pro Caelio, with an Appendix on the In Clodium et Curionem* (Leiden, 1973).

Gerrard, Christine, 'Lyttelton, George, first Baron Lyttelton (1709-1773)', in *Oxford Dictionary of National Biography*.

Gibbons, Luke, *Edmund Burke and Ireland: Aesthetics, Politics and the Colonial Sublime* (Cambridge, 2003).

Gippert, Susanne, 'The poet and the statesman: Plutarchan biography in eighteenth century England' in L. De Blois, J. Bons, T. Kessels and D. M. Schenkeveld (eds), *The Statesman in Plutarch's Works: Proceedings of the International Conference of the International Plutarch Society, Nijmegen/Castle Hernen, May 1-5, 2002*, 2 vols (Leiden and Boston, 2004).

Golden, Leon, 'Reception of Horace's *Ars Poetica*', in G. Davis (ed.), *A Companion to Horace* (Oxford, 2010).

Goring, Paul, *The Rhetoric of Sensibility in Eighteenth-Century Culture* (Cambridge, 2005).

——, 'The elocutionary movement in Britain', in M. J. MacDonald (ed.), *The Oxford Handbook of Rhetorical Studies* (Oxford, 2017).

Grimal, Pierre, 'Cicéron et les tyrans de Sicile', *Ciceroniana* iv (1980), pp. 63-74.

Gruen, Erich S., *The Hellenistic World and the Coming of Rome*, 2 vols (Berkeley, CA, 1984).

Guerra, Lia, '"The great theatre of the world": Edmund Burke's dramatic perspective', in L. M. Crisafulli and C. Pietropoli (eds), *The Languages of Performance in British Romanticism* (Oxford, 2008).

Hall, Jon, 'Persuasive design in Cicero's *De Oratore*', *Phoenix* xlviii/3 (1994), pp. 210-25.

Halttunen, Karen, 'Humanitarianism and the pornography of pain in Anglo-American culture', *The American Historical Review* c/2 (1995), pp. 303-34.

Hampsher-Monk, Iain, 'Rhetoric and opinion in the politics of Edmund Burke', *History of Political Thought* ix (1988), pp. 455-84.

——, 'Edmund Burke and empire', in D. Kelly (ed.), *Lineages of Empire: The Historical Roots of British Imperial Thought* (Oxford, 2009).

Hardwick, Lorna, *Reception Studies* (Oxford, 2003).

Haywood, Ian, *Bloody Romanticism: Spectacular Violence and the Politics of Representation, 1776-1832* (Basingstoke, 2006).
Hindson, Paul and Gray, Tim, *Burke's Dramatic Theory of Politics* (Aldershot, 1988).
Hughes, Joseph J., *Comedic Borrowing in Selected Orations of Cicero* (Ph.D. Diss. University of Iowa, 1987).
——, 'Inter tribunal and scaenam: comedy and rhetoric in Rome', in W. J. Dominik (ed.), *Roman Eloquence: Rhetoric and Society in Literature* (London and New York, 1997).
Ingram, Robert G., 'Conyers Middleton's *Cicero*: enlightenment, scholarship, and polemic', in William H. F. Altman (ed.), *Brill's Companion to the Reception of Cicero* (Leiden and Boston, 2015).
Innocenti, Beth, 'Towards a theory of vivid description as practiced in Cicero's *Verrine* orations', *Rhetorica* xii (1994), pp. 355-81.
Jones, Robert W., *Literature, Gender and Politics in Britain during the War for America 1770-1785* (Cambridge, 2011).
Kennedy, George Alexander, *The Art of Rhetoric in the Roman World* (Princeton, NJ, 1972).
Kent, Eddy, *Corporate Character: Representing Imperial Power in British India, 1786-1901* (Toronto, 2014).
Kramnick, Isaac, *Bolingbroke and His Circle: The Politics of Nostalgia in the Age of Walpole* (Cambridge, MA, 1968).
Laird, Andrew, 'The *Ars Poetica*', in S. Harrison (ed.), *The Cambridge Companion to Horace* (Cambridge, 2007).
Langford, Paul, 'Burke, Edmund (1729/30-1797)', in *Oxford Dictionary of National Biography*.
Lawson, Philip, and Phillips, Jim, '"Our Execrable Banditti": perceptions of nabobs in mid-eighteenth-century Britain', *Albion* xvi/3 (1984), pp. 225-41.
Leeman, Anron D., Pinkster, Harm (and others), *M. T. Cicero. De Oratore libri III. Kommentar*, 5 vols (Heidelberg, 1981-2008).
Leis, Arlene, 'Cutting, arranging, and pasting: Sarah Sophia Banks as collector', *Early Modern Women: An Interdisciplinary Journal* ix/1 (2014), pp. 127-40.
Lintott, Andrew, 'The citadel of the allies', in J. R. W. Prag (ed.), *Sicilia Nutrix Plebis Romanae: Rhetoric, Law, and Taxation in Cicero's Verrines* (London, 2007).
Lock, F. P., *Burke's Reflections on the Revolution in France* (London, 1985).
——, *Edmund Burke, Volume One: 1730-84* and *Volume Two: 1784-1797* (Oxford, 1998-2006).
——, 'Burke's life', in D. Dwan and C. J. Insole (eds), *The Cambridge Companion to Edmund Burke* (Cambridge, 2012).

MacDonald, Michael J., 'Introduction', in M. J. MacDonald (ed.), *The Oxford Handbook of Rhetorical Studies* (Oxford, 2017).

Mahoney, John L., 'The classical tradition in eighteenth century English rhetorical education', *History of Education Journal* ix/4 (1958), pp. 93-7.

Majeed, Javed, *Ungoverned Imaginings: James Mill's The History of British India and Orientalism* (Oxford, 1992).

Mallory, Anne, 'Burke, boredom, and the theater of counterrevolution', *PMLA* cxviii/2 (2003), pp. 224-38.

Marsden, Jean, 'Shakespeare and sympathy', in P. Sabor and P. Yachnin (eds), *Shakespeare and the Eighteenth Century* (Aldershot, 2008).

Marshall, P. J., 'The personal fortune of Warren Hastings', *Economic History Review* xvii/2 (1964), pp. 284-300.

———, *The Impeachment of Warren Hastings* (Oxford, 1965).

———, 'Indian officials under the East India Company in eighteenth-century Bengal', *Bengal Past and Present* lxxxiv (1965), pp. 95-120.

———, 'Warren Hastings as scholar and patron', in A. Whiteman, J. S. Bromley and P. G. M. Dickson (eds), *Statesmen, Scholars and Merchants: Essays in Eighteenth-Century Literature presented to Dame Lucy Sutherland* (Oxford, 1973).

———, *The New Cambridge History of India. Bengal: The British Bridgehead. Eastern India 1740-1828* (Cambridge, 1987).

———, 'The making of an imperial icon: the case of Warren Hastings', *Journal of Imperial and Commonwealth History* xxvii/3 (1999), pp. 1-16.

———, 'Hastings, Warren (1732-1818)', in *Oxford Dictionary of National Biography*.

May, James M., *Trials of Character: The Eloquence of Ciceronian Ethos* (Chapel Hill, NC, and London, 1988).

———, 'Cicero and the beasts', *Syllecta Classica* vii (1995), pp. 143-53.

———, 'Ciceronian oratory in context', in J. M. May (ed.), *Brill's Companion to Cicero: Oratory and Rhetoric* (Leiden, 2002).

McIntosh, Carey, 'Elementary rhetorical ideas and eighteenth-century English', *Language Sciences* xxii/3 (2000), pp. 231-49.

Miles, Margaret M., *Art as Plunder: The Ancient Origins of Debate about Cultural Property* (Cambridge, 2008).

Miller, Peter N., *Defining the Common Good: Empire, Religion and Philosophy in Eighteenth-Century Britain* (Cambridge, 1994).

Moon, Penderel, *Warren Hastings and British India* (London, 1947).

Moss, Jean Dietz '"Discordant Consensus": Old and new rhetoric at Trinity College, Dublin', *Rhetorica* xiv/4 (1996), pp. 383-441.

Mukherjee, S. N., *Sir William Jones: A Study in Eighteenth-Century British Attitudes to India* (London, 1987).

Mullan, John, *Sentiment and Sociability: The Language of Feeling in the Eighteenth Century* (Oxford, 1988).
Murray, Robert, *Edmund Burke: A Biography* (Oxford, 1931).
Musselwhite, David, 'The trial of Warren Hastings', in F. Barker, P. Hulme, M. Iversen and D. Loxley (eds), *Literature, Politics and Theory: Papers from the Essex Conference 1976–84* (London and New York, 1986).
Narducci, Emanuele, *Processi ai politici nella Roma antica* (Roma–Bari, 1995).
———, *Cicerone e l'eloquenza romana. Retorica e progetto culturale* (Roma–Bari, 1997).
Nechtman, Tillman W., *Nabobs: Empire and Identity in Eighteenth-Century Britain* (Cambridge, 2010).
Neocleous, Mark, 'The monstrous multitude: Edmund Burke's political teratology', *Contemporary Political Theory* iii (2004), pp. 70–88.
O'Brien, Conor Cruise, *The Great Melody: A Thematic Biography and Commented Anthology of Edmund Burke* (London, 1992).
Ochs, Donovan J., 'Rhetorical detailing in Cicero's Verrine Orations', *Central State Speech Journal* xxxiii (1982), pp. 310–18.
Ogilvie, Robert Maxwell, *Latin and Greek: a History of the Influence of the Classics on English Life from 1600 to 1918* (Hamden, CT, 1964).
O'Neill, Daniel I., *Edmund Burke and the Conservative Logic of Empire* (Oakland, CA, 2016).
O'Quinn, Daniel, *Staging Governance: Theatrical Imperialism in London, 1770–1800* (Baltimore, MD, 2005).
Percival, MacIver, *The Fan Book* (New York, 1921).
Peters, Julie Stone, 'Theatricality, legalism, and the scenography of suffering: the trial of Warren Hastings and Richard Brinsley Sheridan's *Pizarro*', *Law and Literature*, xviii (2006), pp. 15–45.
Pincott, Anthony, 'The book tickets of Miss Sarah Sophia Banks (1744–1818)', *The Bookplate Journal*, II/1 (March 2004), pp. 3–30.
Pitts, Jennifer, *A Turn to Empire: The Rise of Imperial Liberalism in Britain and France* (Princeton, NJ, and Oxford, 2005).
Pocock, J. G. A., *The Machiavellian Moment: Florentine Political Thought and the Atlantic Republican Tradition* (Princeton, NJ, 1975).
Potkay, Adam, *The Fate of Eloquence in the Age of Hume* (Cornell, NY, 1994).
Reid, Christopher, *Edmund Burke and the Practice of Political Writing* (Dublin, 1985).
———, 'Burke's Tragic Muse: Sarah Siddons and the "Feminization" of the *Reflections*', in S. Blakemore (ed.), *Burke and the French Revolution: Bicentennial Essays* (Athens, GA, and London, 1992).
———, 'Burke as a rhetorician and orator', in D. Dwan and C. J. Insole (eds), *The Cambridge Companion to Edmund Burke* (Cambridge, 2012).

―――, *Imprison'd Wranglers: The Rhetorical Culture of the House of Commons 1760–1800* (Oxford, 2012).

Remer, Gary, 'The classical orator as political representative: Cicero and the modern concept of representation', *The Journal of Politics* lxxii/4 (2010), pp. 1063–82.

Ribeiro, Aileen, *The Gallery of Fashion* (Princeton, NJ, 2000).

Ridley, Glynis, 'Sheridan's courtroom dramas: the impeachment of Warren Hastings and the trial of the *Bounty* mutineers', in J. E. Derochi and D. J. Ennis (eds), *Richard Brinsley Sheridan: The Impresario in Political and Cultural Context* (Lewisburg, PA, 2013).

Robert, Renaud, 'Ambiguïté du collectionnisme de Verrès', in J. Dubouloz and S. Pittia (eds), *La Sicile de Cicéron: Lectures des Verrines. Actes du colloque de Paris, 19–20 mai 2006* (Besançon, 2007).

Robinson, Nicholas K., *Edmund Burke: A Life in Caricature* (New Haven, CT, and London, 1996).

Rogers, Pat, 'Swift and Cicero: the character of Verres', *Quarterly Journal of Speech* lxi (1975), pp. 71–5.

Roman Eloquence: Rhetoric in Society and Literature, ed. W. J. Dominik, (London and New York, 1997).

Romano, Domenico, 'Cicerone e il ratto di Proserpina', *Ciceroniana* iv (1980), pp. 191–201.

Rudd, Andrew, *Sympathy and India in British Literature 1770–1830* (Basingstoke, 2011).

Russell, Gillian, 'Burke's dagger: theatricality, politics and print culture in the 1790s', *British Journal for Eighteenth-Century Studies* xx (1997), pp. 1–16.

Sachs, Jonathan, *Romantic Antiquity: Rome in the British Imagination, 1789–1832* (Oxford, 2010).

Samet, Elizabeth D., 'A prosecutor and a gentleman: Edmund Burke's idiom of impeachment', *ELH* lxviii/2 (2001), pp. 397–418.

Sen, Sudipta, 'Imperial subjects on trial: on the legal identity of Britons in late eighteenth-century India', *Journal of British Studies* xlv/3 (2006), pp. 532–55.

Sichel, Walter, *Sheridan* (Boston and New York, 1909).

Solkin, David H., 'The battle of the Ciceros: Richard Wilson and the politics of landscape in the age of John Wilkes', in S. Pugh (ed.), *Reading Landscape: Country – City – Capital* (Manchester, 1990).

Stanlis, Peter J., *Edmund Burke and the Natural Law* (Ann Arbor, MI, 1958).

Steel, C. E. W., *Cicero, Rhetoric, and the Empire* (Oxford, 2001).

―――, *Roman Oratory* (Cambridge, 2006).

Strauss, Leo, *Natural Right and History* (Chicago and London, 1953).

Suleri, Sara, *The Rhetoric of English India* (Chicago and London, 1992).

Takada, Yasunari, 'An Augustan representation of Cicero', in P. Robinson et al. (eds), *Enlightened Groves: Essays in Honour of Professor Zenzo Suzuki* (Tokyo, 1996).

Taylor, David Francis, *Theatres of Opposition: Empire, Revolution, and Richard Brinsley Sheridan* (Oxford, 2012).

Teltscher, Kate, *India Inscribed: European and British Writing on India 1600-1800* (Oxford, 1995).

Tempest, Kathryn, 'Saints and sinners: some thoughts on the presentation of character in Attic oratory and Cicero's *Verrines*', in J. R. W. Prag (ed.), *Sicilia Nutrix Plebis Romanae: Rhetoric, Law, and Taxation in Cicero's Verrines* (London, 2007).

Theobald, Robin, 'Scandal in a scandalous age: the impeachment and trial of Warren Hastings, 1788-95', in J. Garrand and James L. Newell (eds), *Scandals in Past and Contemporary Politics* (Manchester and New York, 2006).

Thomson, J. A. K., *The Classical Background of English Literature* (London, 1948).

Todd, Janet, *Sensibility: An Introduction* (New York, 1986).

Tompkins, J. M. S., 'James White, Esq.: a forgotten humourist', *Review of English Studies*, iii/10 (1927), pp. 146-56.

Trotter, Lionel J., *Warren Hastings* (London and Toronto, 1925).

Vasaly, Ann, 'The masks of rhetoric: Cicero's Pro Roscio Amerino', *Rhetorica* iii (1985), pp. 1-20.

——, *Representations: Images of the World in Ciceronian Oratory* (Berkeley, CA, 1993).

——, 'Cicero's early speeches', in J. M. May (ed.), *Brill's Companion to Cicero: Oratory and Rhetoric* (Leiden, 2002).

——, 'Cicero, domestic politics, and the first action of the Verrines', *Classical Antiquity* xxviii/1 (2009), pp. 101-37.

Vasunia, Phiroze, *The Classics and Colonial India* (Oxford, 2013).

——, 'Barbarism and civilization: political writing, history and empire', in N. Vance and J. Wallace (eds), *The Oxford History of Classical Reception in English Literature*, 4 vols (Oxford, 2015).

Vince, C. A., 'Latin poets in the British Parliament', *The Classical Review* xlvi (1932), pp. 97-104.

Ward, Addison, 'The Tory view of Roman history', *Studies in English Literature*, iv (1964), pp. 413-56.

Weinbrot, Howard D., 'History, Horace and Augustus Caesar: some implications for eighteenth-century satire', *Eighteenth-Century Studies*, vii/4 (1974), pp. 391-414.

——, *Augustus Caesar in 'Augustan' England: The Decline of a Classical Norm* (Princeton, NJ, 1978).

West, Shearer, *The Image of the Actor: Verbal and Visual Representation in the Age of Garrick and Kemble* (London, 1991).

Whelan, Frederick G., *Edmund Burke and India: Political Morality and Empire* (Pittsburgh, PA, 1996).
White, Jerry, *London in the Eighteenth Century. A Great and Monstrous Thing* (London, 2012).
Wisse, Jakob, *Ethos and Pathos from Aristotle to Cicero* (Amsterdam, 1989).
Woods, Leigh, *Garrick Claims the Stage: Acting as Social Emblem in Eighteenth-Century England* (Westport, CT, 1984).
Wright, Frederick Warren, *Cicero and the Theater* (Northampton, MA, 1931).
Youngquist, Paul, *Monstrosities: Bodies and British Romanticism* (Minneapolis, MN, 2003).
Zetzel, James, 'Plato with Pillows', in D. Braund and C. Gill (eds), *Myth, History and Culture in Republican Rome: Studies in Honour of T. P. Wiseman* (Exeter, 2003).

Web sources

Dent, William, *The Raree Show* (BM 7273): http://www.britishmuseum.org/research/collection_online/collection_object_details.aspx?objectId=1634523&partId=1&searchText=the+raree+show&page=1 (accessed 28 April 2016).
Eagleton, Catherine, *The collections of Sarah Sophia Banks* (Annual Lecture 2013, Sir Joseph Banks Society): http://www.joseph-banks.org.uk/members/research-papers/annual-lecture-2013/ (accessed 13 January 2017).
Gillray, James, *Impeachment ticket. For the trial of W-RR-NH-ST-NGS Esqr* (BM 7277): http://www.britishmuseum.org/research/collection_online/collection_object_details.aspx?objectId=1627140&partId=1&searchText=impeachment%20ticket (accessed 16 January 2016).
Gillray, James, *Design for the New Gallery of Busts and Pictures* (BM 8072): http://www.britishmuseum.org/research/collection_online/collection_object_details.aspx?objectId=1628932&partId=1&searchText=design+for+the+new+gallery+of+busts+and+pictures&page=1 (accessed 20 September 2016).
Sayers, James, *For the Trial of Warren Ha[stings]/Seventh Day* (BM 7276): http://www.britishmuseum.org/research/collection_online/collection_object_details.aspx?objectId=1461440&partId=1&searchText=james+sayers+ticket&page=1 (accessed 16 January 2016).

Index

Page references in *italics* indicate illustrations.

accomplices 96–7
acquittal 2, 7–8, 38, 88, 92
actio (enactment) 69–84, 134–5
Actor, The (Hill) 74
actors/acting 6, 68, 72–4, 80, 82
Addison, Joseph 69
Agricola (Tacitus) 17
Ahmed, Siraj 4
Alexander the Great 116–17
alliteration 77
'*Amicus Curiae*' (pseudonym) 122–5, 126, 181 n.31
animal imagery 99–104
Annual Register (journal) 113
Antiochus of Syria 123–4
antitheses 76
aposiopesis 83
applause 71
Apronius, Quintus 96
Arabic language 41
'Aristophanes' (pseudonym) 118–20
Articles of Impeachment 45, 126, *127*
Art of Speaking, The (Burgh) 70, 156 n.60
Asaf-al-Daula, Nawab Wazir of Oudh (Awadh) 2, 77–8
Asiatick Society (Kolkata/Calcutta) 44
atrocities, accounts of 4, 80–4, 107–8, 135
audacity 94, 96
audience 2–3, 47, *48*, 50–1, 53–5
   applause 71
   attention 5–6, 54, 55, 103–4
   behaviour 64, 66–7
   emotion 6, 32–3, 76, 105–6, 108, 134–5
   Great Chamberlain's Box 51, 66
   management 61–2
   sensibility 33–4
   sympathy 54, 83, 105–6, 161 n.120, 173 n.98
   and theatricality 50–1, 67–9, 79–80
   women 51, 52–3, 55, 67, 82
avarice 94, 98–9, 169 n.67
Awadh *see* Asaf-al-Daula, Nawab Wazir of Oudh (Awadh); Begums of Oudh (Awadh)

Banks, Sarah Sophia 55–69, 154 n.24, 154 n.25
Banks, Sir Joseph 3, 56, 61
Barwell, Richard 44
beasts (metaphorical epithet) 99–102
Begums of Oudh (Awadh) 2, 4, 71–2, 77–8
Bellenden, William, *De Tribus Luminibus Romanorum* 20–1
Bengal 40, 41, 42, 43, 44, 74
Bhagavad Gītā 43–4
Bisset, Robert, *Life of Edmund Burke* 13
Blair, Hugh 23, 74
Blake, William 108
bodies 49–50, 54, 105–6
body language 49, 69, 70, 75, 78, 83, 134, 135
Bogle, George 29
Boyne, John, *Cicero against Verres* 126, *128*, 134
Breval, John 26
bribery 74, 80–1, 89, 165 n.19, 166 n.25, 168 n.48, 180 n.18
Britannia (symbol) *128*, 129
British Empire 89–93, 103–4
   criticism of 114–15, 136
   and law 36–7, 42, 119–20
   Rome, equated with 42–3, 88–9, 121–2, 136
Broome, Ralph, *Letters from Simpkin the Second to his Dear Brother in Wales* 73–4

Brüggemann, Ludwig Wilhelm, *A View of the English Editions, Translations and Commentaries of Marcus Tullius Cicero, with Remarks* 23–4
Brydone, Patrick, *A Tour to Sicily and Malta* 26
Burgh, James, *The Art of Speaking* 70, 156 n.60
Burke, Edmund 2, 17, 30–9, *60*, 75, 136
  animal imagery, use of 99–102
  biographies of 13
  Cicero, contrasted with 124–5
  Cicero, equated with 13, 115, 118–22, 126–9, *127*, *128*, 134
  Cicero, influence of 6–7, 30, 133, 134
  criticism of 34–5, 124–5
  and geographical morality 36–7, 119–20
  Latin, use of 96
  oratorical powers 30, 32, 80–4, 86, 108–9, 135, 164 n.9
  A Philosophical Enquiry into the Origin of our Ideas of the Sublime and Beautiful 31
  political career 35, 38
  and Rangpur oration 80–4, 135
  Reflections on the Revolution in France 38
  rhetorical skills 33–4, 93, 99–111
  satires of 32, 124–5
  Select Committee on Bengal 37
  'Speech on American Taxation' 35
  'Speech on Conciliation with America' 35
  'Speech on Motion for Papers on Hastings' 89–90, 120
  'Speech on the Opening of the Impeachment' 36, 85–111, 134
  'Speech on the Use of Indians' 32–5
  theatricality 4–5, 5–6, 32–5
Burney, Frances 3, 53–5, 66, 164 n.9
Burrell, Sir Peter 56, 58, *60*, 61
Butler, Charles 135

Calcutta (Kolkata) 40, 41, 43, 44, 74
Calcutta Chronicle: And General Advertiser (journal) 16
Calcutta Gazette; or, Oriental Advertiser (journal) 116–17
Campbell, George, *The Philosophy of Rhetoric* 70
Campbell, John, *The Travels of Edward Brown, Esq* 27
Canter, H. V. 7, 85
capital punishment 74, 106–7, 109
caricatures 14, 100
Carnall, Geoffrey 7, 85
Carnatic province (India) 114–15
Catherine II of Russia 14
Cato's Letters (Gordon and Trenchard) 16
Chait Singh, Raja 2, 117, *127*, *127*
Chambers, Sir William 65, 66, 155 n.41
Character and Conduct of Cicero, Considered (Cibber) 20
Chennai (Madras) 115, 179 n.9
Chesterfield, Earl of 6
Cheyt Singh, Raja *see* Chait Singh, Raja
children, pathos of 97–8, 109–10
Cibber, Colley, *Character and Conduct of Cicero, Considered* 20
Cicero, Marcus Tullius 14, 17–27
  and actors/acting 72–3
  biographies 17–23, 158 n.74
  Burke, compared to 13, 124–5
  Burke, equated with 13, 115, 118–22, 120–2, 126–9, *127*, *128*, 134
  Burke, influence on 6–7, 30, 133, 134
  criticism of 20, 22–3
  and cruelty, accusations of 102–3
  dehumanization of adversaries 99, 101–2
  De Oratore 75, 80
  and emotional affect 6, 75, 80
  familiarization of the exotic 110–11
  imperative form, use of 93
  and moral law 36–7
  ocular demonstration 107
  in press 114–15, 121–2, 179 n.6
  in satires 15
  sound, use of 108
  and sympathy 161–2 n.121
  translations 23–4, 114–15, 121–2, 129–30
  and tyranny, accusations of 102–4
  vanity 18, 22

Cicero, Marcus Tullius, *Verrines (In Verrem)*
  Actio Prima 7, 25
  Actio Secunda 92, 97–8, 173 n.103
  animal imagery 99, 101–4
  Burke's oratory, influence on 7, 36–7, 85–91, 93–104, 107–11
  descriptions, vivid 104–7, 108, 109–11
  familiarity of 24–7, 92–3, 123, 133–4, 135–6
  translations 24–5, 129–30
  and travel writing 26–7
  vocabulary 94–5
Cicero against Verres (Boyne) 126, *128*, 134
classical culture
  allusions 117–18
  education in 11–12, 26–7, 31
  familiarity of 16, 24–7, 92–3, 123, 133–4, 135–6
  and governing classes 26–7, 133, 135
  Roman 31
Clavering, General John 44, 45
Clive, Robert 40
clothing 51, 52–3, 126, *127*, *128*, 129
coats of arms *60*, 61
Code of the Gentoo Laws (Halhed) 42–3
College of Fort William (Kolkata/Calcutta) 41
colonialism *see* imperialism
Cornwallis, Charles, 1st Marquess (Lord Cornwallis) 43, 119
corruption
  of Hastings, alleged 44, 95, 99
  and imperialism 89–91, 114–15, 181 n.25
  judicial 88–9, 123, 166 n.25, 166 n.26, 168 n.48
  and the Orient 89–91, 102
  political 90–1, 101
  risk of 87–9
  of Verres 94–5, 123, 134, 165 n.19, 166 n.25
  of Walpole, Robert, alleged 101
Cortés, Hernán (Ferdinando Cortez) 116–17, 118, 180 n.18
Course of Lectures on Oratory and Criticism, A (Priestley) 70
Courtenay, John 116–17, 118, 180 n.18
Craftsman, The (journal) 101

crucifixion 106–7
cruelty 95, 106–7, 134, 172–3 n.97, 182 n.41

Death of M-L-N in the Life of Cicero, The (satire) 19–20
death sentence 74, 106–7, 109
dehumanization 99–102
demonstration, ocular 107
Demosthenes 14, 15
Dent, William, *The Raree Show* 100
De Oratore (Cicero) 75, 80
  descriptions, vivid 104–11
Design for the New Gallery of Busts and Pictures (Gillray) 14
despotism 95, 102–4
De Tribus Luminibus Romanorum (Bellenden) 20–1
Dio of Halesa 123
duels 45
Dundas, Henry 92
Dunning, John 12
Dupont, Pierre-Gaëton 38

East India Company 5, 37, 40, 44, 90–1, 98
Elliot, Sir Gilbert 50, 67–8, 72, 74–5, 79–80, 137 n.7
eloquence 32–3, 69–72, 75, 76, 79, 135
emotion
  of audience 6, 32–3, 54, 76, 105–6, 108, 134–5
  ipse ardere 75
  lack of 75–6
  of orator 74, 75, 77–8, 82–3, 105–6
  simulation of 73–4
enactment (*actio*) 69–84, 134–5
Encyclopaedia Britannica 21–3
evidence 110–11, 177 n.138, 178 n.140
exaggeration 34–5
Examiner, The (journal) 25
execution 74, 106–7, 109
exhortation 93
extortion 97, 104–5, 123

fainting 73–4, 77, 79, 82
familiarization, of the exotic 110–11
fans, as souvenirs 47–9, *48*
fashion 51, 52–3
Fitzgerald, Lady Sophia 51

Flood, Henry 15
food, at trial 61, 62–3, *62*
Foote, Samuel, *The Nabob* 90
forgery 56–8, 74, 97
For the Trial of Warren Has[tings]/Seventh Day (Sayers) 58–61, *60*
Fort William, College of 41
Fox, Charles James 14, 38, *60*, 117, 118, *128*, 129, 183 n.58
Francis, Philip 30, 44, 45, *60*, 81
French Revolution 37–8, 99–102
frivolity 55

Garrick, David 68, 79
Gavius of Consa 106–7
General Advertiser (journal) 120–1
geographical morality 36–7, 119–20
gesture 69, 129, 183 n.57
Gibbon, Edward 3, 79, 91
Gillray, James
  Design for the New Gallery of Busts and Pictures 14
  Impeachment ticket *For the Trial of W-RR-N H-ST-NGS Esqr* 58–61
  Very Slippy-Weather 126
Godwin, William 92–3, 167 n.46
Gordon, Thomas, *Cato's Letters* 16
governing classes
  in audience 51
  and classical culture 26–7, 133, 135
  education 11–12, 31, 135
Grand Tour 26–7
Greece 102
Grey, Charles 117, 118
Gurney, Joseph 86–7
Guthrie, William 24

Halhed, Nathaniel Brassey 43
  Code of the Gentoo Laws 42–3
Haluntium 104–5
Harris, James 34
Hastings, Warren 39–45, 79
  accomplices 96–7
  acquittal 2, 7–8, 38
  Alexander the Great, compared with 116–17
  appearance 53–4, 137 n.7
  Articles of Impeachment 2, 45, *127*
  and Asian languages 41–2
  avarice, alleged 98
  beast, described as 99–100
  bribery, alleged 80–1, 89, 180 n.18
  British laws, opposes introduction to India 42–3
  caricatures of 100
  corruption, alleged 44, 95, 99
  Cortés, equated with 118
  cruelty, alleged 95, 172–3 n.97
  dehumanization of 99–102
  as despot 95
  as dramatic hero 54
  and Indian culture 39, 43
  monster, described as 100
  as 'nabob' 91
  as oriental 'threat' 95, 100, 126, *127*
  portrait 40, 41, 42
  praise of 124
  Proposal for Establishing a Professorship of the Persian Language in the University of Oxford 41
  rapacity, alleged 98, 100
  and satire 118–20
  support for 116, 120–5, 182 n.42
  tyranny, alleged 102–4
  Verres, contrasted with 124
  Verres, equated with 24, 87, 92–3, 115–16, 120–2, 126–9, *127*, 133
  wealth 41, 98, 151 n.65
Henna (Enna, Sicily) 105
Hicky's Bengal Gazette; or the Original Calcutta General Advertiser 114–15
Hill, John, *The Actor* 74
Hircarrah, The (journal) 17
History of the Life of Marcus Tullius Cicero (Middleton) 19–21, 123
homoteleuton 77
Hood, Lord (Samuel Hood) 116
Horace 17
horror 80–4
House of Commons 2, 32, 35, 71
House of Lords 2, 3, 7–8, 38, 47, 93
Howard, Charles (10th Duke of Norfolk) 47, 56, 57
Hume, David 90
  Of Eloquence 69–70
hyperbole 81

Idea of the Modern Eloquence of the Bar (Mackenzie) 26
identification, sentimental 77–8
illness 82–3, 160 n.101
  fainting 73–4, 77, 79, 82
  simulation 4, 73–4, 134–5
imagery 75, 76, 77, 99–102, 175 n.119
immediacy 103–4, 105–6, 107–8
Impeachment, The (Sayers) 126–9, *127*, 134
Impeachment ticket For the Trial of W-RR-N H-ST-NGS Esqr (Gillray) 58–61
imperative form 93
imperialism
  and corruption 89–91, 114–15
  criticism of 114–15, 116–17, 118, 129–30
  and geographical morality 36–7, 119–20
  guilt 4–5, 138 n.12
  and justice 88–9
  and legal systems 37, 42
  Roman 42–3
  and status of colonized 93–4
  and wealth 89
Impey, Sir Elijah 74–5, 79
India
  Bengal 40, 41, 42, 43, 44, 74
  and Burke, Edmund 35
  Calcutta (Kolkata) 40, 41, 43, 44, 74
  Carnatic province 114–15
  clothing, traditional 39
  English-language press 16–17, 114–17, 179 n.6, 180 n.20
  and geographical morality 36–7
  Greece, equated with 43
  importance 103–4
  Madras (Chennai) 115
  in satirical prints *128*, 129
  Sicily, equated with 114–15, 121–2
India Gazette: Or, Calcutta Public Advertiser (journal) 16, 115–16
Indians, representation of 93–4
ipse ardere 75
irony 25, 118–20, 121

Johnson, Samuel 41
Jones, Sir William 12, 31, 41, 43, 152 n.78
judgment 74, 76
jurors 87–8, 93

justice 87–9, 106–7, 166 n.23
  and corruption 88–9, 123, 166 n.25, 166 n.26, 168 n.48
Justinian 43
juxtaposition 120–5

Kant, Immanuel 31
Knight, Richard Payne 26
Kolkata (Calcutta) 40, 41, 43, 44, 74

Langhorne, John 17
Langhorne, Thomas 17
languages 41, 44
  English 16–17, 114–17
  Latin 11, 13, 16, 31, 40, 96
Latin language 11, 13, 16, 31, 40, 96
law and legal systems
  and British Empire 37, 42, 44, 74
  and geographical morality 36–7, 119–20
  and justice 87–9, 106–7, 166 n.23
  moral law 36–7, 119–20
lawyers 72–3
Lectures on Rhetoric and Belles Lettres (Smith) 70
Lee, Charles 32
Letters from Simpkin the Second to his Dear Brother in Wales (Broome) 73–4
Life of Edmund Burke (Bisset) 13
Linley, Elizabeth Ann 3, 82
litotes 76
Lives (Plutarch) 17–18, 158 n.74
Lock, F.P. 4, 98
Locke, John 11
London Magazine (journal) 30
luxury 89, 90, 91
Lyttelton, George, *Observations on the Life of Cicero* 18

Macaulay, Thomas Babington 3
McCrea, Jane 32–4
Mackenzie, George, *Idea of the Modern Eloquence of the Bar* 26
Madras (Chennai) 115, 179 n.9
madraseh (Kolkata/Calcutta) 43
Malleolus 97–8
Mansfield, 1st Earl of (William Murray) 13
Martin, Claude 41–2

Melmoth, William 24
memorabilia, of trial 47–9, *48*, 55–69
metonymy 76
Middleton, Conyers 142 n.35, 143 n.50
  *History of the Life of Marcus Tullius
  Cicero* 19–21, 123
Mill, John Stuart 11, 139 n.5
money 89, 90–1, 98
Monson, Colonel George 44, 45
monsters/monstrosity 99–102, 134, 171 n.82
morality, geographical 36–7, 119–20
Morning Chronicle and London Advertiser 33–4, 34–5
Morning Post and Daily Advertiser (journal) 14
mourning, language of 103, 105, 174 n.110
movement 108
Mucius (pseudonym, William Godwin) 92–3
Mucius Scaevola, Gaius 92
Murphy, Arthur 17
Murray, William (1st Earl of Mansfield) 13

Nabob, The (Foote) 90
'nabobs' (East India Company employees) 90–1
Nandakumar, Maharaja 74
Narrative of a Five Years' Expedition against the Negroes of Suriname (Stedman) 108
Nawab of Bengal (Siraj ud-Daulah) 40
Nawab Wazir of Oudh (Awadh) (Asaf-al-Daula) 2, 77–8
newspapers 16–17, 113, 114–17, 121–2, 179 n.6
Niobe 82, 163 n.135
Nixon, James 55
Norfolk, 10th Duke of (Charles Howard) 47, 56, 57
North, Lord (Frederick North) *128*, 129, 183 n.58
North, Thomas 17

Observations on the Life of Cicero (Lyttelton) 18
Ochakov crisis 14
ocular demonstration 107
Of Eloquence (Hume) 69–70

O'Quinn, Daniel 4
orators 6, 13–17, 82
  emotion of 74, 75, 77–8, 82–3, 105–6
oratory
  and actors/acting 68, 72–4, 80, 82
  body language 49, 69, 70, 75, 78, 83, 134, 135
  classical 5, 133
  delivery 70–1
  education in 12, 31, 135
  emotional effect 32–3, 73–4, 75, 79–80
  identification, sentimental 77–8
  illness, feigned 4, 73–4, 134–5
  publication of 72, 86–7, 157 n.72
  rational 69–70, 75–6
  and sensationalism 33–4, 80–4
  and sensibility 32–3
  sound, use of 69, 70, 75, 108–9
  theatricality 3–4, 5–7, 32–5, 49, 79–80, 134–5, 157–8 n.80
  transcriptions 72, 157 n.72
  and voice/vocalization 69, 70, 75
  see also rhetoric
Orient, as 'corrupting' influence 89–91, 102
orphans, pathos of 97–8
Oudh (Awadh), Begums of 2, 4, 71–2, 77–8
Oudh (Awadh), Nawab Wazir of (Asaf-al-Daula) 2, 77–8
Oxford, University of 41

pamphlets 25, 124
Parliamentary Register (journal) 33
Parr, Samuel, *Prefatio ad Bellendenum* 21
Paterson, John 4
pathos 77–8, 83, 97–8, 109–10, 173 n.98
Persian language 41
persuasion 71, 80, 162 n.123
Philosophical Enquiry into the Origin of our Ideas of the Sublime and Beautiful, A (Burke) 31
Philosophy of Rhetoric, The (Campbell) 70
Pitt, William (the Elder) 91
Pitt, William (the Younger) 14, 45
Pizarro (Sheridan) 118
Plassey, battle of 40
Plutarch, *Lives* 17–18, 158 n.74
Political and Herald Review (journal) 92–3

politics/politicians 12–17, 35, 38, 72–3, 90–1, 101
Polybius 89
Powell, John 126–8, *127*
power 36, 44, 110
Prattent, Thomas, *A View of the Court Sitting on the Trial of Warren Hastings Esq* 47–9, *48*
Prefatio ad Bellendenum (Parr) 21
press
 British 120–5
 Cicero translations, publication of 114–15, 121–2, 179 n.6
 Indian 16–17, 114–17, 179 n.6, 180 n.20
 newspapers 16–17, 113, 114–17, 121–2, 179 n.6
 periodicals/reviews 113
 reports of trial 86, 113–17, 120–5, 134
 and theatricality 52–3, 121
Priestley, Joseph, *A Course of Lectures on Oratory and Criticism* 70
prints, satirical 14, 58–61, 126–31
propaganda 113
Proposal for Establishing a Professorship of the Persian Language in the University of Oxford (Hastings) 41
pseudonyms, classical 16, 92–3, 118–20, 122–5, 126, 181 n.31
Public Advertiser (journal) 14–15, 33, 35, 121, 122–5, 126
publication of oratory 72, 86–7, 157 n.72
public speaking *see* oratory

queues, for trial 14–15, 66–7
Quintilian, Marcus Fabius 6, 109–10, 183 n.57

race 95
racism 100
Rangpur 'atrocities' 4, 80–4, 97, 107–8
rapacity 98, 100, 134
rape 34, 108–9
Raree Show, The (Dent) 100
rationalism 69–70, 75–6
reception 86
 emotional 6, 32–3, 76, 105–6, 108
 in press 113–25
 in satirical prints 126–31

and sympathy 105–6, 161 n.120, 173 n.98
 theatrical 4
Reflections on the Revolution in France (Burke) 38
refreshments, at trial 61, 62–4, *62*
Regulating Act (1773) 44
relativism, moral 36–7, 119–20
repetition 76, 77, 169 n.68
Reynolds, Sir Joshua 3, 39, 41, 42
Reynolds's Turk's Head Club 31
rhetoric 6, 12, 49, 130, 133, 134–5
 alliteration 77
 antitheses 76
 aposiopesis 83
 dehumanization 99–102
 descriptions, vivid 104–11
 eloquence 32–3, 69–72, 75, 76, 79, 135
 and emotional affect 70, 80
 exaggeration 34–5
 exhortation 93
 homoteleuton 77
 hyperbole 81
 identification, sentimental 77–8
 imagery 75, 76, 77, 99–102, 175 n.119
 immediacy 103–4, 105–6, 107–8
 imperative form 93
 ipse ardere 75
 irony 25, 118–20, 121
 juxtaposition 120–5
 litotes 76
 metonymy 76
 mourning, language of 103, 105, 174 n.110
 pathos 77–8, 83, 97–8, 109–10, 173 n.98
 persuasion 71, 80, 162 n.123
 repetition 76, 77, 169 n.68
 understatement 76
Rohilla war 44–5
Roman empire 31, 42–3, 88–9, 121–2, 126, *128*
Romanticism 107–8
Rumbold, Sir Thomas 115, 179 n.9

Sanskrit language 44
satire 19–20, 134
 of Burke 32, 124–5
 of Cicero 15
 of Hastings 118–20

Index

prints 14, 58–61, *60*, 126–31, *127*, *128*
  of Sheridan 73–4
  of Verres 24–5
Sayers, James
  The Impeachment 126–9, *127*, 134
  For the Trial of Warren Has[tings]/ Seventh Day 58–61, *60*
Schreiber, Lady Charlotte Elizabeth 47
Scott-Waring, John ('Major Scott') 113, 121
seals 42, 56, *59*, 66
Select Committee on Bengal 37
sensationalism 33–4, 80–4
sensibility 32–3, 33–4, 161 n.120
sexual violence 34, 108–9
Sheridan, Richard Brinsley 2, 4, 38, 68, 157 n.69, 160 n.101
  Begums of Oudh oration 71–2, 75–80
  Pizarro 118
  satires of 73–4
Sheridan, Thomas 78
Sicily 26–7, 102, 105, 121–2, 172 n.92
Siddons, Sarah 3, 79, 82
sight/seeing 53–4, 108
Singh, Devi 80–1, 96, 97
Singh, Ganga Govind 96, 97
Singh, Raja Chait 2, 117, 127, *127*
Siraj ud-Daulah (Nawab of Bengal) 40
Smith, Adam, *Lectures on Rhetoric and Belles Lettres* 70
sound 69, 70, 75, 108–9
souvenirs, of trial 47–9, *48*, 55–69
spectacle 3, 4–5, 47–9, 107–8
Spectator, The (journal) 16
spectators *see* audience
speeches *see* oratory
'Speech on American Taxation' (Burke) 35
'Speech on Motion for Papers on Hastings' (Burke) 89–90, 120
'Speech on the Opening of the Impeachment' (Burke) 36, 85–111, 134
'Speech on the Use of Indians' (Burke) 32–5
Stedman, John Gabriel, *Narrative of a Five Years' Expedition against the Negroes of Suriname* 108
Supreme Council of Bengal 44
Supreme Court of Calcutta 74
Swift, Jonathan 25, 121–2, 134, 181 n.26

Swinburne, Henry 22–3
sympathy 54, 83, 105–6, 108–10, 161 n.120, 161–2 n.121

Tacitus, Publius Cornelius, *Agricola* 17
taxation 80–1
Taylor, David Francis 6
tears 79, 109–10
tea trade 103–4
theatricality
  and audience 50–1, 67–9, 79–80
  of Burke 4–5, 5–6, 32–5
  of oratory 3–4, 5–7, 32–5, 49, 79–80, 134–5, 157–8 n.80
  and press reporting 52–3, 121
  of Westminster Hall 50–1, 67–9
theft 105, 123–4
tickets, for trial 47, 56–67, *57*, *59*, *65*
  anti-forgery measures 56–8
  demand for 66–7, 72, 157 n.67
  design 57–8
  parodies 58–9
  'pass and repass' 61, *63*
Timarchides 96
Times, The (journal) 121–2
torture 81, 107–8
Tour to Sicily and Malta, A (Brydone) 26
trade, imperial 103–4
transcriptions 72, 86–7
translations 16, 17, 31, 43–4, 139 n.8
  of Cicero 23–4, 114–15, 121–2, 129–30
  in newspapers 114–15, 121–2, 179 n.6
Travels of Edward Brown, Esq, The (Campbell) 27
travel writing 26–7
Trenchard, John, *Cato's Letters* 16
Trinity College 31
tyranny 95, 102–4

understatement 76
upper classes
  in audience 51
  and classical culture 26–7, 133, 135
  education 11–12, 31, 135

vampire imagery 100
Verres, Gaius 6–7, 22, 24–5, 85–111, 123–4, 133–4, 169 n.63

accomplices 96
avarice 94, 99, 123
British imperialism, equated with 114–15
corruption 94–5, 123, 134, 165 n.19, 166 n.25
cruelty 102–3, 134, 182 n.41
dehumanization of 99
extortion 104–5, 123
and Gavius of Consa 106–7
greed 94, 99, 123
Hastings, contrasted with 124
Hastings, equated with 24, 87, 92–3, 115–16, 120–2, 126–9, *127*, 133
as monster 101–2, 134
rapacity 134
in satires 24–5
symbolic value of 24–5
theft 105, 123–4
as tyrant 102–4, 124
Verres and his Scribblers: A Satire in Three Cantos (pamphlet) 25, 134
Verrines (In Verrem) (Cicero)
Actio Prima 7, 25
Actio Secunda 92, 97–8, 173 n.103
animal imagery 99, 101–4
Burke's oratory, influence on 7, 36–7, 85–91, 93–104, 107–11
descriptions, vivid 104–7, 108, 109–11
familiarity of 24–7, 92–3, 123, 133–4, 135–6
translations 24–5, 129–30
and travel writing 26–7
vocabulary 94–5

Very Slippy-Weather (Gillray) 126
victims 97–8, 107–9
View of the Court Sitting on the Trial of Warren Hastings Esq, A (Prattent) 47–9, *48*
View of the English Editions, Translations and Commentaries of Marcus Tullius Cicero, with Remarks, A (Brüggemann) 23–4
violence, accounts of 4, 80–4, 107–8, 135
Virgil 97, 100, 169 n.62
voice/vocalization 69, 70, 75
Voltaire 15

Walpole, Horace 33–4
Walpole, Sir Robert 25, 101, 134, 171 n.85
Ward, John 70
Warton, Joseph 20
wealth 89, 90–1, 98
weeping 79, 109–10
Westminster Hall 2–3, 47–9, *48*, 50–5, 61–9, *62*, 153 n.9, 153 n.12
Wharton, Thomas (1st Earl) 25, 134
Whig party 14, 18, 37–8
White, James 24
Wilkes, John 116
Wilkins, Charles 43–4
witnesses 109, 178 n.140
women
    at trial 51, 52–3, 55, 67, 82
    as victims 107–8, 108–9
World, The (Indian journal) 118–20, 180 n.20

Zoffany, Johan 41

www.ingramcontent.com/pod-product-compliance
Lightning Source LLC
Chambersburg PA
CBHW052042300426
44117CB00012B/1940